Beyond Glasnost

Jeffrey C. Goldfarb

Beyond Glasnost

The Post-Totalitarian Mind

Foreword by
Jan Jozef Szczepanski

The University of Chicago Press   *Chicago and London*

JEFFREY C. GOLDFARB is associate professor of sociology at the New School for Social Research. He is the author of *The Persistence of Freedom: The Sociological Implications of Polish Student Theater* and *On Cultural Freedom: An Exploration of Public Life in Poland and America*, the latter of which is also published by the University of Chicago Press.

The University of Chicago Press, Chicago 60637
The University of Chicago Press, Ltd., London
© 1989 by The University of Chicago
All rights reserved. Published 1989
Printed in the United States of America
98 97 96 95 94 93 92 91 90 89   54321

LIBRARY OF CONGRESS CATALOGING-IN-PUBLICATION DATA

Goldfarb, Jeffrey C.
  Beyond glasnost.

  Includes index.
  1. Politics and culture—Europe, Eastern.
2. Communism and culture—Europe, Eastern.   3. Europe,
Eastern—Intellectual life—20th century.   I. Title.
DJK50.G64   1989   306'.2'0947   88-27857
ISBN 0-226-30097-8

For Brina and Sam

Contents

Foreword

JAN JOZEF SZCZEPANSKI

IN HIS PENETRATING ANALYSIS of totalitarianism, Jeffrey C. Goldfarb illuminates the difficulties in understanding this phenomenon, and addresses the confusion in Western approaches to it. I feel that this is exactly what we, in this part of the world, and in this time, have been waiting for. Never before has anyone so seriously attempted to overcome the gap between Western and Eastern attitudes. The book will make a fundamental contribution to mutual understanding.

Reading Goldfarb's book, I am reminded of a personal experience, during my first visit to the West after the war, in 1957—in the time of Khrushchev's thaw. In Paris, I met a French journalist, a member of the French Communist Party, who tried to convince me that the workers' revolt in Poznań of May 1956 was an invention of the reactionary mass media, and in fact did not happen. When asked what made him think so, he replied that it is illogical for workers to rebel against a workers' state. The application of logical principles, based on ideological theory instead of facts, seems to me crucial to a definition of the totalitarian mentality.

This incident might have been a random case. I promptly discovered, however, that this attitude—although in a more nuanced form—prevailed among French intellectuals, despite the recent disclosures of the aberrations of Stalinism. It should be stressed here that in the West, and particularly in France, in those times to be an intellectual meant to profess leftist convictions. If not, one was automatically labeled a reactionary, and according to a simplified political classification, a fascist. This crude dichotomy, enforced by wartime propaganda, was mainly based on a conception of progress, characterized by a scientific and rational attitude toward social and political problems. As such, it embodied a continuation of the tradition of the eighteenth-century Enlightenment.

To people sharing the experience of my part of Europe, this frame of mind seemed completely out of touch with reality—a sort of irrelevant nominalism.

The arbitrary way of deciding what is progressive, and what is not, seems to me to be one of the main obstacles to identifying the difference between traditional tyranny and the totalitarianism of our times. Once you accept the notion that progress is linked to an ideological theory, enshrined in a political power structure, there is no way out of a vicious circle of wishful thinking, coercion, historical mystification, and, eventually, a reign of terror. Therefore, the ideological component has to be considered one of the basic denominators of totalitarianism. Two distinctive features of totalitarian ideology (whether it is of the leftist or rightist orientation) are the aspirations to create a "new man," and the quest for legitimization in the supposed will of the "masses." Here the cherished logical principle of the intellectual works according to its own (natural) rules. The concept of the "new man" inevitably adopts the shape of a docile subject of the regime, and the will of the "masses" is formulated by the ruling elite according to its political and class interests.

Goldfarb observes rightly that, to achieve its aims, a totalitarian regime has to devise a totalitarian culture. This is essential to the formation of the personality of the "new man." This culture, supposed to fulfill the aspirations of the "masses," has, paradoxically, not much in common with the idea of progress. To the contrary, it favors the mediocrity of traditional conventions and discriminates against every form of modern inventiveness. Again this is typical for both left-wing and right-wing totalitarianism. In Hitler's Germany, the artistic avant-garde was scoffed at as "entartete Kunst." In the Soviet Bloc, socialist realism (a copy of nineteenth-century academism) was the officially enforced style. Similarly conservative patterns apply to other realms of the "superstructure," especially science and economics, although in those cases the sacrosanct model is furnished by the orthodox interpretation of the scriptures of the founding fathers of Marxist ideology. Not progress, but stagnation, is the inevitable result of the application of such principles. And instead of the "free society of producers," predicted to emerge from the "withering state," an immobile etatism with an overblown bureaucracy and an all-pervading coercive system is the epitome of the progressive vision.

The processes we are witnessing today, generated by Gorbachev's "glasnost" and "perestroika," are an attempt to break out of stagnation without endangering the very existence of the system. Goldfarb sees in them manifest symptoms of an oncoming post-totalitarian era. But he correctly refrains from presenting them as a clear-cut reversal of existing trends.

The gradual destruction of the established totalitarian patterns began much earlier in the so-called People's Democracies, and in the Soviet Union itself.

The eagerly anticipated "new man" emerged as a party aparatchik or an opportunist, paying lip service to the ideology, while in the seemingly shapeless masses, the aspirations to privacy, dignity, and initiative did not die out. The consecutive upheavals in East Germany, Hungary, Czechoslovakia, and Poland, viewed by many Western observers as melodramatic episodes in the history of an empire, were in fact repeated evidence of the nonviability of the utopia. This was strikingly visible in Poland during the time of "Solidarity." Here the "old man" with old anxieties and spiritual needs, and a craving to shape his own fate, appeared hand in hand with the reformer and the rebel. Many progressive Westerners felt scandalized by the alliance of the trade unionists and the Catholic Church. But this alliance was not just a tactical maneuver. It illustrated also the deep need to restore the full dimension of a humanity that had been shaped for ages by its own cultural and spiritual tradition.

The post-totalitarian era does not necessarily mean the abolition of the political status quo and a return to liberal principles, to a market economy, and to parliamentary practices.

On the other hand, it certainly does mean a far-reaching relaxation of ideological constraints. This would amount to the
emergence of a society of citizens, though still within the
boundaries of an enlightened etatistic system.

   Goldfarb chooses a most appropriate vantage point, seeking his clues in the experience of the so-called dissident movements of Eastern Europe. Stressing the importance of culture
to the formation of the totalitarian mentality, he notices at the
same time its basic inadaptability to a system built on officially promulgated truths. These truths were never generally
accepted in the European countries swallowed up by Stalin's
empire. The relaxation of ideological principles, epitomized
by Gorbachev's "glasnost," undoubtedly develops under the
impact of the longstanding resistance of the societies of this
region. In trying to envision the shape of a post-totalitarian
era it is essential to watch these processes carefully because,
as Goldfarb says: "Post-totalitarian culture precedes post-
totalitarian politics."

Acknowledgments

I BEGAN THIS inquiry as a continuation of a conversation I had in the private apartment of an extraordinary man in Warsaw. I continued and developed the inquiry as I was challenged during serious and sometimes contentious discussions with my colleagues in New York at the New School for Social Research. My goal in this inquiry is not to reveal some political or social scientific truth, but to stimulate further critical discussions about sustaining the ideals of democracy, culture, and justice beyond totalitarian certitudes.

My first and most provocative interlocutor was Adam Michnik. I thank him for our friendship and for his example. His is an archetypical post-totalitarian mind. When we at the New School gave him an honorary degree, he became our colleague. Because of his inspiration, regular exchanges among Hungarian, Polish, American, and other colleagues address problems of politics and culture in the ongoing Democracy Seminar of the New School. This manuscript is the first of what I imagine will be a series of works to come out of that seminar.

Of the seminar participants I wish to acknowledge, I am especially indebted to Osborne Wiggins and Elzbieta Matynia. I discovered the central theoretical ideas in this manuscript during lunches, dinners, and coffee breaks with Wiggins. I discovered Poland, over a fifteen-year period, with the help of Matynia. I finally feel free to acknowledge her invaluable and long-term assistance.

The New York seminar participants informed this work by challenging me to rethink my position, by providing me with new information and perspectives, and by prodding me to substantiate and strengthen my analysis. I thank specifically

Andrew Arato, György Bence, Anne Bowler, José Casanova, Juan Corradi, Ferenc Feher, Nina Gladziuk, Agnes Heller, Ira Katznelson, David Ost, and Eli Sagan, active participants who influenced the writing of the following text.

I also wish to acknowledge the assistance of friends and colleagues in Poland who demonstrated to me not only that such a thing as a post-totalitarian mind exists, but that it has something to say to us in the political West about our world. For their friendship, invaluable assistance, and intellectual exchange, I acknowledge Roman Stachyra, Aldona Jawlowska, Jerzy Szacki, Pawel Spiewak, Helena Datner, Basia Szwedowska, Janek Litynski, and many others who helped me during my recent, sometimes difficult, visits to Poland.

For assistance in the preparation of the manuscript, I thank Dorothy Mullen, Michele Dykhuis, Nancy Stoll, Andrew Metz, and Thomas Obrzut.

Most profoundly, I am indebted to Naomi Gruson Goldfarb for twenty years of partnership in the exploration of the politics of culture, and to my father, Benjamin Goldfarb, who taught me how and why to think about politics.

Introduction

A SPECTRE is haunting Eastern Europe—the spectre of glasnost. All the powers of the present day try to make sense of it. Its reality is far from assured; its permanence even less so. But something has clearly changed in Communist-dominated and -controlled social orders. Most significantly, there now exists a post-totalitarian mind.

In this study I shall account for this new mind deliberately. If we try to understand Mikhail Gorbachev, his orthodox opponents, his officially accepted critics, and his independent opposition, in Soviet Russia and beyond, without understanding the distinctive nature of modern tyranny and its development, we are doomed to superficiality. We must reconsider both the essential qualities of the totalitarian order and the development of political and cultural alternatives in the Soviet bloc. This reconsideration is exploratory and necessarily unorthodox. When we discover something new—and something truly new is emerging in the Soviet bloc—we often must use unorthodox means for charting the new terrain. Otherwise, the uncharted terrain may be confused with the more familiar; the new can too easily be fitted into existing patterns of thought and be lost. We must focus on the appearance of newness and carefully seek both to account for it and to act with imaginative understanding.

Gorbachev has become a worldwide celebrity, fitted into a typical celebrity mold. His popularity in the West is probably greater than any previous Soviet leader's; he rivals all Western leaders in popularity. His book *Perestroika,* written in an official Newspeak, is a bestseller.[1] He is *Time* magazine's Man of the Year (1987). The relationships between his wife and the first ladies of the world are the source of constant journalistic gossip, as is her lack of popularity in the Soviet Union. All this seems to have its foundation in a new Soviet shrewdness in public relations.

It also displays Western superficiality. To be sure, there are among Western experts, policy analysts, opinion leaders, and the informed public careful calculations concerning recent Soviet promise and performance. But lacking is a theoretical understanding of the change in the Soviet leadership as a manifestation of the changes in totalitarianism and the opposition to it over a long period of time in many parts of the world. Put succinctly, the complex relationships between glasnost and totalitarianism, and glasnost and Solidarność, must be addressed.

What is most remarkable about Gorbachev in comparison with his immediate predecessors is that he is responding to the economic, social, political, and cultural realities and problems of the Soviet order. What most characterizes the Western response to Gorbachev is the inability to understand the fundamental nature of that order—both as it is officially rendered and as this rendering is resisted. To understand the official order, I analyze sociologically the history of the concept of totalitarianism and account phenomenologically for the everyday reality of totalitarianism as a cultural form (in part 1). To understand the resistance, I closely read and interpret the political and cultural works of oppositionists as they are embedded within and secede from the official order (in part 2). I tell stories of repression and liberation, some of which I have personally observed, and present interpretations, so that we may substantiate our understanding of the continuities and changes in totalitarian orders.

My approach is unorthodox. Most studies of the Soviet Union or Soviet-type societies follow the method of either the sciences (presenting hypotheses drawn from general theories concerning the nature of the existing socialist order, and confirming or disconfirming the hypotheses and theories in investigation) or the humanities (intensively analyzing a particular problem or set of problems in a particular country or group of countries). The latter kind of study has been primarily conducted by area specialists, the former by social scientists. Both have yielded substantial results. But even taken together and combined with the available fiction, poetry, films, and theater from the "other Europe," a theoretical understanding of the fundamental contours of the social order linked with an appreciation of the experienced realities of everyday life is hard to come by. In my judgment, by *systematically* combining social-scientific and humanistic approaches, by analyzing the experience of living in existing socialist societies as revealed through direct observations and literature, and combining this analysis directly with social theorizing, we can come to appreciate the deep changes in the Soviet bloc and how they relate to our world. In this way, I attempt to demonstrate the degree to which the changes are a manifestation of profound, long-term resistance and systemic change beyond Party personalities and the politics of news headlines.

The spectre of glasnost, perhaps even more than Marx's spectre of Communism, is best understood from the bottom up. Whereas Communism has proven itself to be a movement of vanguardism and dictatorship, it is my contention that glasnost, as an official policy of openness and publicity, is an official imitation of the struggles and accomplishments of subjugated people—people working in isolated country cottages (Vaclav Havel) and in antiquated industrial factories (Lech Walesa), expelled students (Adam Michnik) and academicians (Andrei Sakharov and Bronislaw Geremek), voluntary and involuntary political exiles (Milan Kundera and Aleksander Solzhenitsyn). These well-known, along with not so well-known, oppositionists are the true authors of glasnost, the instigators of the post-totalitarian mind. To discover the meaning of what these authors of fundamental political and cultural change have to say, I attempt to portray their world as they understand and experience it, presenting theoretical interpretations along the way. We will move from lived experience as observed and portrayed in cultural and political works to a theoretical attempt to specify the broad contours of a new societal frame of mind with direct implications for us in both thought and action.

Poland is a logical point of discovery of the post-totalitarian mind. It shares with its neighbors political movements against the Communist party monopoly, a dissident culture, official economic and political experiments, and the development of independent cultural and political public life. But in Poland all of this in the past decade is most advanced.[2] Poland, of course, does not represent the future of the Soviet bloc. Different national traditions, political cultures and experiences, and economic situations suggest very different prospects for the different nations of the bloc. Yet, because of the advanced nature of its independent public life, Poland attests to how far the post-totalitarian mind has already come.

But even during the course of the Polish events of the seventies and eighties, their very special significance was often overlooked. The proceedings of an international conference I attended on alternative modes of development and alternative ways of life, held in Poland in June 1980, illustrates this point. The conference participants were primarily from Germany, England, Scandinavia, and Poland. I was invited by the Poles as an expert on Polish youth theater. From conception to conclusion, the conference was permeated with confusion and misunderstanding. Remember, this was Poland, two months before the Gdansk strikes, with sporadic strikes already spreading around the country. We met in the midst of a revolutionary situation, but the Westerners did not seem to understand.

The very calling of the conference was based on misunderstanding. Those from the West were primarily interested in alternative modes of development. Among them were policy analysts and political activists interested in ecological issues, active in "green" politics. They were concerned with alternatives to capitalist industrial development. The Poles were interested in alternative ways of life as means for establishing alternative zones free of the dominant command structures—thus their interest in youth theater.

The youth theater presentations and the interpretations of

them seemed quaint but relatively trivial to the Westerners. They, after all, addressed big issues—the imminent ecological disaster fostered by capitalism and enforced by U.S. geopolitics, with its potential for igniting a thermonuclear catastrophe—while the Poles presented a seemingly marginal avant-garde art movement. To the Poles, the Westerners seemed equally ignorant. The Poles had no doubt that the world faced potential ecological and nuclear dangers, but their economy and social order were collapsing. Severe political repression was not a distant threat. It was represented at the conference by members of the internal security forces (i.e., secret police). When the Poles spoke of youth theater, they spoke of a free zone that was being extended by the democratic opposition, which they also explained.

One Polish scholar bravely described the beginnings of independent unions, a woman's movement, and an ecological movement. She also emphasized that the repressive forces were in the conference. The Westerners did not realize that they themselves were in a Polish zone of tolerated autonomy which could be repressed at any moment and for which the Poles might have to pay after the Westerners left. Two Englishmen were particularly absurd. After presenting an Althussarian critique of Western politics, they spoke informally. What particularly irked them were the privileges they received with hard currency in socialist Poland. That a black market exists in a purported socialist state suggested to them that socialism did not really exist in Poland. For the Poles, the black market was, rather, proof of socialism's reality, one which they and their compatriots were forthrightly challenging.

One such challenge to established authority was in a street theater. Its works were represented to the conference in a slide presentation. The theater, the Academy of Movement (Akademia Ruchu), has been active throughout the eighties, but it was particularly significant in the late seventies and 1980. The artistic expression of the Academy was (and is) very much up to date. Though Wojciech Krukowski, the director, did not speak about his academy in Western terms, in those terms his is a performance group, mixing media: film, dance, recitations of poetry, sculpture, painting, and theater. They present works in conventional and unconventional settings as disruptions of social, cultural, and political conventions. In one work he described, *News of the Day* (which I elsewhere observed), the theater party goes to huge housing blocks, making a racket with makeshift drums, kazoos, tambourines, and microphones. They announce a theater performance. Their audiences are workers just returned from work, children from playgrounds, mothers and fathers from food lines. The theater members recite poetry and news excerpts as the subtext of pantomime. They present a simple, straightforward parody of life in People's Poland. But their medium was more important than their message, Krukowski explained. They created theater where none had existed, without official support. Indeed, they used bureaucratic inefficiencies and local, petty political conflicts to their advantage: no one said they could not perform, so they did. Playing such games led to many official reprimands, but the group nonetheless persisted.

Another performance illustrates the Academy's ingenuity in their street actions. They presented a mime performance in the center of Warsaw, without authorization. When the militia came to stop the disruption of traffic, the group pretended to be making a film. The militia then redirected the traffic so that the filming could proceed. The Academy and militia both knew that, whereas theater is censored before performance, film is only censored after filming.

At the conference, Krukowski showed a series of slides documenting a citywide performance at a theater festival in Lodz. They mimicked socialist realist statues, played on and around public transportation, flew nonsensical banners, and, most politically provocative, formed lines leading out of meat shops to complement the real and frustrating lines leading into those shops.

When Krukowski fielded questions, the chasm that separates the political East from the political West became most apparent. Krukowski was attacked for mocking the plight of ordinary Polish citizens and for imposing theater upon them without their consent. He tried to explain that he and his group, through an innovative use of movement in unusual contexts, were freeing space from official definition and coercion, not only for themselves but for ordinary people. But the Western Europeans could not conceive of the totality of official definition affecting all people in all realms of their daily lives, and therefore they could not appreciate the Academy of Movement.

Two months later, in the shipyards of Poland, a working-class movement directed against the workers' state demonstrated more forcefully the struggle against the Party-state for an autonomous civil society, upsetting not only politics as usual in the Soviet bloc, but also the conventional understanding of politics in the West. Communists in business suits, anti-Communists in overalls, revolutionary workers attending mass during an occupation strike, secular leftists reconciling with the Catholic church, the church providing refuge for non-Communist secularists, and a self-declared, self-limiting revolution: these were among the appearances and realities of Poland's democratic opposition and of Solidarity which challenged conventional political understanding. Prevailing dichotomies— conservative and liberal, Left and Right, progressive and reactionary, capitalist and socialist—no longer were helpful in understanding political events.

Solidarność, Polish martial law, glasnost, and perestroika are now part of our political experience and vocabulary. But they are there as a challenge to our understanding, not yet understood. Totalitarian culture and its opposition have changed over time. Here I analyze those changes as a way of understanding the new frame of mind they reveal and promote.

The post-totalitarian mind, I will show, is the cultural complex initiated by autonomous agents who directly reject totalitarian culture. Most crucially, these agents deconstruct the distinctive totalitarian amalgamation of force and a purported absolute truth. They also bring into being very significant changes in the politics and language of officialdom and officially accepted critics. All these cultural changes—in autonomous culture, in officially accepted, somewhat independent culture, and in official culture (the so-called policy of glasnost)—are features of the post-totalitarian terrain, which includes the looming presence of totalitarian culture, the promise of the post-totalitarian mind, and the dangers of a neototalitarian state.

Before proceeding to the analysis of each of these components of the post-totalitarian terrain, I would like to discuss a book, Czeslaw Milosz's *The Captive Mind*. In that book Milosz reveals the deep totalitarian structure in an earlier cultural context. He sought "to create afresh the stages by which the mind gives way to compulsion from without, and to trace the road along which men in people's democracies are led on to orthodoxy."[3] Here we reconsider his rich account as an introduction to the analysis of how people are beginning to travel that road in the other direction.

Milosz's bleak book was written in bleak times, the late forties and early fifties. The wounds of the Nazi horrors still festered. Stalin's reign of terror, interrupted only by the war, was again in high gear. There was little reason to believe that totalitarianism would not be permanently characterized by such terror. Milosz's task was to explain how intellectuals with and without Communist, or even leftist, pasts came to support the new order and think in its prescribed way; how they came to have captive minds.

Milosz shows how human frailties and ambitions meet and support modern tyranny. All sorts of people come to support the new tyranny; their plurality strengthens the new order until there is no difference among them. Milosz tells of public delusions and private resistance. He explains how artists and intellectuals reap benefit from the new order. They are paid well, brought to new academies, and, following an official script, given a key role in the making of the new socialist man. As long as they follow Party dictates, they overcome artistic and intellectual isolation and are enticed by their new effectiveness. This Milosz calls "the Pill of Murti Bing." Though having swallowed the pill, the captive minds maintain some semblance of their individual integrity by gaming with censors and cultural commissars. They tell themselves that the true meaning of their work is the deep subtext, which sometimes only they can recognize.

Milosz tells us that officially provided pleasures and bad faith combine to explain the lives of writers Alpha (Jerzy Andrzejewski), Beta (Tadeusz Borowski), Gamma (Jerzy Putrament), and Delta (Konstanty Ildefons Galczynski). The stories of their lives were written in Stalinist Poland, where Gamma is a hack turned cultural commissar. Alpha, Beta, and Delta are first rate, but somehow convince themselves, willingly, that the sacrifice of their talents and individual viewpoints is desirable.

Alpha is a moralist. Before the war, he was a fairly well-known Catholic writer, who published in nationalist journals. During the war he wrote impassioned tragic stories about the non-Communist underground. After the war, he switched sides. He wrote a renowned moral tragedy with subtlety (not in the style of socialist realism), but his hero now was not a priest, as in the past, but a Communist. While he did not betray his sensibility as a moralist, he accepted the official view of historical inevitability and revolutionary resistance. Having gone that far, with the stiffening of Stalinism he joined the Party, published a self-criticism, and lost sight of any truth other than that which the Party dialecticians declared.

Beta's story is strikingly different. A survivor of Auschwitz, he was without any faith or belief even before his imprisonment. Upon return from the camps, he told stories of the living hell from the viewpoint of an accessory. He portrayed the nakedness of survivors. He described in detail the hierarchy of oppression and brutality of the "concentration universe." He purposively did not tell of the moral exemplars. He led his readers to believe that he himself became a brute, while in fact, according to fellow prisoners, he was selfless and heroic. The hardness of his view, his toughness, led him to accept official ideology in a highly idiosyncratic way. His was a revolt against Western civilization: "Christianity equals capi-

talism equals Hitlerism." This accounted for his attraction to
the new order and his acceptance of it as an inevitable execu-
tioner. Eventually he wrote journalistic party propaganda and
then committed suicide.

Gamma's route to captivity is familiar. A mediocre writer,
he gladly gave up writing for politics as a way of avoiding the
blank page.

The case of Delta again demonstrates how talented intellectuals willingly supported the powers organized against their
talents. Delta was a kind of trickster. An alcoholic with an exu-
berant imagination, he took little seriously, especially politics.
Before the war he counted Jews among his close friends and
associates, yet he wrote anti-Semitic diatribes in support of
forceful nationalism. He served the ascendant popular prince
then and after his release from a POW camp in Germany—
first in the West for a right-wing emigre audience, then, upon
his return to Poland, for the new order. His verbal dexterity
and poetic sensibility, according to Milosz, made him an en-
tertaining troubadour. As long as the Party could use him as
proof that all factions of the nation, even Catholics and rightists, supported People's Poland, he was supported lavishly.
Once Stalinist control was secure, he was silenced and dis-
counted, to be reused when required.

Milosz's portraits are of real writers, not types. He is interested in how artists and intellectuals with distinctive voices
become types, fulfilling roles serving totalitarian powers.
Galczynski (Delta) died in 1953. Borowski's (Beta's) suicide
was in 1950, though his renown has since spread; a broad
international public has studied what he so fearlessly accomplished in *This Way to the Gas Chambers, Ladies and Gentlemen*.[4] Jerzy Putrament (Gamma) became a literary official.
Andrzejewski (Alpha) found a new life as a moralist in the political opposition. He was a founding member of KOR (the
Committee to Defend Workers), the first major institution of
the democratic opposition.

Many others whose minds were captured then have since
freed themselves, most spectacularly Tadeusz Konwicki, Po-

land's leading senior novelist. He has formed a number of his major works around his shame of that period and the doubt it casts upon his present convictions.

The movement from the captive mind to a post-totalitarian mind is highly individualistic and leads in many directions. Milosz shows that when authors, artists, and intellectuals succumb to captivity they move from individuality to type, from pluralism to monism. When authors, artists, intellectuals, workers, and peasants move beyond totalitarianism they find new pluralisms, not all necessarily desirable. Milosz shows how nationalism, racism, and self-indulgence came to strengthen the totalitarianian order. Now, with post-totalitarianism, not only democracy, free expression, and human rights come to the fore. Along with these advances, the negative cultural, political, and personal motives that had been used by the totalitarians in their rise to power appear again. We should not be overly optimistic or utopian about the changes in the Soviet bloc.

Yet there is reason for hope. In the post-Stalinist era, when totalitarian terror was replaced by a totalitarianism without terror, criticism became possible, but primarily as a more open interpretation of official ideology (see chapter 3). This was the era of Marxist humanism. People of many different viewpoints could speak, but the speech had to be channelled through some version of the official syntax. For this reason, people with different views did not rationally and openly confront each other. The great advance of the post-totalitarian oppositionists is in making such rational and open confrontation a first principle (see chapters 4 and 5). With such a first principle, the politics and culture of xenophobic nationalism, racism, and self-indulgence are less likely to prevail. With glasnost this oppositional force of free public deliberation may even become an aspect of official culture. But we should not underestimate the obstacles. In this inquiry, I proceed soberly.

Over the past fifteen years I have studied the development of independent culture and politics in the "other Europe"—

East Central Europe, where independent intellectuals and artists, despite repression, have been most committed to the European Enlightenment ideals of critical inquiry, freedom, and self-governance. My major goal during this course of study was to develop a theoretical framework for understanding the sociological constitution of one manifestation of these ideals—cultural freedom. In *The Persistence of Freedom: The Sociological Implications of Polish Student Theater* and in *On Cultural Freedom: An Exploration of Public Life in Poland and America,* I analyzed the conditions that support the development of cultural works which are creatively critical of societal constraints and engage in inventive conversations with works of the past and present, keeping cultural traditions alive and promoting the formation of autonomous publics. I further attempted to apply this analysis of autonomous cultural life to an understanding of the political cultures of present-day Poland and America. I considered a specific set of theoretical issues as it persists through changing cultural, political, and economic circumstances, in order to gain a better understanding of both circumstances and issues.

Polish political changes which were directly applicable to my inquiries were much more radical over the years than I or anyone else could have imagined. I started my inquiries for relatively esoteric academic and personal reasons: I wanted to do a comparative study of theater and, living in New York and learning about the cultural and political significance of Polish theater, decided on Poland as my point of comparison with America.

In Poland, another world was opened to me, one little known in the West. It was one where cultural and political freedom were treated as lost treasures to be excavated and carefully restored. The excavation and restoration proceeded quietly, under totalitarian shadows. Few understood the importance of the enterprise. Most outsiders noticed only when the workers and intellectuals "suddenly" and directly confronted the totalitarian order in Gdansk.

Unfortunately, most often the confrontation in Gdansk was

perceived as a melodrama played out between good guys and bad guys. For Ronald Reagan, here again were freedom fighters facing the evil empire. For Leonid Brezhnev, the counterrevolution had begun. As melodrama, the story was ended by the Polish authorities with the declaration of a state of war against Polish society.

I am uncomfortable even with the serious variations on this melodramatic interpretation for three reasons. First, it does not confront the nature of totalitarianism and its limits. Second, it fails to understand the sources of collective resistance. And third, it does not consider the lasting effects of political and cultural resistance. For these reasons, I began working on this manuscript.

I shifted my analytic focus. Instead of considering a stable set of theoretical questions concerning cultural freedom, I focused on the political and cultural changes in the Soviet bloc. In order to appreciate the emerging cultural and political alternatives in that part of the world, I sought to understand the new democratic theories of politics propounded by people such as Adam Michnik, Miklos Haraszti, and Vaclav Havel and the new cultural works of authors such as Stanislaw Baranczak, George Konrad, and Milan Kundera. To understand their world, I sought to develop a more adequate understanding of totalitarianism, its continuities and changes.

My treasured association with people active in the posttotalitarian cultural and political life of Poland inspired this work. My goal is to make sense of their world for those in my world. Such a task is not as difficult as it may appear; we share fundamental ideals of democracy and democratic culture. Stanislaw Baranczak shows us again what a public poem is, in the tradition of Walt Whitman. Adam Michnik reminds us what democracy is and what democratic commitment can mean, in a sense combining the intellectual and moral traditions linking Martin Luther King, Jr., to Abraham Lincoln and Thomas Jefferson. The democratic struggles against totalitarianism bring something new into the world, but it is linked to the democratic struggles of the past. Thus we can identify it, and the freshness of their democratic commitments may serve as an inspiration for us to reinvigorate ours.

On a more practical plane, the post-totalitarian oppositionists demonstrate in their writings and actions the facticity of totalitarianism, and they can help us understand the nature of the changes in Gorbachev's Kremlin. In my previous work I began with the premise that the notion of a complex totalitarian society made no sense. I took as proof of this that opposition to totalitarianism was a persistent component of the purportedly totalitarian social order. Here I do not overlook this observation, but more closely consider the phenomenology of official cultural life and its penetration into everyday life. I thus seek to understand the distinctive qualities of the official totalitarian culture and its relationship to civil society.

I start by trying to answer one difficult question: what is totalitarianism? I close by trying to answer another difficult question: is totalitarianism withering away? In between I explore the world of modern tyranny, judge the prospects of its opposition, and consider a new frame of mind—the post-totalitarian mind.

I

Totalitarianism

O N E

What is Totalitarianism?

CONSIDER A WORLD where the publicly spoken word and the published written word have a single, official set of meanings, sanctioned by the state; where political authority is legitimated through disbelief; where contact between individuals is regularly qualified by political suspicion and paranoia; and where the norms of daily life are constantly subject to official revision. In this world, the past is routinely rewritten; only the future is officially certain. This is today's totalitarianism. It is a world poorly understood. As a result, no cure has been developed other than radical transformation—which seems impossible in the nuclear age.

In the East Germany of 1953, the Hungary and Poland of 1956, the Czechoslovakia of 1968, and the Poland of 1980–81, subjects turned citizens attempted to achieve fundamental political transformations but failed. Yet behind such extraordinary actions are ongoing struggles to sustain alternatives to totalitarianism in everyday life. In the pages that follow I analyze such struggles, both as they emerge from and develop within the official totalitarian order and as they are constituted autonomously and directed against the order. I consider the social and political dilemmas of everyday life and their official rendering, Newspeak. I investigate closely the constitution of autonomous public life through the collective action of Solidarity and the literary imagination and political thought of East Central European artists and intellectuals.

My chief goal in this inquiry is to illuminate the cultural and political alternatives to modern tyranny. To do this we must first understand what totalitarianism is. This is no small matter. The term is often used too freely by politicians and overly tendentious thinkers. Confusion reigns about the concept, and cautious political and social scientists have all but abandoned it. Here, then, I analyze the concept's shifting meanings and the changing sociopolitical worlds to which it refers. I will attempt to demonstrate that totalitarianism is best understood as the cultural form necessary for modern tyranny. While societies may not, and indeed probably cannot, be completely controlled or totalized, and polities inevitably will not proceed along one simple chain of command, the projects of totalization and absolute command emanate from totalitarian culture.

The social project of totalization and the culture of totalitarianism distinguish modern from old-fashioned tyranny. I hope to demonstrate this through a careful analysis of political actors and creative artists. Such inquiry necessarily starts with political judgment. It is my strong conviction that we must develop social and political theories that sensitize us to modern barbarism so that we can effectively oppose it. Theories which minimize or ignore the distinctive qualities of modern tyranny lead not only to ignorance, but to apathy and inaction. With this in mind I will make some simple, though not uncontroversial, judgments. I hope that their soundness will be evaluated not only on the basis of political prejudice, but on a careful reconsideration of the cultural constitution of totalitarianism and free public action, i.e., of Newspeak and its alternatives.

Life really is different in an old-fashioned tyranny than in a totalitarian order. Though traditional autocracies may sometimes be more unpleasant and brutal, human ontology is not undergoing a conscious, politically enforced systematic redefinition. Conventionally, some spheres of autonomy are respected by traditional tyrants. It is exactly these spheres—of friends and family, education and religion—which are the primary targets of the totalitarians. However, to substitute totalitarianism for traditional tyranny is not a mark of human progress; to support traditional tyranny in the name of democracy as a means to avoid totalitarianism is the height of hypocrisy. This essay seeks to demonstrate that we must distinguish between traditional autocracy and distinctly modern tyranny so that we can search for and understand alternatives to both.

The Emergence of the Concept

The neologism *totalitarianism* was coined to name a monstrous human creation and a tragic set of human experiences. The ongoing struggle to capture its meaning results in shifting usages and referents, suggesting scientific unreliability. Thus, in the 1968 edition of the *International Encyclopedia of the Social Sciences,* the entry under *totalitarianism* dismisses the notion.[1] The persistence of the term as part of our political vocabulary, however, indicates a practical, though not unproblematic, wisdom. It involves a groping search to understand the new tyranny so that it may be resisted.

The first critical referent of totalitarianism was Nazi Germany. Central features of nazism were generalized and applied to the Soviet Union and at times to the fascist regimes of Italy and Spain. Such generalization was a response to new historical experiences that challenged both social and political theory, as well as organized political practice.

Faced with a series of pressing political questions, the dominant perspectives of liberalism, conservativism, and Marxism confronted the interwar political experience awkwardly at best. For liberals: could nazism be considered a new form of reaction, fundamentally conservative in orientation and identifiable with the fascism of Italy and Francoism in Spain, while Soviet Communism is set apart as a new form of jacobinism? For conservatives: could the threat of bolshevism, with its atheism, destruction of tradition, and the obliteration of human distinctiveness, be distinguished from nazism, which was purportedly grounded in the experience of a nation? For Marxists: could nazism, along with Francoism and fascism, be adequately labeled as an advanced form of capitalism in its final crisis? Could the similarity between the repressive practices and cultural productions of these regimes, and the practices and productions of the Soviet Union, be ignored? For many—liberals, conservatives, and Marxists—the Left/Right, progressive/conservative, capitalist/socialist dichotomies formulated in the political contexts of the late eighteenth and nineteenth centuries did not adequately serve as a guide to new historical phenomena. A radically new political theory was called for.

Could conventional social science, with its theories of progress, modernization, and differentiation, address this need? Could it account for mass terror, party rule, secret police, concentration camps, heroes of labor and race, and genocide? Could it analyze the prevailing situation of European life of the late thirties and early forties? Clearly the answer to each of the questions was and is no. A different approach to the experience of Western civilization is in order if we are to comprehend the totalitarian challenge.

For the liberal, the total loss of individual freedom in the Soviet Union and Nazi Germany may be of the greatest concern. For the conservative, the disregard for traditional value and the cumulative accomplishments of Western civilization may be the most pressing. And for the Marxist, the greatest problem may be perceived as the frustration of class liberation and self-determination. But despite the differences, each of these political projects held by social scientists as citizens was challenged by new sorts of political and social movements. The first task was to ascertain how these movements and the regimes they brought into being were related to each other and to previous sorts of political movements, parties, and regimes. This then provided the basis for an examination of the origins and life of totalitarianism. It was and is not only an empirical problem, but a normative one as well.

When the central fact of the new era was defined as the demise of the liberal economy, with the development of new managerial techniques that control economic, political and social life, nazism, Soviet communism and New Dealism could be identified and purported to be historically inevitable. Yet this thesis, advanced by James Burnham,[2] not only ignored central features distinguishing nazism, Soviet communism, and New Dealism, it fit no existing political project and no prevailing set of normative judgments. Such historical inevitability was simply not accepted, and people, indeed nation-states, acted according to other judgments.

Judgments articulated during the war must be distinguished from those made before and after the war; not simply because the totalitarian objects changed during and after conflict, but because alternative political projects changed. The invasion of Poland forced Western liberals and conservatives to reconsider any notions of nazism as a lesser evil than, or even a bulwark against, bolshevism, or as fundamentally a nationalist movement with some unpleasant qualities. The Nazi advance into the Soviet Union forced the Soviet Marxists to abandon the identification of nazism as an advanced stage of capitalism and the characterization of the war as an intracapitalist struggle. It was only after the war that liberals, conservatives, and some Western radicals were again willing to identify their wartime allies with nazism, and that Soviet Marxists remembered that nazism was an advanced stage of capitalism in crisis.

Such shifts of appraisal have more to do with the changing structure of geopolitics than with changes in the totalitarian object or serious changes in intellectual perspective, judgment, and interpretation. During the war fascism could become a general term applicable to Italian, German, and Spanish systems, and it was viewed as distinct from Soviet socialism. After the war, and for some, especially in the French intellectual world, a good deal after the war, the Soviet gulag and the Nazi system of concentration and death camps were publicly declared to be of the same generic type.

When the enormity of Soviet terror comes to be perceived as comparable to Nazi terror, the idea that fascism is a rightist phenomenon, encompassing the experiences of Italy, Spain, and Germany, absolutely distinct from Stalinism, viewed as an unfortunate degeneration of the positively humane socialist ideal, becomes untenable, even for those on the Left. With this perception the notion of totalitarianism gains cogency. The

Soviet and Nazi cases are seen as being archetypical. The Italian and Spanish experiences, while horrific, appear to be of a different order, as do the people's republics of Eastern Europe.

But the sociological definition of *totalitarianism* is still far from transparent. Two distinct strategies of characterization have been presented: one reveals the nature of totalitarian orders according to their origins, the other according to their everyday function. The study of origins has led to profound insights, but makes difficult an understanding of the persistent totalitarian challenge. The study of everyday functions has tended to be too facile, presenting models of totalitarian politics and society that have had questionable empirical validity and normative consequences. Here we shall critically review these positions as the sociological prelude to a cultural approach. Guiding our inquiry is the fact that the totalitarian world is ever-changing, and the search for an understanding and for practical alternatives should be informed by a broad variety of political norms. Any adequate theory of totalitarianism, then, must address the problems of change and plurality. As we shall observe, the chief problem with some approaches to totalitarianism is that they focus upon one moment in its history. Other approaches fail even more fundamentally because they are dogmatically attached to only one political alternative to the new tyranny. Today it is primarily the neoconservatives who substitute one dogmatism for another.

Genetic Definition

Hannah Arendt provided the classic formulation, *The Origins of Totalitarianism.*[3] In her work, totalitarianism is an alternative outcome of Western modernization. Central factors contributing to its origins are the development of the nation-state, modern anti-Semitism, race thinking and pan-national social movements, imperialism, the rise of the masses, and the loss of fixed ethical standards, which are replaced by terror and the celebration of violence. These elements of the origins are presented as a demonic tale of modernization, very much tied to the distinctive development of Western social, economic, and cultural practices. As do modern democracies, totalitarian movements reach out to elements of the population previously excluded from political practice. But the inclusion is of a perverse sort. At the center of the totalitarian world are the primary commitments of modernity—individualism, release from tradition, change as a positive value, moral relativism, instrumental rationality, even enlightenment—but these are reorganized and deformed to support totalized domination.

The deformation of the emancipatory project of modernity and enlightenment is processed, according to Arendt, through an elaborate, onion-like structure of Party organization designed to support a fictitious ideology in the face of an inconvenient observable world. Individualism becomes the loss of self. Traditions are abandoned, and all morals are viewed as relative, because the Party theory, as interpreted by the Party elite, has discovered the underlying mystery of the chaotic, immoral world. Party practice, be it racial purification or struggle against class enemies, confirms scientific prediction. Genocide takes on a semblance of normality because it is a clear instrumental means to an end determined to be inevitable by Party theory.

The theoretical knowledge deeply embedded in the onion's core is insulated from the world outside by the differentiation of elite structures, Party memberships, and Party front organizations. The elites are most committed to the theory and most detached from the world, while front members are most in touch with the world but merely sympathetic and least committed to the theory. In such a fashion, theorists of millenia comfortably ignore the observable world, and those who must live in the world come to imagine the profound wisdom of those who ignore it. Repetition of the wisdom indicates its inner consistency, which comes to be recognized by the elite and the masses as the basis of wisdom's truth.

Yet for the elite the system of control, of organizational discipline, is the theory; the actual content of the theory is of little import, being completely malleable. "What binds these men [the elite] together is a firm and sincere belief in human omnipotence. Their moral cynicism, their belief that everything is permitted, rests on the solid conviction that everything is possible."[4] Such cynicism leads from the ideational terror of propaganda with occasional outbursts of violence to a political regime with its basis in terror. The archetypal locus of the political order is the concentration camp. As a pure institution of terror, it is the definitive institution of the totalitarian order.

Arendt's great accomplishment was to bring onto center stage the uniqueness of totalitarianism. She forthrightly demonstrated that the orders of Stalin and Hitler cannot be considered as manifestations of something else. She showed the connections between the development of totalitarianism and the previous experiences of the modern West, but clearly delineated the juncture between these and the totalitarian experience.

However, the demise of national socialism and moderations in Soviet repressive practices have obscured her delineation, leading some to modify the concept of totalitarianism, others to abandon the notion completely, and still others to use the notion as descriptive of the discrete horrific experiences of the recent past. Arendt herself knew that post–World War II political developments presented a renewed challenge to political theory. Revised editions of *The Origins* included her reflections on the Hungarian revolution and the liberalization of Soviet practice. For her, totalitarianism only occurred when tyrants acted as if there were no constraints; they acted on the premise that everything is possible. Qualification, therefore, had to be applied to both the experience of the Soviet satellites, given the Hungarian evidence that citizens (no longer subjects) were capable of free political action in opposition to the Communist order, and Khrushchev's Soviet Union, given the flowering of a critical culture during the thaw.

Theoretical Modification: Political and Empirical

The cold war, the pursuit of peaceful coexistence and detente, and the new cold war between the superpowers have shaped

modifications of the concept of totalitarianism. The idea of
totalitarianism without terror was constructed to convey a
relative normalization of life in the Soviet bloc without abandoning the cold-war notion that the contemporary world is
divided between the free and unfree worlds.[5] Models of convergence linked industrialization with democratization (understood as the development of Western political institutions)
and promised that totalitarian society would become more
pluralistic, given the technological necessities of industrial
society and peaceful coexistence.[6] Detente promised a new
world order on the basis of such ideas, with the pluralistic imperatives of industrial growth undermining totalitarian rule.
An understanding that these ideas substituted hopefulness for
reasoning provided the intellectual grounds for the pursuit of
the new cold-war ideology of the eighties, though the ideas
surfaced again among the new cold-warriors when they proposed engaging the Soviets in an intensive arms race for the
purposes of promoting a Soviet economic breakdown.[7] They
maintained that the incompatibility between economic vitality
and the totalitarian order would lead to such a breakdown.

More is involved in these understandings of the totalitarian
world than the shifting contours of geopolitics. Models of
convergence and notions of totalitarianism without terror are
products of more rigorous empirical investigation of the Soviet bloc. After Stalin's death, the relaxation of the international tensions and Soviet repression did not only change
the totalitarian object. It changed, as well, the possibilities of
the investigation of the object. Not only the policies and ideological pronouncements of the political elite, but the everyday
life of families, schools, and factories could be examined.

Arendt elegantly connected totalitarianism with a special
type of scientistic ideological reasoning, a reasoning which
starts with one simple premise that unlocks the key to history
and the nature of the human order. Every and any aspect of
the future and the nature of the human world is then deduc-
ible. The connection between the premise and reality sometimes must be enforced in the most brutal fashion. Racial theory reveals that the Jewish people are members of a dying

race, *therefore,* genocide. But this connection between ideology and practice does not only take such horrific forms. It
also helps order daily life. Thus the private lives of Communist party members, and theoretically of all other members of
Soviet-type societies, are monitored according to the dictates
of official ideology. All sorts of private activities, from child
rearing to dating, follow correct and incorrect patterns. This
led early theorists of totalitarianism to posit the existence of a
totalitarian society. The problem with this material deduction, however, is that a closer look reveals the existence of a
problematic distance between Party norms and pronouncements and the practices of everyday life. From a distance,
without empirical investigation, it seems that the goal of political control of every aspect of social life, public and private,
is realized. Upon closer investigation, the variable social resistances to control become objects of inquiry. The Party
does not simply impose its will; it attempts to impose its
will on a group of human beings engaged in stable relationships that often resist control and direction in both subtle
and not so subtle ways. These relationships include those of
the family, of schools and universities, of communities and
churches, specific factories and bureaucracies. Empirical studies of Communist-controlled and -directed societies reveal significant variation in malleability, both among societies and
within each society from one institutional sector to another.[8]

Sensitivity to such findings has shaped recent theories of totalitarianism as much as changes in the geopolitical atmosphere. Beyond a reductive understanding of the changing
political fashions of political theory lies solid material which
challenges the usefulness of positing the existence of totalitarianism in contemporary societies of the Soviet bloc.

There were and are a variety of responses to this challenge.
The most straightforward was simply to abandon the very notion of totalitarianism.[9] Even in the most extreme circumstances, such as concentration camps, resistance to control
persists in predictable patterns.[10] In less difficult circumstances,
such as in the nation-states of the Soviet bloc, there flourishes

resistance of both grand (e.g., the Hungarian revolution and Polish Solidarity) and petty varieties (e.g., the Soviet black and gray markets). Such empirical evidence reveals that totalitarianism may be at most an ideological boast. Elevated to a theory of society, it does little more than take seriously the repressive aspiration of the repressive force.

Model Construction

A methodological variation on this empirical critical theme involves the construction of models of totalitarianism which seek to measure degrees of totalitarianism versus pluralism. It is conceded that totalitarian society is a construct, simplifying a more complicated reality. But it is explained that this simplification represents the propensity of certain modern tyrants to assert total control on the basis of an ideology. Pluralistic society is presented as the alternative, where a plurality of social, political, and cultural forces coexist in one order. This too is understood as a simplification, in that some shared common ground, other than civil war, must exist—a consensus regarding values, contractual arrangement, rules of conflict. Comparison is facilitated through these simplifications.

According to this methodology, a totalitarian society has a highly concentrated power, legitimated by the intensive ideological commitments promoting radical social transformations; in a pluralistic society, power is dispersed, though based in consensus, and politics does not promote a univocal teleology. The ideal types of totalitarian and pluralistic society are presented as being qualitatively different, but differences are empirically confirmed through quantitative measures. Thus the notion of totalitarianism can be kept alive as it accounts for differences in everyday life of contemporary societies. The key difference is the degree of state control of social activities. It has been observed that in a pluralistic society such as the United States, only military forces are totally or nearly totally controlled by the state, whereas in a totalitarian society such as the Soviet Union, a broad set of activities is so controlled, ranging from the military to education, mass media, health services, housing, and sports. In the Soviet Union, for all intents and purposes, no activity is free of the state; whereas, in the United States, a broad range of activities is.[11]

Given that this approach illuminates vast differences between modern societies and overcomes the problematic empirical referent of genetic theories of totalitarianism, such comparisons have clear advantages over earlier formulations. But from the point of view of a normatively animated political and social theory,[12] these advantages are counterbalanced by an enormous disadvantage: *such empirically grounded modeling washes out the historical distinctiveness of twentieth-century totalitarian movements and regimes, and too readily severs their connection with the project of modernity.*

When the notion of totalitarianism is abandoned, the distinctiveness of totalitarianism and its connection with modernity are directly lost. Ironically, the totalitarianism/pluralism modeling, largely constructed to avoid such a loss, bestows it. The primary normative reason for considering totalitarianism as a new sort of political and social phenomenon is the uniqueness of twentieth-century barbarism. But if we follow the totalitarianism/pluralism models, all sorts of ancient autocracies might come to be labeled totalitarian. The only specifically modern attribute which such models include is the use of advanced technologies for mass communications and surveillance.[13] The German death camps, the Soviet gulag, and the "depopulation" of Cambodia become incidents in the modern world, not events which constitute the modern human condition.

Arendt demonstrated that totalitarian practice redefines the relationship between reason and violence. She presents these changed relationships as they emerged in *The Origins*. The prisoner Eichmann personifies these relationships phenomenologically.[14] Eichmann was reasonable and normal. He had an abililty to use a language that hid his own evil deeds not only from others but also from himself, so he understood himself as a good man who actually had affection for the Jewish people. He illuminates the link between the normal man of the modern world and the modern monster. By frankly and pro-vocatively speaking about this link, Arendt aroused a great deal of controversy.[15] But she presented as well a theoretical and practical challenge: to think and act remembering that the worse than imaginable happened, *and* that the world that brought it into being—the modern world—is our world. Are we, or our neighbors, potential Eichmanns? Is a politics legiti-mated by a silent majority an ominous foreboding of the mass movements of the interwar era? Has the liberalized post-Stalinist order abandoned its totalitarian roots? Can we think about such matters and still act reasonably in a complex tech-nological order? To answer these questions requires the nor-mative sensibility of theorists such as Arendt along with the tough-mindedness of the critics of theories of totalitarianism. The neoconservatives aspire to this position. They know well that distinctions must be made between modern tyranny and traditional autocracy. But they make distinctions for narrow political purposes, ignoring the crucial connection between modernity and totalitarianism.

The Neoconservative Approach

The heyday of totalitarian theories was in the forties and fifties; the critical empiricists had their day in the sixties and early seventies. In the United States over the past ten years, the idea of totalitarianism has been abandoned to the neoconser-vatives. In the hands of Norman Podhoretz, Irving Kristol, and especially Jeane Kirkpatrick, totalitarianism has again been contrasted with more traditional forms of tyranny.[16] They argue that, whereas totalitarianism presents no capacity for internal reform, traditional tyranny has such capacity. The geopolitical referent for this argument is transparent. Present-day Marxist politics or Soviet-supported movements and states are said to be totalitarian and incompatible with democratiza-tion. Anti-Communist dictatorships, on the other hand, are traditional autocracies and reformable. Therefore aid to right-wing dictators in opposition to Communists serves democratic purposes.

On its own terms this sort of argument is debatable. In
Hungary (1956), Czechoslovakia (1968), and Poland (1981),
the limits on the societal transformation were set most directly by the Red Army, not the totalitarian system.[17] Nonetheless, the distinction Kirkpatrick makes is not exclusively
ideological. It serves more than the interest of Reagan's mili-
tarization of American foreign policy. In Kirkpatrick's proposition that "totalitarianism is utopianism come to power,"[18]
she attempts to reflect again upon modern horrors, and in
doing so she recaptures the critical element of the theory of
totalitarianism. But by her definition, utopianism seems to include all potential this-worldly alternatives to the status quo,
and totalitarianism seems to include all tyrannies that seek to
correct injustices instead of accepting them. It follows from
her argument that Tito was totalitarian, while Franco was
not. She identifies herself with the Burkean conservative tradition and takes any reasoned critiques of existing customs as
proto-totalitarianism. From this perspective, all political projects of the left appear totalitarian.

Kirkpatrick, unlike Arendt, writes from a politically comfortable position quite similar to Burke's.[19] One can more easily
sing the praises of habit and political customs when these include traditions of tolerance, pluralism, and self-governance.
From a position of such comfort, in that totalitarian movements do encompass radical political projects, any radical political project may appear dangerously totalitarian. But when
democratic traditions are understood to be enfeebled or under
duress, as they must be understood in the twentieth century,
radical projects appear to be in order.

Arendt's political theory is based on a radical republican
project; this is most evident in her writings on the ancient
polis, the American revolution, and the Hungarian workers'
councils.[20] She knew that the constitution of such a project
was necessary because the civilized political and cultural traditions of the West had ruptured in the twentieth century.[21]
Without tradition, and being "in dark times," we must create
a new beginning. "Beginning, before it becomes a historical

event, is the supreme capacity of man; politically, it is identical with man's freedom."[22] This is a call for radical action as a fundamental postscript to totalitarianism.

Kirkpatrick knows that totalitarianism is an important analytic term because it "demystifies modern tyranny,"[23] but by considering the term from a narrow, conservative perspective within a liberal society, she avoids confronting the connection between totalitarianism and modernity. In fact, by focusing analysis on the problem of distinguishing unpleasant friends from unpleasant enemies, she obfuscates the place of totalitarianism in modernity.[24]

Totalitarianism, Modernity, and Solidarity

We can perceive this failure clearly by serious reflection on past experiences and future possibilities; by thinking, as Arendt put it, between past and future.[25] In such a way we can achieve a critical perspective on modernity. Our reflections must involve more than simple projections from the present. Such projection, in fact, is part of the cultural problem, being an instance of the link between modern culture and totalitarian culture.[26] A special combination of historical and utopian thought is necessary. We need to consider a meaningful past that frees us from the limitations of the present. We must imagine alternative futures not as necessities but as possibilities. In that way the present historical condition need not seem natural, the way things have always been and always will be.

This approach to past and future contrasts with the positivism of modernization and of futurist studies which purport to know the future by projecting trends forward, never escaping the logic of the present. It contrasts as well with the totalitarian approach, which uses the key to past and present—some simple proposition concerning race or class relations—to unlock the future.

The fallacy of the positivist approach is that it assumes a mechanical stability in human relations leaving no room for freedom, for a new beginning. The totalitarian imagery is mechanical as well, but much more brutally so. In it the machine is a deep structure, its underlying logic illuminating the truth of empirical world, present and past. Force must be used in bringing about the inevitable working out of the logic in the future. Not only is there no room for the freedom of political action, the only available political action is repressive. Freedom is defined by the perceived necessity of realizing the inevitable future.

The totalitarian confrontation with modernity involves a simple acceptance of some of its aspects, ones which facilitate the manufacture of the prescribed version of humanity (the Soviet man, the proper Aryan) and the brutal rejection of its liberating aspects, which may run counter to prescription. The liberal and conservative critiques of totalitarianism reject the brutality but never consider its connection with modernity. Recent political and cultural developments in East Central Europe do address these connections in an empirically sound way, with full awareness of the uniqueness of totalitarianism. In addressing the connections in this fashion, they may be interpreted as outlining a post-totalitarian theory of totalitarianism.

Solidarity and Post-Totalitarian Theory

From the point of view of earlier theories of totalitarianism, a movement such as Solidarity should not appear in a totalitarian order, nor should theories on the nature of the totalitarian order appear, nor should subtle political strategy be developed. But all of this did happen, and most of the agents who brought these events into being self-consciously understand that they live in a totalitarian order.

Here we face not one simple paradox but a complex of paradoxes. The people of the Soviet bloc have been deeply damaged by the political order under which they have lived for the last forty years or more. A historical darkness surrounds them. They dimly perceive the world outside their immediate social orbit, where social appearances may often be masks rather than symbols of social realities. They have not quite occupied the world of Orwell's 1984, but that work of fiction does build on a lived experience.

In the experience of ordinary people of the Soviet bloc, world history is regularly rewritten. Censorship and propaganda not only control perception but distort it in complicated ways. Information is limited, and available interpretation is skewed in the direction favorable to officialdom and its ideology, which is commonly known. This leads to a straightforward lack of knowledge and perspective, and also to assumptions by the critically predisposed that information is probably available for opposing perspectives, which therefore *must* be correct. Contemporary examples of the latter include: the death squads of El Salvador must be a fabrication, and the Sandinista revolution is simply an example of Soviet imperialism, since official information and interpretation point to the opposite conclusions; the Soviet Union must be the source of all that is wrong with Eastern European societies, since officially it is responsible for all that is right; the United States must be completely free of responsibility for the arms race, since it is officially responsible for it.

The deepest shadow cast over the people of the Soviet bloc is found in the realm of interpersonal relations. Communication in factories and universities, in schools and government bureaus, is mediated by an official language which is referential almost exclusively to itself. "Everyone knows" that a promotion in the workplace is determined by political patronage and favor exchange, but this is communicated officially through catch phrases such as "work for society," "Party spirit," and "committedness to the building of socialism." Though "everyone" may know this, exactly how these official phrases indicate real political workings is always problematic. A broad array of human relationships is based, therefore, on uncertain grounds. From the point of view of Eastern Europe, Orwell's most striking achievement in *1984* very well may be his depiction of how a totalitarian order perverts human relations. When a person gets involved in the workings of the official order, as almost everyone must, it is never certain who can and who cannot be trusted, what the meanings of spoken words are, and how distanced an individual is from the jargon he is forced to use. The way Kremlinologists must scan official statements for hints of the real intent of the Soviet leadership is a reflection of the way Eastern Europeans must interpret their everyday social lives.

From the midst of these shadows comes a most effective approach to a theory of totalitarianism. It is shaped by a deep sense of fallibility and insecurity, given the Eastern Europeans' perception of their world. It may be best labelled as post-totalitarian social theory. It is empirically sound because it is an approach to a lived, everyday experience. It is normatively sound because it builds upon an understanding that this everyday experience is radically rotten. This post-totalitarian frame of mind is my primary object of investigation. We can observe how it became the collective experience of a society.

The very basis of the empirical revision of the theory of totalitarianism is the starting point of post-totalitarianism. The distance between the ideological conception of the social order and the actual workings of the social order (pluralistically understood) is a lived experience of every subject of a totalitarian order. Officially, the Party theory of Marxist Leninism may hold the key to industrial planning and economic well-being, setting prescribed production levels. Yet mechanics know they must use unofficial markets if they are to keep the industrial plants functioning, and workers know that without the unofficial economy, they and their families would not have sufficient food, clothing, and shelter. All who must act unofficially (i.e., contrary to prescribed demands by official ideology) understand that doing so can lead to negative sanctions ranging from loss of pay or work to the extreme instance of official terrorism, that is, loss of life.

The operation of the order in ways contrary to official prescription is a necessary, but not sufficient, proof of liberalism or pluralism. Officialdom may tolerate a great deal of unorthodox activity, but the unorthodox know the nature of official prerogative. At any moment their activity could be terminated. In this way the juncture persists between the official ideology of social life and social life itself. Functional pluralism of the economy, culture, political bodies, and other social institutions leads a precarious existence alongside totalitarian control. Totalitarian control and functional pluralism are not opposites, but component parts of a single social order.

The starting point of the Polish democratic opposition, and later of Solidarity, was an understanding that the totalitarian Party-state and Polish society, though forcibly interrelated, must be analytically distinguished. Politically the social forces must be strengthened, narrowing the reach of, and eventually extinguishing, totalitarianism. The guiding social imagery was that of the state versus civil society—in the language of Solidarity, the authorities versus society. The means for the strengthening of society varied and were heatedly debated.

This was all sparked by a spontaneous food riot in 1976. Such reactive protests to arbitrary official policies have been common enough in the Soviet bloc. Illegal strikes are regular occurrences in Yugoslavia; they existed on a mass scale in Romania in 1978 and have even occurred, with little publicity, in the Soviet Union. In Poland such strikes have been the primary precipitant of regime change in the postwar era.

But the strikes of 1976 were different. The regime quickly retracted proposed increases in food prices, officially after "consultations with the nation," but actually in response to the riots. Protestors were punished. Dissident intellectuals organized first a relief fund for the punished, then an information bulletin concerning their fate and the conditions of Polish workers.

Rapidly such activity expanded. Small unofficial unions were established. A broad spectrum of underground news bulletins, magazines, journals and books was published; distinct political movements were formed; alternative educational institutions were established. All of this was built on the image of the society versus the state.

The activity was amazingly broad, given the repressive ambitions and apparatus of the regime. In other Communist-controlled and -directed societies of Eastern Europe and the Soviet Union, nothing approaching the activity in Poland had ever existed. Still, this activity had more in common with the dissident movements of the Soviet Union and its bloc than with the social movements of the West. Though the activists, publishers, writers, and editors openly included their names, addresses, and telephone numbers on publications and invited broad participation, opposition activity remained confined to a relatively narrow social circle.

Then, in the summer of 1979, John Paul II visited Poland. Suddenly society saw itself set apart from the authorities. The strategy of the opposition was to act as if Poland were free: to engage in opposition activity openly and to write and speak without regard to censorship or political taboo. This strategy became the lived experience of a great majority of the Polish people. They celebrated a religious, cultural, and even political commitment which was contrary to the dominant political order. In the absence of officialdom at John Paul's processions and masses, they themselves collectively observed the juncture between society and state. What everybody had been subjectively and privately experiencing in an atomized fashion in all official interactions was collectively experienced and shared.

Solidarity built upon this experience in August of 1980. It sought to represent society against the totalitarian order. It did not propose overt political change; rather, it sought to expand a zone of independence from totalitarian definitions of control, to detotalize parts of the social order. Formally, this was a modest reform program. The repeated assertion that Solidarity was a simple trade-union movement was a representation of this modesty. But of course a great deal was involved in this "simple" assertion. Polish society sought to get official recognition for the coexistence of pluralism and totalitarianism, and in so doing it sought to unmask the fictive ideology of totalitarianism.

In Solidarity, an alternative center of authority had developed. The issue was how expansive this center was to be and on what ground it should meet the authorities. Before August 1980, the opposition sought to be autonomous from the state. But since they were on the peripheries of consequential economic and political life, they did not have to contemplate where the realm of society ended and authority began. They could even take advantage of the gray zone between the world of officialdom and the world of opposition. A group of officially well-placed intellectuals and officials organized their own frontlike organization, DiP (Experience and the Future), which sought to mediate between the forces of society and officialdom. After August 1980, the zone between officialdom and society was used by the former to reassert its control over the latter. Even after the "state of war" was declared, new state-controlled unions were formed which were said to be formally independent of the Party-state apparatus and have a right to strike. The Solidarity leadership and membership knew what this meant. They understood that it was not an attempt to compromise with the forces of society, but to compromise these forces. The new unions have been remarkably unpopular, even though membership facilitates access to scarce resources such as housing, schooling, and opportunities to travel abroad and take paid vacations.

This is not the place to tell in detail the story of Solidarity's struggle.[27] Here we need to move on to the general understanding of totalitarianism which emerges from these struggles. The understanding revolves around a dichotomy: not of empirical totalitarianism versus empirical pluralism, nor of totalitarianism versus authoritarianism, but of totalitarianism versus a free public domain. To appreciate post-totalitarian theory as it emerges from practical struggles, we must recognize that the earlier theories of totalitarianism are connected to present-day practical politics.

Totalitarian Theories and Political Policy

The alternative theoretical dichotomies concerning totalitarianism present alternative links between past and future and, as such, alternative plans for practical action.

The empirical opposition of pluralism and totalitarianism, already described, implies that a single process of modernization lies between past and future. Modernization is generally viewed as a social good. It includes such processes as secularization, urbanization, social differentiation (functional and structural), increased economic productivity, democratization, individuation, and rationalization (organizational and technological). These processes come into being in opposition to traditional ways of life, as resistance. The manner in which the traditions are attacked defines the political character of the modernization process, i.e., the movement between the premodern past and the modern future. While some theorists of totalitarianism posit that its repressive structures are necessary simply to unlock the restrictive hold of the past, and that subsequently liberal, individualistic, democratic practices will flourish (i.e., once the deviant societal types catch up),[28] other theorists posit that modern democracy and dictatorship represent alternative political economies for modern social orders.[29] Theories of convergence are based upon the first position; theories of competition between the free and Communist worlds are based upon the second. Common to both theoretical positions is a progressive evolutionary theory of social development leading to modernity (presented in a more or less subtle manner). But the positions do lead to different sorts of practical politics, in the arena of international relations and for opposition movements within totalitarian orders. On the international front, economic development of totalitarian societies should be promoted if we posit that the restrictive policies would no longer be necessary with such development. But if we posit the possibility of two sorts of modernity, economic development would only serve to strengthen oppression. The totalitarian threat, then, must be faced politically. The same lessons hold for the internal opposition to totalitarianism. If modernity naturally leads to the devolution of totalitarian controls, the best policy for the opposition is to bide its time, to let social development take its natural course, even to promote the rationalization of the system. But if the possibility of a totalitarian modernity is acknowledged, such a position must be forcefully opposed, along with the policies of the totalitarian polity.

The neoconservative opposition of totalitarianism and

authoritarianism concedes the viability of a totalitarian modernity and calls for battle against it. The battle, not modernization, lies between past and future. In fact, as we have observed, many aspects of modernity are identified with the totalitarian project by conservative theorists. The emancipation from traditional constraints (the family, locality, class, etc.) is viewed with suspicion, because without such constraints insatiable rising expectations can lead to a "twilight of authority" and a totalitarian fever.[30] Premodern social relations come to appear to embody an ancient wisdom. Ironically, in the name of democracy and a very modern conception of (liberal) freedom, traditional forms of autocracy and despotism are included as part of the free versus the totalitarian world. International politics take on the aspect of a moral crusade. The evil of totalitarianism not only overshadows the unpleasantness one might find in the free world, but it overshadows the complexities of the totalitarian world. The varieties of opposition to totalitarian rule are ignored. Afghan fundamentalists, Nicaraguan Contras, and Polish labor activists are all identified as freedom fighters, while those who oppose traditional oppressions are condemned as terrorists.

In this mode of thought, anti-Communism, as the battle against the evil empire, takes precedence over all other political and ethical commitments. The Western battle over international human rights is largely fought between the modernist liberals, who maintain a positive, normative commitment to individual liberty and some form of representational democracy worldwide, and the neoconservatives, who view the world as engaged in a moral anti-Communist crusade and cannot concern themselves too deeply with the problem of liberty in foreign lands.

The contrasting post-totalitarian position has liberal elements but involves significantly more than this. It is a real alternative to neoconservatism and modernizing liberalism. Between past and future is neither a moral crusade nor modernization, but a struggle for a public domain, where people can speak and act freely in the presence of others. The resemblance to the normative position of Arendt is striking. But whereas Arendt's analysis focuses upon the transformation of totalitarian movements into totalitarian regimes, post-totalitarian theory focuses upon the transformation of totalitarian regimes into totalitarian societies.

At issue is how the fictive world of totalitarian ideology not only motivates social movements and regime politics but becomes a basis for societal consciousness and activism. To use the official rhetoric, the new "Soviet man" becomes a sort of reality. Terror and the führer principle are no longer necessary, because the Party definition of the human world has become a primary orientation of the mass of totalized subjects. The official script of social life, totalitarian culture, becomes a hegemonic component of the societal situation. Totalitarianism provides a grotesque political culture of modernity. The opposition movement in Poland since 1976 and, with lesser success, those of Hungary and Czechoslovakia, have fought against this grotesque culture.

We find ourselves at the primary paradoxical juncture: explaining totalitarianism from the point of view of its opposition. The paradox tells us much about the nature of the object of inquiry. Now, the term *totalitarian* does not refer to the successful completion of the totalitarian political project, as opposed to that of pluralism or Western modernization. Rather it refers to a cultural penetration of all aspects of social life, where that social life maintains an interaction with its totalitarian definition. Specifically in Poland, the society crystallized in opposition to the official definition, but the odds against this are very great. Party-state monopolization of the means of both positive and negative coercion plays a key role, but this is the normal aspiration of the traditional tyrant. The added totalitarian element involves the Party's official monopoly on truth and the relationship between official truth and coercion in social life. The relationship emerges from the very texture of everyday life and its connection with official ideology.[31]

In a famous aphorism Lenin once declared, "Soviets plus electricity equals socialism." The statement is clearly simplistic from the point of view of the history of socialist struggles, but it points to an underlying tension in Soviet totalitarian modernity. The Chinese opposition of Red versus Expert during the Cultural Revolution points to the same tension.

Official Communist ideologies link the realization of a political utopia with industrialization: the possibility of a classless society depends on the formation of an industrial working class. Under the leadership of a vanguard, the Party, this class creates the good society. The good society, though, depends not only upon such leadership, but upon the material abundance of a modern economic and technological order. The tension between the functional demands of that order and the political and cultural imperatives of Party leadership leads to three primary systemic attributes of the (Soviet) totalitarian modernity: totalized political aspiration, industrialization, and functional differentiation.[32] These are mutually supportive attributes from the point of view of official ideology. Party leadership helps bring about industrialization, and industrialization supports the achievement of Party goals. Scarce resources are distributed according to the functional needs of economic and social sectors, and rewards are parceled out for contributions to building the good society. But outside of the official view everything does not work so smoothly. The technical rationality of industry and the articulation of interests among functional groups do not run absolutely parallel with the ideological Party vision of social life. The special features of totalitarian culture manifest themselves at this point. They involve the simultaneous appearance of the official version of the occurrences of everyday life and the actual occurrences, and the official power to force all to give credence publicly to the official version. In this manner an official truth prevails.

Even at the moment of Solidarity's greatest power, following its victory at the Gdansk shipyards, in a strategic move of

conciliation, the workers recognized the "leading role of the
Polish United Workers' party" (the Communist party). In this
formulation the labor movement acknowledged both harsh
geopolitical realities and its limited political ambition. It was
clearly understood that the existence of "neighbors" (as the
Solidarity activists ironically called the Soviets) made a fundamental transformation of the entire system impossible. Further, the strength of Solidarity to begin with was to turn away
from such ideas of fundamental transformation and to focus
instead on concrete and immediate problems and their resolution. Yet a great deal was conceded, because the act of conciliation was formulated in the language of official ideology.
The ambiguous phrase "leading role of the Party" is the cultural face of totalitarian oppression. The phrase has been used
in justifying censorship and the system of Party patronage
(*nomenklatura*) for practically all leadership positions in the
society, and explaining the viability of centralized planning
and the desirability of using terror to ensure public confor-
mity to official doctrine. By accepting this formulation, the
labor leaders set the stage for struggles between themselves
and the Party. The well-institutionalized logic of totalitarian
culture met the newly institutionalized logic of a free public domain.

What the members of the free public domain had to face
was that the logic of totalitarian culture penetrated practically
every nook and cranny of the social order. The Party had an
official script revealing the truth of the situation, and the
means of repression to enforce the truth. Thus, it could cite
the presence of antisocialist elements in resisting any proposal
for local change, from the changing of management or work
conditions to the elimination of special perquisites for the
Party elite.

The struggles during the Solidarity period followed this pattern. Ultimately, with the monopoly over the means of violence, the Party declared a state of war, following the script.
The imprisonments and internment camps of the state of war

validated the official truth. Here we have a quintessential instance of totalitarian culture. Violence defines truth. Today
that truth, which is believed by no one, permeates the social
structure, contaminates language, and becomes the destructive resource of modern tyranny. The post-totalitarian mind
emerges with the fundamental rejection of this truth.

T W O

Newspeak and the Politics of Force

THE PRIMARY GOAL of Solidarity was to uncouple civil society from totalitarian culture.[1] Despite the linguistic concession at the nationwide level, when the unionists recognized the Party's "leading role," a major task of the movement was to free the workings of the differentiated social order from official definition, to allow people to get on with work, family, and cultural activities free of Party definition and control. Before August 1980, social activists could take advantage of the gray area between the authorities and society. Afterwards the activists sought to define clear boundaries, so that a delimited realm of free public action would be possible. Where the boundaries should or could be drawn was an open question. A great deal of internal disagreement in Solidarity arose over this issue, and the authorities capitalized on the controversy. There was agreement, though, that a new culture and language had to be formulated, free of official definition and used for understanding both recent history and future projects.[2]

With the practical actions and accomplishments of Solidarity in mind, it becomes clear that totalitarianism should not be understood as an accomplished fact, but as a cultural project which penetrates and dominates. Its opposite is not simply a specific form of institutionalized pluralism or the free world, but a political and cultural project for the constitution of a free public domain. The exact form such a project would have taken in Poland was not known. Its complete realization was understood to be utopian. The form it might take elsewhere certainly cannot be described in advance. For the present purposes it is important to observe that the notion of totalitarianism can now be based upon an analytic distinction which people have acted upon. The analytic distinction allows for both a clear view of the unique repressive forces of the totalitarian order and an appreciation of the countervailing forces of potential public resistance.

A totalitarian project is politically institutionalized in a prerogative state, and a project for the free public domain seeks to institutionalize political agreements, ultimately in law, to limit repressive prerogatives. Between the projects of totalitarianism and of public freedom are everyday life and the state as battlegrounds. The totalitarian project seeks absolute, ideologically justified prerogatives even when the ideology loses its cogency for the rulers and the ruled. The other side seeks liberalism and formal legality. Political, civil, and individual freedoms are its political projects. Civil legality is its immediate political task.

Political projects exist as part of ongoing, everyday human relations, many of which are far from determined by the projects. A great deal of family life, friendships, and even civil law, daily economic activity, and education are only marginally influenced by the most dramatic political changes. People grow up, study, marry, raise families, buy apartments, that is, conduct fairly normal private lives, under the most diverse political conditions. They are not untouched by politics, but part of their struggle for personal identity involves a turning away from politics at strategic, and often highly significant, moments in their lives. The projects of totalitarianism and public freedom react to this quite differently. The totalitarian seeks to obliterate privacy and autonomy in social life. His opponent defends them.

Totalitarian culture, through the identification of its fictive world with the everyday world, establishes institutionalized state structures with the prerogative of political coercion, ideologically justified as necessary. Many of the public deliberations of Solidarity and other public forums of the Polish democratic opposition have focused on establishing protection against this prerogative. The underground Solidarity

leadership's apparently presumptuous identification of itself
with society is grounded in its sense that it is supported by the
Polish people in undertaking such defensive action.

Here we confront a major theoretical problem. The totalitarians consciously confuse force with reason; thus, there is an
official truth (politically enforced) about everything. Liberals
attempt to maintain the fiction of an absolute distinction to
protect reason from even sovereign, legitimate force; thus the
"social contract" theory of the state. These fictions must be
considered critically so that modern tyranny may be understood, along with the social and cultural aspects of resistance.

Force and Reason

In order to confront the politics of the modern world and of
totalitarianism, we must liberate ourselves from the simple
conceptual dualisms and polarities which were developed to
explain premodern or early modern orders. We have juxtaposed superstructure against infrastructure, norm against fact,
economy against politics, ideology against material conditions
for so long that we fail to see that human reality regularly defies
such dichotomies. As Arendt has noted, the political categories we still use today are simply the Platonic division between
unchanging essences and changing realities turned upside
down. If we view social praxis as the foundation of theory, we
merely invert the Platonic doctrine that the theory of the philosopher king must shape and ground everyday praxis. If we
explain cultural norms as determined by their material circumstances, we simply reverse the relationship between norm
and materiality that Plato proposed. Today, we assume, it is
history which shapes principles, whereas for Plato it was principle which governed and illuminated history. We have no
more escaped from Plato by turning him on his head than
Marx escaped from Hegel by turning him rightside up.[3]

Our problem, the relationship between political reason and
political force, is a pressing case in point.[4] The utopian elements of totalitarianism and the concept of an absolutely free
public domain arise from the illusion that political reason and

force are mutually exclusive opposites. On the contrary, existing political cultures are amalgamations of approaches to reason and force (and their relationships to each other).[5] The political cultures of totalitarianism and public freedom must be analyzed as such amalgamations. To specify the character of political cultures dispassionately, we must first appreciate the general but variable interconnectedness of force and reason. Totalitarianism, then, can be defined precisely as a specific, pernicious variety of interconnectedness.

Political reason and language are usually seen as addressing the higher faculties of the citizen such as deliberation and the critical intellect. Force is viewed as aimed at the lower faculties such as the instinct for self-preservation and our fear of pain or death. Hence governmental language and governmental violence are dichotomized, just as the mind is divided into the part that thinks and the part that feels and desires. Accepting such polarities, we are led to distinguish between liberal and traditionally despotic governments.

Liberal regimes pride themselves on the persuasiveness of their principles. Compliance with these regimes is supposedly motivated by the citizen's belief in the legitimacy of their norms. Liberal rule is the rule of pure reason. Force proves unnecessary because citizens obey voluntarily.

Despotic regimes seemingly bypass persuasion and reason and rely on brute force. If the police are strong enough, the government need not appeal to the intellect. People who fear for their safety and survival will obey even laws they deem abhorrent. After all, in securing compliance, fear works just as well as belief.

The mechanics of obedience seem to hinge on this either/or of brute force and rational persuasion: either the government persuades rationally and dispenses with force, or it forces through threats and violence, in which case persuasion is superfluous. But even in liberal regimes, principles and values coerce actions as well as persuade intellect. Citizens who cannot express their grievances in terms defined by these principles find themselves strangely without power; in addition to being unable to speak, they realize they are also unable to act. Principles not only have a meaning; they also exercise a force and restrain human behavior. Similarly, in despotic regimes force quickly takes on meaning. When the citizens watch the police act with violence, they immediately begin to make sense of it. Force is never naked, because it is clothed in meaning and significance for those who witness it. Political violence always makes a statement; it tells the onlookers what the government means.

The power of words and the meaningfulness of force may be illustrated by referring to the recent history of the United States. During the civil rights demonstrations of the sixties, we saw the claims of black Americans encounter the clubs and tear gas of the police. The arguments of blacks, no matter how well founded on traditional principles of human rights and equality, seemed to prove the powerlessness of all words and principles when confronted with the real physical weapons of the police. And yet these scenes of police violence were transmuted when shown on nationwide television. Now, what was the reality of these scenes on television? Nothing but a fleeting display of images, words, and pictures sometimes out of focus. And yet these images and words entered into a war against the clubs and tear gas of the Alabama police, and the images and words won. The policemen watched as their ugly weapons had all power sucked out of them by a few newsreels and front-page headlines.

But words can prove more powerful than a policeman's club only because the club, in addition to being a weapon, makes a public statement. The Alabama authorities themselves sensed this, for when they sent the police to disperse crowds, they armed them with tear-gas canisters and not with machine guns. A machine gun is not merely an instrument of brute force; it is a symbol with a meaning. It has a meaning which, when it appears in public, must fit in logically with those other meanings that people grasp when they speak of the value of human life and the freedom to petition the government. Likewise, throwing tear gas is not simply a deed of violence; it is also an act of speech in the political vocabulary. The Alabama officials were constrained by a system of definitions in which liberal principles contradicted machine guns, and they had to contend that tear gas signified a respect for human safety.

In politics it is never simply a matter of persuasion through speech, or mute coercion through violence. For words can rob the police of their weapons,[6] and weapons always function as meaningful signs in a system of political reason. Accordingly, violence moves at the same level as language, namely, the level of meaning and persuasion. Weapons address our intellects just as much as they do our instincts and fears. And language speaks directly to our primal drives for self-preservation as well as to our reason.

The fundamental correlation between reason and power comes in diverse and manifold forms. These different forms, however, determine the nature and variety of politics in the modern world. In places like the United States, when public discourse loses its own power to shape events, when democracy is viewed as an equilibrium of mute contrary forces, conservative, liberal, and radical politics are reduced to the free market, economic redistributions, and material conditions. And when meaning itself becomes a machine for manipulation, when appearances, images and words—by defining "the good" as consumer goods—enslave rather than liberate, mass society has emerged.

At this point some commonalities and differences between my approach and Michel Foucault's to the problem of politics and culture should be noted. Foucault also understands the intimate connection between power and knowledge and force and reason. He too sees an intimate connection among the culture of modern tyranny, totalization, and subjection. He also knows that the relationships between reason and power, or as he more technologically puts it, "systems of communication and power relations," come in "diverse forms, diverse places, diverse circumstances or occasions." He too recognizes, though, that "there are also 'blocks' in which the ad-

justments of abilities, the resources of communication and
power relations constitute regulated and concerted systems."[7]
This leads Foucault to his central analytic and normative
structure of "agonism," which I share, but with a crucial
difference.

In his researches of "power and freedom's refusal to sub-
mit," Foucault strategically takes as his central task the deconstruction of power and reason as they are "blocked" in
specific "disciplines" in order to discern the powers. His central critical focus is on state bureaucratic power and subjection. He attempts to show that the king is naked so that we
may "partially transform and improve our 'relations to authority,' relations between the sexes, the way in which we perceive insanity or illness." He chooses this path because he
knows that utopian politics and practical inquiry, based on
claims of grounded truth and a teleology of total transformation, are key factors in twentieth-century catastrophe. In his
critique of such enlightened dreams, he observes:

> In fact we know from experience that the claim to es-
> cape from the system of contemporary reality so as to
> produce the overall programs of another society, of
> another way of thinking, another culture, another vi-
> sion of the world, has led only to the return of the
> most dangerous traditions.[8]

But he goes too far by conflating modernism with totalitarianism. Whereas neoconservatives such as Jeane Kirkpatrick ignore the link between modernity and totalitarianism, Foucault
does not sufficiently contrast them. He seems to disavow modern hopes for reasonable democracy and democratic reason.

In proceeding with his critical inquiry, Foucault identifies all
institutions as embodiments of power and knowledge and then
finds questionable *any* alternative cultural claim—because "an
important part of the mechanisms put into operation by an
institution are designed to ensure its own preservation."[9] He
thus does not sufficiently appreciate the possible link between
alternative autonomous (enlightened) discourse and autono-

mous social and political practices as they may constitute free
and democratic alternatives. Showing in his life's work that a
specific king is naked (the modern bureaucratic and professional one), he confuses his life's work with human fate. The
post-totalitarian culture analyzed below indicates that there
are still positive possibilities of significant, large-scale change.
In order to appreciate this we must now analyze the specific
correlation of truth and violence as they define today's totalitarianism so that the post-totalitarian alternatives may be adequately understood.

Force Defines Truth

Totalitarianism with and without terror: these are the two political varieties of a single cultural species. In both violence
defines truth; force overwhelms meaning. It is the extreme
brutality of terror which first distinguished totalitarianism in
Hitler's Germany and Stalin's Russia. Yet, though distinct brutality identified the species, it also complicates analysis. Brutality is central to the human experience, from ancient Greek
civilization[10] to European imperialism.[11] Indeed, today old-
fashioned oligarchs of the Western Hemisphere probably gen-
erate greater brutality than European totalitarians. It is with
such facts in mind that we have become confused about totalitarianism as a political concept. By examining how totalitarian culture looms behind today's totalitarianism, as well as
behind totalitarian terror, and by considering the continuing
relationship between totalitarianism and terror, the confusion
can be clarified. The focus of our inquiry is the definitive and
unchanging totalitarian relationship between truth and force.
It is this specific relationship which distinguishes modern
from traditional tyranny.

The Nazi death camps and the Soviet gulag present the essential character of totalitarianism. In such settings the human capacity for evil is starkly revealed. As distinct political
settings, they are unique in their combination of this brutality
with rationality, abnormality with normality, wickedness with
banality. Hannah Arendt tried to capture this in her "report

on the banality of evil." Eichmann, she tells us, was not the monster the Israeli prosecutor depicted, but an unusually normal (banal) character, whose amoralism and quiet efficiency characterize the Everyman of the modern world. Eichmann, a man who was responsible for the most monstrous deeds known in history, appears in Arendt's account as an innocent, a simple bureaucrat who did his duty, concerned more about the advancement of his career than the consequences of his actions. His rationalizations of his actions were not simply convenient conceits cynically invented to avoid responsibility, but were, as Arendt forcefully demonstrated, built into the very structure of the totalitarian death machine.

Ideology explained that some beings who gave every appearance of being human were not. When this led to genocide, and when visceral human reaction to their own inhumanity might have exploded the ideological facade of the murderers, grand but empty phrases were coined to cure reality. Himmler counseled the commanders of the *Einstazgruppen* and the higher SS and police leaders:

> To have stuck it out and, apart from exceptions caused by human weakness, to have remained decent. That is what has made us hard. This is a page of glory in our history which has never been written and is never to be written. . . . We realize that what we are expecting from you is "superhuman," to be "superhumanly inhuman." [12]

By being assured that they were taking part in a historic moment of monumental significance, a significance explained ideologically, ordinary humans became modern beasts. They knew that theirs was "a great task that occurs once in two thousand years." The human remorse and instinctive reactions against carnage, then, were effectively used to console the self. In light of the historical context, instead of saying, "What horrible things I did to people," the murderers were able to say, "What horrible things I had to watch in the pursuance of my duties, how heavily the task weighed on my shoulders." [13]

Brutality is rationalized and placed within a world historical context. In this way, humans become capable of anything. Words mean anything, can mean almost everything, but really mean nothing. This is totalitarian culture. It penetrates the political, social, and cultural spheres of totalitarian orders. Force defines reason as the means to an absolute truth about the world: past, present, and future. In each sphere of life, force defines reason differently, more or less absolutely. The relationship between these spheres of life determines the variety of the species: with and without terror. Totalitarianism has a common political culture, but there are differences among totalitarians. They arise from the process of social differentiation and the totalitarian attempt to undermine it.

While a central fact of modernity, recognized by a broad consensus of social theorists, is its social complexity,[14] with greater specialization in politics, economics, culture, and religion, totalitarians brutally deny this fact. They attempt to create a dedifferentiated society on the grounds of a super-simplistic view of the world. The dedifferentiation of society has ideological, social structural and linguistic dimensions. The Party-state as a political apparatus interferes with the functions of relativity autonomous social institutions, from economic units like factories and farms to cultural bodies like genetic research institutes and university social science departments. This is motivated and justified ideologically—the Party is playing its vanguard role in the making of the revolution or the building of socialism. Once the political intervention in the nonpolitical social sphere is firmly established, its routine justification fosters the development of Newspeak, which is a fundamental cultural instrument of totalitarianism. Ideology is the core of totalitarian culture. By being the official culture, it is primarily perpetuated by force. By being the truth, it is a substitute for reason.

A simple key unlocks the mysteries and ambiguities of all human experience. Tragedy becomes unnecessary. Disappointments are explained and resolved. This all requires that the complex modern world be brought into accord with the prescription the dogma suggests. All history is explained. The truth of the world is thus revealed. Then the world must be made and remade according to the truth. We have already observed how this yields inhumanity: individuals become expendable, people in millions are annihilated, generations are sacrificed for the realization of utopia. Totalitarian simplicity also fundamentally transforms the organization of everyday life. Science and art, economics and politics, philosophy and industry, sexuality and morality, and much more are guided by the key idea.

Biology and genetics, for example, cease to be autonomous disciplines of scientific inquiry. Instead a great achievement of modernity, modern science freed from extrascientific dogma, is denounced as a bourgeois means to enslave the proletariat and confine historical materialist science. Lysenkoism, the Soviet materialist biological science, conformed to the amateurish speculations of Engels instead of the real development of scientific investigation. Agricultural disasters resulted, with starvation. But the totalitarian culture expressed through Party-state policy and the organization of scientific institutions ignored these inconvenient facts for thirty years.

In this case the move from classic totalitarianism, with terror, to today's totalitarianism comes into clear view. It is perhaps the most spectacular, tendentious Soviet attack upon the autonomy of science and art, but it is as well rather typical. The general consequences of totalitarianism for the overall social structure and for everyday life are graphically revealed by this well-known case.

Lysenkoism

In the late twenties a debate raged in the Soviet Union between those who advocated the inheritance of acquired characteristics and those who advocated the reality of genes and of genetic transmission. As in other fields, from literature to history to social science, each side in the genetics debate sought to demonstrate the ideological correctness of its position, i.e., its consistency with Marxism and dialectical materialism. Trofim Lysenko, an undistinguished agronomist, proved to be a skilled opportunist. He transformed a questionable, simple experiment of vernalization, an agronomic practice that attempted to obtain winter crops through summer planting, into a properly proletarian botanic science. He turned scientistic quackery into totalitarian dogma.

In the thirties Lysenko was a significant force on the Soviet cultural scene, one that persisted through the early sixties. Without any scientific accomplishment he dominated the world of natural science as a quintessential totalitarian. Confusing truth with coercion, he destroyed genetics as an independent field of scientific investigation. A totalitarian science was born, with Lysenko as its chief midwife.

Genetics and the new science faced each other. Zhores A. Medvedev, the first Soviet historian critical of Lysenkoism, observed the situation in 1936:

> On the one hand we see a serious branch of science, the big area of world genetics, a harmonious edifice of interconnected, theoretical concepts, logically following from a colossal amount of factual material, and represented in our country by a large group of qualified specialists in genetics. On the other hand, we meet an embryonic idea, lacking serious scientific content, not corroborated by sufficient reliable data, and supported by a small group that did not include even a single geneticist. But the representatives of this group were distinguished by a close solidarity, great self-confidence, and an inclination to demagoguery and political analogies.[15]

The small group was armed with official ideology and intimately connected with the repressive apparatus. With such armament and connection, autonomous science was attacked over a long period of time. Both the sustained attack and the persistence of science tells a great deal about the totalitarian social structure.

In the thirties Lysenko had to destroy his enemies, a well-developed and institutionalized group of genetics researchers. Here is an interchange between Lysenko and Nikolay

Ivanovitch Vavilov, the first geneticist singled out for ideological attack. Lysenko sought to dismantle institutions for genetics research. His means was to attack the ideological purity
of the researchers and their findings.

V[AVILOV]: Evolution is an oversimplification of
specific events. This is a fact you could verify.

L[YSENKO]: I don't question that evolution is a fact.
But is it true that evolution is an oversimplification,
an unwinding? Is it true or not?

V: It's an undisputable fact. Take the 100 percent
Darwinist Severtsov (I myself am under suspicion by
you). There is a law of reduction; often many animal
groups had a history of the reduction of many organs
towards a vestigial state. There is also a law of in-
crease in complexity. . . .

L: I understand from what you wrote that you
came to agree with your teacher, Bateson, that evolution must be viewed as a process of simplification. Yet
in Chapter Four of the history of the Party it says that
evolution is in complexity. . . .

V: In short, there is also reduction. When I studied
with Bateson . . .

L: As an anti-Darwinist.

V: No. Some day I'll tell you about Bateson, a most
fascinating, most interesting man.

L: Couldn't you learn from Marx?

V: Recently a book of Haldane's came out. He is an
interesting figure, a member of the British communist
party, an outstanding geneticist, biochemist and philosopher. He wrote an interesting book entitled *Marxism and Science,* in which he tried . . .

L: (interrupting): And got a dressing down.

V: Of course he got a dressing down in the bourgeois press, but he is so talented that he was admired
even when he was scolded. . . . He said that Marxism
is more applicable to evolution in history . . . that it
can foresee much, just as Engels foresaw fifty years
ahead many contemporary discoveries. I must say

that I am a lover of Marxist literature, not only ours
but of the foreign too. There too, many attempts at
Marxist validation are made.[16]

Vavilov turned to evidence to sustain his argument. He
looked for verification and referred to Marxism as a powerful
model and theory with a specific range of application, to be
tested and compared with other theories. Lysenko looked for
purity: "Marxism is the only science." All that led to Marxism, such as Darwinism, was good but prescientific. Fidelity
to the "true theory," not verification, was the ultimate scientific criterion. For Lysenko, scientific dispute about the nature
of evolution was resolved by referring to the history of the
Party. Vavilov carefully attempted to separate argument from
its individual source, while to Lysenko it was the source which
decided the quality of the argument.

The debate was between two men, both with ambitions and
interests. Lysenko sought to vanquish, Vavilov to survive.
Lysenko struggled for ideological purity, Vavilov for ideological acceptance. Lysenko asserted, repeated and condemned;
Vavilov reasoned. Vavilov strove to maintain official recognition for the scientific status of genetics; Lysenko wanted genetics condemned. Self-interest was connected with those
positions. The careers and livelihoods of those men (and many
other men and women) depended on the outcome of their
conflict. But more was and is involved than a clash between
two men, or between their principles and interests or debating
styles. We may see that the clash and its outcome represent
totalitarian culture and the temporary defeat of an alternative.
The defeat was only temporary to the degree to which the
vanquished maintained a mode of reasoning and a scientific
life in opposition to totalitarian culture.

Vavilov lost. He was arrested in August 1940 and died in
prison in 1942, soon after his election to the Royal Society of
London. However, Lysenko did not win absolutely. The battle
subsided during the war, when practical exigencies slowed

Lysenko's attack. Like Vavilov, other scientists languished and died in prison for their defense of science in the thirties, but no new attacks were launched.

In 1945 Lysenko again went on the offensive, with the publication of an article questioning the cornerstone of Darwinism, the notion of intraspecific competition. When his article was criticized in a scientific journal, he countered in *Pravda* and *Literaturnaya Gazeta*. "How [do we] explain why bourgeois biology [sic] values so highly the 'theory' of intraspecific competition?" He answered his own question with a scientific non sequitur: "Because it must justify the fact that in capitalist society, the great majority of people, in a period of over-production of material goods, lives poorly." [17]

Ideologies, based on the existence of a true key to history's past, present, and future, were used to destroy not only scientific propositions but many botanists, morphologists, zoologists, and evolutionists who came to be identified as bourgeois ideologists. "Menshevizing idealism" by "Mendelists-Morganists-Weismannists" was denounced by the "new Michurinist-Soviet biology," and "reactionary philosophy" was denounced by dialectical materialists. A scientific cold war was declared. Theories and findings developed in the United States were discredited. [18]

In the late forties and early fifties, Lysenko was the absolute victor. The practical application of his ideas led to agricultural disaster, but this was ignored. He became the object of a minor personality cult. His portrait hung in all scientific institutions. Art stores sold his busts. A hymn in his honor was in the repertoire of the State Chorus:

> Merrily play on, accordion.
> With my girlfriend let me sing
> Of the eternal glory of Academician Lysenko.
>
> He walks the Michurian path
> With firm tread.
> He protects us from being duped by Mendelist-
>   Morganists. [19]

The Lysenko cult coincided with Stalin's revival of totalitarian terror in the postwar period. In the post-Stalin era, de-Stalinization included de-Lysenkoization. Change came slowly, and not without serious problems. Lysenko fought on well into the sixties. Ultimately, however, science prevailed. The victims of Lysenko's attack, including Vavilov, were rehabilitated. The new alchemy in all its varieties was denounced. Full official support was given to genetics.

Lysenko's Legacy: An Instance of Totalitarian Culture without Terror

The story of Lysenkoism is not a simple Soviet melodrama with a scientific happy ending. Lysenko's legacy includes, perhaps most fundamentally, the linguistic distortion of critique and reason. At first Lysenko's opponents referred primarily to scientific criteria, using straightforward scientific reasoning to refute his claims. But in the end they too used official euphemisms, e.g., the "cult of Stalin," and they attempted to use Marxist-Leninist orthodoxy to sustain their positions. In chapter 3, I will analyze sociologically and in detail the strategic reasons for this. For now we should observe that by appropriating official dogma for an autonomous cultural project (freer science, in this case), some autonomy has been achieved, but at considerable practical expense. The critics of Lysenko unintentionally supported a totalitarianism without terror.

In the opening of his well-documented monograph on Lysenko, Zhores Medvedev attempted ideologically to set the limits of his political interpretation. He wrote: "Marx, Engels and Lenin aspired to the creation of the democratic forms of socialism, whereas Stalin, finding himself in power in the then solitary socialist state, took another path—that of the concentration of power in the swollen apparatus of repression, political dictatorship, arbitrary rule and personality cult."[20]

Medvedev was involved in a real and tragic practical project. Because he viewed Soviet socialism, that is, the socialism of Stalin *and* of Marx, Engels, and Lenin, as immutable, he

sought to justify scientific autonomy in the language of officialdom. But by using the language of officialdom, he suggested significant restrictions on the autonomy of science.

The ideologues Medvedev opposed wanted to subordinate
science to the "scientific doctrine" of Marxism-Leninism.
Medvedev scrupulously documented the grave theoretical,
practical, and human consequences of this. One could easily
draw from his report the conclusion that Marxism-Leninism
lacked a claim to the status of science. But Medvedev cautiously avoided this conclusion. He proposed that:

> Karl Marx, Friedrich Engels, and Vladimir Ilich Lenin
> were above all great thinkers and scientists; they were
> creating communism as a science concerned with the
> forms of development of human society. The scien-
> tific proof of Marx, Engels and Lenin was the method
> of proofs, the method of analysis of facts and of arriv-
> ing at truth. It is precisely because of this that Marx-
> ism has always attracted the minds of progressive
> scientists.[21]

Here we have Newspeak, the linguistic form of totalitarian culture, formulated to show that the victims of Lysenko,
not Lysenko and his colleagues, were the true progressive
scientists.

But science remains politicized following this formulation.
Each sentence represents an apparently clear assertion which
upon closer examination is neither clear nor truthful. Significantly, this is probably intentional. It may or may not be true
that Karl Marx was above all a great thinker and scientist, especially given contemporary understandings of the nature of
science. But Lenin's talents clearly lay primarily in his capacities as a strategist and political leader, and Engels mostly simplified, explicated, and propagated Marx's views. Lenin was
creating Communism not as a science, but as an outcome of
civil war. He was concerned with a revolutionary struggle for
political power, not with an investigation into future forms of
human society. Even Marx and Engels did not give much

thought to such forms. Whether Marx and Engels used primarily and systematically positivist methods of proof and analysis as the means toward truth has been hotly debated among Marxists, but surely Lenin did not. The purported scientific basis of Marxism has no doubt been a component of its attraction to some scientists, but who is or is not progressive is not at all transparent, and whether Marx's appeal is based on scientific accomplishment or totalitarian certainty is not a trivial question.

Although Medvedev may have been a convinced Marxist-Leninist when he wrote that text, he is not and was not a fool. Surely he understood the problems with his statements. But he made them with purpose: he wanted to claim the importance of scientific method, the method of an autonomous science. In a society with an official truth, he legimated his own ends as a scientist by referring to that truth and its sanctified leading lights. He showed that Marx, Engels, and Lenin were scientists, and that today's scientists support them because of it. He might have wanted to write, "Like Marx, we seek to be scientists. Give us the freedom he had in the British library. Let us follow our own distinct methods." But he could not be straightforward. He had to blame Lysenkoism on an unexplained fanaticism, the cult of Stalinism, and the eccentricities of Khrushchev. He analyzed science as science as far as he could, but he could not be unambiguous in his critique. He had to hide (albeit minimally) behind ideology to oppose totalitarian tyranny.

This tyranny, as modern tyranny, occurs in a modern or modernizing society. Modernity requires some degree, indeed a great degree, of social and cultural differentiation. People must do different things according to different principles and standards. To engage in science is to engage in activity set apart from religious dogma and political beliefs. When dogma and belief supersede free inquiry and predetermine the interpretation of research findings, science cannot flourish.[22]

This was both recognized and attacked in the Soviet Union. The imperatives of building an advanced industrial economy,

278039

a key element of socialist construction, led to tolerance of scientific freedoms, but the imperatives of official ideology, of a totalitarian culture, led to frontal attack on them. The audacity of Lysenko, and a key to his success, was to attack science in the name of science. The tragedy of his victims and their defenders was that they were forced to use ideology to defend science. In the Soviet Union, and in other totalitarian orders without terror, the arts and sciences are problematically differentiated from the domain of totalitarian culture and totalitarian command.

The tension between ideology on the one hand, and the economic, cultural, and social spheres on the other, can be understood as a systemic characteristic growing out of the imperatives of totalized political aspiration, industrialization, and functional differentiation.[23] The precise social constitution of the tension can also be analyzed much more closely in everyday social interaction. We observe this spectacularly in the Lysenko case. When Lysenko railed against his opponents, when he denounced them, research institutes were disbanded. A totalitarian terror functioned.

Today, as with Lysenko's critics, totalitarian cultural interaction without terror proceeds in less spectacular but no less consequential ways. Censorship and political review of artistic activities and scientific projects, citizenship criteria for passport control and career mobility, and the proliferation of Newspeak are instances of totalitarian penetration into differentiated everyday life.

Totalitarian Culture and Newspeak

Newspeak is of central importance. It is the linguistic equivalent of the master idea of the official ideology. While the simple idea of class struggle or racial hierarchy is the ideational core of the official truth, Newspeak is its linguistic structure. It is a language fictively scrutinized by Orwell, but very much a reality. Newspeak, as Orwell observed, is not only a medium of expression for a world view and mental habits, but it is a medium which makes the expression of other types of thoughts difficult if not impossible.

Orwell imagined that Newspeak would pervade all social interaction of the political elite. In fact it has penetrated official public interaction of the entire population. It is often forgotten that the world of Orwell's hero, Winston Smith, was the world of the Party bureaucrats. In *1984* the public as a whole was ignorant of official ideology, *IngSoc*. They, the "proles," existed in a sort of primordial private domain; only Party members spoke Newspeak and thought "newthink." In today's totalitarianism, things are different. No one uses official language privately among friends or relatives. No one believes in all the details of the official ideological renderings of the social order. But just about everyone must use the language of the official ideology for official social interactions.

Consider closely one such interaction as a case in point. In May 1980 a Polish university lecturer was under a promotion review by his department. He was particularly vulnerable politically: he was the only junior professor in the social science faculty who was not a member of the Party. One afternoon while he was picking up mail with a friend,[24] his department chairman called him aside and told him that a problem had come up in the review. Though his academic accomplishments were beyond rebuke, evidence of civic responsibility was lacking. (The phrase in Polish, *praca spoleczena,* translates literally to "social work," which I will use here for precision.) The chairman then asked his young colleague to supply such evidence at his earliest convenience.

In Poland, as in the West, academic success is based on a variety of criteria. In the United States teaching, serving the university, and scholarly publications are the formal grounds for academic promotion. We know that quite often (more often than is desirable) success or failure in the university hinges upon other factors—personality, demeanor, deference, acquiescence, etc.—but is justified by the formal criteria. An "officialese" is then used to explain decisions on promotion or tenure. At first glance the Polish lecturer was facing a minor variation on this theme. Yet the practices he faced were much more pernicious, fundamentally rooted in the basic constitution of the totalitarian order.

First observe the similarities to American practices. As
would happen on American ground, the chairman was telling
the young Polish scholar, none too subtly, that there were
problems with the review. Otherwise the lecturer would not
have been approached. But was the apparent problem the real
one? Again the issue would arise in both Poland and the
United States. If the answer were yes, in both settings the case
could be closed. The documentation would be provided and
the decision rendered. But when the answer is no (as was the
case here), the fundamentally totalitarian nature of Polish society becomes more evident. In American society, when the answer is no, the real behind the apparent could be any number of
things. It could have to do with personal animosities between
the junior faculty member and his seniors. It could result from
departmental or university politics, or from broader issues, research style, theoretical orientation, macropolitics, etc. This
may be contrary to explicit academic ideals, but it is not systematically and directly related to the systemwide structure of
domination in American society. Such is the case in Poland
and other societies of the political East.

When the young Polish academic was approached, the official Newspeak phrase *praca spoleczena* (social work) had
clear enough Newspeak reference but was not easily translatable outside the restricted linguistic and ideological code.
When Party members "voluntarily" sacrifice a day off to work
on various public works (cleaning a park, preparing a parade
ground, working on a construction site, etc.) they engage in
social work. The phrase refers to such officially sponsored,
purportedly selfless activity. It refers to cleaning up after a
May Day parade, but not to cleaning up after a church procession on Corpus Christi. It refers to planning a protest film
festival concerning American involvement in Central America,
but not to a protest against the Soviet presence in Afghanistan.
The phrase *social work* articulated within an official context
has apparently clear meaning, but there is a world beyond
official definition, and here the ambiguity of the phrase becomes apparent.

The seemingly simple interaction between the junior faculty member and the chairman could refer to a multiplicity of real problems, all of which revolve around the tension between totalitarian culture and social differentiation. The request for evidence of social work could refer to political problems of the junior colleague or to political problems of his closest senior associate in the social science faculty, the social science faculty, or the university as a whole. It might also emanate from political changes, from the most local to the most centralized Party apparatus. Perhaps the issue was simply that the young social scientist was not a Party member. Perhaps it had to do with his father's anti-Communist past. Or more ominously, perhaps it had to do with his reputation for allowing free discussion in the classroom, accepting theses which referred to illegal literature, and personally supporting independent culture.

Hours after his meeting with the department chair, the young scholar consulted with groups of friends and colleagues, to share interpretations of the event and to devise a strategy for action. They agreed that on a number of counts the scholar, his primary senior mentor, and his institute were vulnerable: the scholar for his connections with unofficial (illegal) cultural activities; his mentor for being an independent-minded scholar active in a semi-clandestine, unofficial initiative, DiP, which was objectively examining the Polish economic and social crisis; and the social science institute as a whole for ever more boldly sponsoring autonomous social research and for teaching independent of and often in opposition to Marxist ideology.

In sum, the scholar, his mentor, and his institute were functioning according to the dictates of a modern scientific ethic which was tolerated but at any point could be officially called into question and repressed. The request for further evidence of social work could indicate the beginnings of such questioning and repression.

Even if it did indicate such questioning and repression, the agent of the repression was unknown. Perhaps it was the

department chair, or another department social scientist serving as Party ideologist, or Party groups in the university or
locality, or even the Central Committee. The scholar and his
colleagues speculated at length about this. No one knew for
certain. If the evidence of social work is deemed insufficient by
officialdom, there is often an ongoing battle, especially if the
repressive agent is at a lower level. There the scientist can face
the Party hack and win. In this case, however, no battle occurred; the evidence was deemed acceptable.

This did not happen automatically. Given the ambiguity of
the phrase *social work,* it was not at all clear what sort of evidence should be submitted. All knew that on strict, Party-
minded grounds, the scholar did no social work, but they
assumed that other evidence might do. Stalinism, the era of
totalitarianism with terror when cultural commissars such as
Lysenko reigned, had passed. The outcome of the battle between totalitarian culture and relatively autonomous spheres
of life was not predetermined. An invitation existed to test the
expansiveness of the real referents for Newspeak terms such
as *social work.* In close consultation with his colleagues, the
academic submitted a report which emphasized his activities
with student groups. Clearly he could not include his work in
underground publishing, though "really"—that is, outside the
world of Party definition—this is perhaps the most profound
contribution a scholar can make to the public good. But even
his reference to the officially recognized and officially supported student groups was not without political irony and
tension.

In the late seventies Poland was rapidly developing an alternative cultural world and alternative social institutions, and
official cultural groups faced a challenge: to *compete* or to *associate* with unofficial, autonomous cultural life. Such association could range from outright crossover to clandestine
support, but open support of the unofficial by the official led
to problems with the authorities, and our young scholar had
helped advise a group through such problems. He was an ad-
visor to an official student cultural group that was ignoring

official directives and cooperating with illegal cultural groups. Of course the character of the advice, and the problems of the group, were not mentioned in the report. The report was submitted and apparently accepted; the scholar was promoted; the crisis passed without public notice. All those involved in the case soon forgot its details. Weeks later, Poland was engulfed in one of the most spectacular nonviolent revolutions of the twentieth century: Solidarność was born.

To understand Solidarity and its enemies, we must understand in detail small events like the one described. They reveal the persistence of totalitarianism without terror, the totalitarianism of everyday life. The contrasts with the Lysenko case are great, but so are the similarities. At the root of the similarities is the social function of Newspeak, for when Lysenko faced his opponents, and when the chairman faced the young social scientist, they used an official language and official reasoning. Truth and force were confused. Totalitarian culture prevailed.

In explaining away genetic theory, Lysenko asserted, "Bourgeois biology by its very essence, because it is bourgeois, neither could nor can make any discoveries that have to be based on the absence of intraspecific competition."[25] The details of scientific reasoning and evidence were not used. Rather, the "Grand March"[26] of the proletariat was extended to the field of biology. The simple idea of class struggle, the key to all history, was extended into the realm of scientific investigation. Given the Party-state monopoly of force, and given official claims to universal truth, such extension decides discussion when one discussant has official support. Once Lysenko defined his opponents as bourgeois biologists, they were vanquished.

When the young Polish scholar was asked for evidence of social work, the same sort of defeat appeared imminent. Not engaging in social work is retrograde behavior. The practical circumstances of Party struggles decide how retrograde behavior is defined. In the late forties and early fifties, the definition and consequences were very much like those in the

Lysenko case. In the late fifties and early sixties, lack of evidence of social work was defined as anti-Polish, and the consequences were not as severe; the evidence was sometimes ignored, or used to fight micro- or macro-political struggles. This most clearly marked the change from the Stalinist to the post-Stalinist period.

In the seventies, more often than not, such evidence of anti-socialist behavior was ignored. Jadwiga Staniszkis, a prominent Polish sociologist, in a remarkable phrase, calls this period one of socialist repressive tolerance.²⁷ Though such changes are significant, the underlying confrontation between totalitarian culture and sociocultural autonomy remains stable. The undermining of an autonomous sphere persists. The ambiguous meaning outside the Newspeak linguistic system is a primary tool of totalitarian control. The official monopoly of force defines truth through the use of Newspeak.

In his dystopia, Orwell imagined the eventual complete expansion of Newspeak usage into everyday life as well as public life. But instead strategic differentiated usage has developed (as we have seen), with a clear social grammar. All sorts of activities and events, from international affairs to teachers' conferences and agricultural updates, are reported in Newspeak in the official press. In the state bureaucracy, Newspeak is freely used in memoranda and reports. Among Party officials, Newspeak must be used as an affirmation of political identity. Between Party-state authority and political subject (the case analyzed above), Newspeak is used strategically to enforce political control. Such interactions occur throughout the society: in entrance examinations to all sorts of schools, in examinations at the schools, in application for passports, in job interviews, etc. When all parties to such interactions consistently use Newspeak it gains a significant life; in the process, the social order, dominated by the totalitarian party, is legitimated.

To demonstrate this crucial point, we return briefly to the social science faculty. From a certain practical point of view, the case reported seems to be trivial. No negative sanctions resulted from the request for social work. The young scholar was promoted, and the social science faculty maintained a high degree of autonomy. Though it may be appreciated that a certain unfortunate linguistic pattern was sustained by the review—a pattern which formally reproduced Stalinist practices—the lack of repression makes it seem like an archaic vestige of little importance. But when we shift focus from the agent of repression to the object of repression and the repressive interaction, we see that more is involved than a repressive vestige. Exactly because of its seemingly benign aspects, the case illustrates the depth and power of totalitarian culture.

The chairman's use of the phrase "social work" paralleled Lysenko's word usage. The chairman's request for evidence of social work was part of a code of political control. The need for scholars to be upstanding citizens was justified as the key to a bright socialist future. Committed scholarship was presented as an extension of the accomplishments and legacy of the best of the Polish intellectuals, the "guardians of the national soul." Apart from the repressive state apparatus, this makes no sense.

In this system, the official version of the proper balance between scholarship and citizenship is not open to question; it is declared and enforced. For example, when Wladyslaw Gomulka, the Communist party chief in the late fifties and early sixties, contravening the traditional Polish notion, declared that the Party, not the independent creative intellectuals, was the new guardian of the national soul, the statement was not a political judgment to be weighed along with others. It was an aggressive attack on independent and critical Polish intellectuals of the early sixties.

In today's totalitarianism, the link between the linguistic code and violence produces less dramatic consequences than in the times of terror. It is not life on the line, but freedom. The actions of the social scientists unwittingly demonstrated this. In order for the scholar to maintain an academic career, and in order for him and his colleagues to struggle for the limited autonomy of the academy, the academics sought to expand the real referent of the Newspeak phrase "social work." But by playing the game, they gave life to the repressive code and legitimacy to the political order which sustains it.

The scholar and his colleagues tried to be included in the official script, but the inclusion strengthened it. "Social work" may refer to unorthodox officially accepted behavior, but not to officially proscribed behavior. The citizenship responsibilities of the scholar are linguistically tightly constrained. At this point Orwell's dystopia and everyday life are quite similar. What Orwell took to be the potential major danger of Newspeak is in fact its major danger. In concluding his reflections, Orwell notes:

> From the foregoing account it will be seen that in Newspeak the expression of unorthodox opinions, above a very low level, was well nigh impossible. It was of course possible to utter heresies of a very crude kind, a species of blasphemy. It would have been possible, for example, to say *Big Brother is ungood*. But this statement, which to an unorthodox ear merely conveyed a self-evident absurdity, could not have been sustained by a reasoned argument, because the necessary words were not available. Ideas inimical to Ingsoc could only be entertained in a vague wordless form, and could only be named in very broad terms which lumped together and condemned whole groups of heresies without defining them in doing so. One could, in fact, only use Newspeak for unorthodox purposes by illegitimately translating some of the words back into Oldspeak.[28]

An essential though exaggerated truth of everyday totalitarian life is being revealed here. "Social work," "*Truth*" (the name of a newspaper), "peace," "progressive," "Workers' Party," and "freedom," are among many words which have been robbed of any critical meaning. They appear in public to serve the powers. Any other usage is censored, or indeed becomes unimaginable. People may know that the official truth is a lie, but they begin to lose their capacity to seek the truth, which is not simply the opposite of lies. The little event in the Polish social science faculty is an instance of the process by which this incapacity is produced. "Social Work" becomes meaningful only within the restricted linguistic code, visible public action only within the confines of official ideology.

Newspeak itself is socially differentiated. It is used with consistency in the official press, most purely in Party dailies and weeklies, less so in Party theoretical journals, and even less so as apparently required periodic expressions of ritualistic fealty to the powers in journals of the various arts and sciences. In the broadcast media and the performing arts, generally the greater the audience the more intense the use of Newspeak; television more than radio broadcasts, the most popular films more than art films, films more than theater. In social interaction the use of Newspeak varies systematically. It is practically unknown in private conversations. Party members may use some of its formulations as a personal expression of their identities, but even then it is limited to circumstances of intense political mobilization. In nonintimate, unofficial social interactions, people who use Newspeak are distancing themselves from the persons being addressed. Since Newspeak formulations are not the norm, using them becomes a clear expression of noncommunication. Contrary to Orwell's imagination, most people, including Party members, speak to each other without using official language. Because of this, the bleakness of his vision must be rejected.

Newspeak is the norm only in official public interaction. But as we have observed, this is not unproblematic. The underlying social conflict between differentiated social and cultural spheres of life and official, ideologically inspired political projects leads to linguistic ambiguities and tension. Consider another example. Even at the height of socialist realism, for one painter to speak about another's painting in the language of Newspeak without mentioning autonomous qualities of painting would be an insult. Though at times it might be the better part of discretion to refer to Party-spiritedness (the painting's embodiment of the heroic proletarian struggle on the road to socialism, etc.), discussion about the use of color and line becomes nonsensical when put in these terms. Yet certain colors, shapes, and lines are censored, and censorship is justified in Newspeak.

The interaction between censor and painter resembles our social scientist's case. Party artistic canons have little to do with painting. Once strict socialist-realist cartoons are not demanded, there is a great deal of uncertainty as to what will and what will not be permitted, what will and will not be encouraged. An allergy to the modern and experimental is often a given, as is a love for sentiment and kitsch, but such conservative—one might even say petit-bourgeois—tastes are explained in terms of agitprop, worker's struggles, and socialist ideals. Often artists must interact with censors using Newspeak, but they actually seek to know and test the limits of official conservative tastes. As in the social scientist's case, more open limits are desirable from the point of view of an autonomous artistic enterprise, but blending such "liberalism" with the official rhetoric compromises the art.

The official ideology, with its unique identification of force with reason, together with Newspeak, embeds totalitarian culture in state practices and in everyday life. The terror is gone. But the distinctive stamp of totalitarianism is solidified. As a part of daily life people must adjust to the irrationality of speaking about the world in a language that obscures rather than illuminates. They must lead schizophrenic existences, where following the official script is impossible (a proletarian or a bourgeois science?) but a necessary pretense. They must live in bad faith, performing official duties justified by official ideology, using an official language, all of which is foreign to them, to their true selves. But publicly those true selves cannot be revealed.

The state, following the logic of totalitarianism, engages in an unending project of enforcing and applying the official truth throughout the social order. In this sense, the social order is completely politicized (more precisely, statized). While Foucault and the poststructuralists imagine that state control and domination extend subtly and clandestinely to all realms of the modern social order, from the private realms of sensuality to the august realms of human reason and science, and Habermas and the new critical theorists [29] fear the covert colonization of the life world in late capitalism, those who live in totalitarian orders do in fact knowingly face the open penetration of the Party-state into all realms of their social and private lives.

Yet the notion of complete politicization can be confusing. It has often been cited as the definitive characteristic of totalitarianism. When it has been demonstrated that vast segments of social life escape control, it is asserted that there is no such thing as totalitarianism. It is this definition and assertion that I question here. Totalitarian politicization must be understood as a persistent propensity arising from totalitarian culture. Official "knowledge" of the whole truth about past, present, and future (whether it is believed or not) is aggressively expansive in its political application. Though social and private life become fields for expansion, resistance arises based on differentiated social and private life, from the bonds between family and friends to the imperatives of modern science, technology, and economics. Such resistance is in a sense natural and of little direct systemic significance. It leads to minor and major corruption, inefficiency, and private unhappiness. Someone who works for a construction company trades scarce lumber for access to a preschool for his child or to an apartment, sacrificing official construction goals for family needs. Others—who therefore do not gain access to preschools for their children or get apartments on time—are unhappy. The practicalities and complexities of daily life limit the reach of the state, but the state's character is merely revealed by such resistances and tensions; it is not transformed in any way. The politicizing Party-state, working out the imperatives of totalitarian culture, is only frontally resisted when a real alternative culture is developed.

The autonomous culture of Eastern Europe and the developing autonomous politics gain their distinctiveness, their poetic and democratic power, because they address such issues. They seek an alternative to Newspeak, its ideological background, and the social and political world in which it is spoken. To seek such alternatives is an extremely difficult task. Newspeak, the conflation of force with reason, and the de-differentiation (that is, the destruction) of autonomous cultural and social institutions through ideological and linguistic attack, present not only momentary distractions, but lasting confusions. Even where autonomous political ethics once existed, one must reinvent them. Where they existed only in rudimentary form, such as in much of Eastern Europe, the obstacles are even greater. To be against totalitarianism, to be anti-Communist and anti-Soviet, is not enough. It is merely to declare, like an Orwell character, that Big Brother is ungood.

THREE

The Limits of Newspeak

WE HAVE SEEN that official politics and culture in totalitarian orders are based upon an official truth that is both required in all public discourse, and, nonofficially, generally viewed as the official lie. The most radical cultural and political alternatives are best understood as those which seek to be set apart from the official truth and its culture and politics. Such alternatives are not simply negative in their composition, directly set against repressive agency and censorship. They attempt as well to build a more truthful political culture set apart from the world of officialdom. In the process, they build an alternative, independent public life.

The independent public life emerges in a tortuous fashion. In the main it has appeared within the interstices of command, as officially accepted critical expression. In this chapter we will consider the social bases of embedded public culture, its meaning and limitations. Then we will turn to the democratic political culture. Completely independent, it is the most substantial alternative to totalitarian culture.

The embedded culture has ambiguous social, cultural, and political meanings. It is both socially autonomous and dependent. It addresses the discourse of national and international cultural traditions, while these are blocked by the veil of censorship and official ideology. And while it seems to make possible autonomous public life, it legitimates the totalitarian order, making political autonomy impossible. To observe the ambiguity clearly, we visit the production of a Polish theater in the seventies, a particularly revealing example of tolerated critical culture. Then I will try to demonstrate how the supports and accomplishments of such a culture also point to its limits and deconstruction.[1]

A Theater Performance in Poland

Poland. The city, Lodz. A snowy December. Midnight. The many guests invited to the "art opening" are waiting for the doors of 77 Piortkowski Street to open. As their anticipation of the night ahead mounts, so does their impatience, and everyone experiences the involuntary pushes and shoves of an anxious crowd. The third major premier of Theater 77 is about to take place, and all are aware of the great artistic and political importance this theater has had in Polish life since the ousting of the Communist Party leader, Wladyslaw Gomulka, in December 1970. Tonight begins *Retrospektywa*. An art opening? A play? An event, certainly. The audience is speculating on what its role will be. They have followed the instructions on their invitations and have read the attached excerpt from the controversial personal diary of Witold Gombrowicz (the late Polish avant-garde playwright, novelist, and man of letters) in which he asserts that Poles ought to abandon their history and turn to the future, irrespective of past problems and complexes. What does all this mean? Finally the large doors squeak open, but only enough for one person at a time to escape the jamming mass and enter the stately, subdued atmosphere of what appears to be an art opening.

Wine is being served. Coca-Cola, smoked fish, cheeses, breads, and all the embellishments are present, as are the host and, most importantly, the art works: groups of actors assuming the poses of famous historical paintings. After nearly half an hour of talk, food, and drink, the host interrupts what proves to be the first phase of the evening's events. He welcomes the guests to *Retrospektywa* and asks them if they all have their ballots, which were handed out at the door. Reading the ballot aloud, he asks: do you agree or disagree with Gombrowicz's assertion that Poles should abandon their historical traditions? He tells the audience: if you disagree, hand in your ballots, so marked, and go upstairs to the room on the right; if you agree, so indicate and go upstairs to the room on the left; if you are undecided, remain on the first floor holding your ballots. There will be two separate performances upstairs, after which everyone will return for another common meeting downstairs. A discussion will follow that meeting.

Upstairs, the action centers on a song. The song is "Red Poppies on Monte Cassino" ("*Czerwone maki na Monte Cassino*"), which celebrates the heroics of the Polish army not aligned with the Soviet Union in the Second World War. Banned in Poland in the fifties, it carries nationalistic and even some anti-Russian overtones. For those who wanted to disregard Polish history and traditions, the song is sung half in Polish and half in Russian, a presentation disquieting almost to the point of disbelief to a Pole. In the next room the people are standing in darkness. They hear the voice of a man whom they can barely see. He is speaking to them as a commander would to his troops before a battle. Then suddenly a fire is lit in an old pot-bellied stove in the corner of the room. Shadows dance around the walls, and everyone naturally moves closer together, seeing each other's faces again. There is a temporary break in the mood as a closed circuit television set is turned on. The program is the members of Theater 77 singing "Red Poppies on Monte Cassino." They sing proudly, perhaps a bit too proudly. Each session disconcertingly plays to the professed belief of the audience.

After these presentations the groups separately return to the main room on the first floor. There, Polish history is re-enacted, from liberation following the Second World War to 1956, the year of the fall of the Stalinist regime in Poland. The play takes the audience through the events leading to the Communist victory: the liberation of Polish territory by the Red Army and the Polish People's Army, the establishment of the coalition government dominated by the Communist Worker's Party, and the liquidation of all coalition foes. The process of Stalinization is underscored. Ideological discussions—on such fine points as the meaning of cosmopolitanism and internationalism, the difference between anticosmopolitanism and anti-Semitism, and the nature of the classless society and the role of the workers in it—are reiterated. Self-criticism sessions are shown, as are prosecutions of enemies of the people, each serving as an example of the dogmatic excesses that character-ized the political life of that time.

During all of this, the continual plight of ordinary people is presented by 77 through personal conversations directed at members of the audience by the actors. Grand speeches are made in the center of the room, while members of the audi-ence are directly confronted by the actors sitting among them who comment on everyday problems—problems of procuring food, proper housing, clothing for children, and so forth. The actors ask individual members of the audience their opinions and advice for solving these problems. Conversations result which sound like many such conversations held on the streets, in cafeterias, and in homes.

The simultaneous, but separate, enactment of the politics and struggles of the political elite of the nation, and the every-day problems of common people, without any apparent effect of one upon the other, is a clear dramatization of a most im-portant problem in Poland. The parallel between the histori-cal presentation and the contemporary situation of Poland is not missed by the audience. The action in the center of the room continues. The debate goes on, each participant more vigorously citing Marx to make his or her point. Yet slowly, following the lead of the members of 77 in the audience, people leave the action to go to the discussion upstairs.

After the scene downstairs, it is clear that the prevailing opinion of the members of 77 is that Poland must confront its history and come to terms with it in order to plan for the fu-ture. Zdzislaw Hejduk, the director of the theater, in intro-ductory remarks before the discussion that follows the full performance, bluntly states this and suggests that it is a good time to discuss the problems presented during the art opening, those dealing with Gombrowicz's statement and any other problems that seem important.

The audience is confronted and uncomfortable, and discus-sion begins nervously. This has more to do with the appropri-ateness of public discussions of this sort than with the issues involved. The uneasy atmosphere created by the confrontation is itself a testament to the importance of the evening's message. Theater 77 seems to be suggesting that the sorry legacy of Stalinization in Poland resulted partially, at least, from too many people passively accepting it, that the deadening "stabilization" of the Gomulka period in the sixties occurred because effective resistance was not mounted. If particular problems had been confronted forthrightly, the mistakes of the past might have been avoided. In the discussion, 77 encourages an honest look at this legacy, but more importantly, it encourages an open examination of similar problems that continue to exist.

The discussion lasts for hours, developing toward openness and honesty, though ultimately achieving neither. People discuss history, Gombrowicz, specifics of the play—some people denounce certain aspects and some approve. Yet the leap from the hypothetical to real and deeply felt contemporary issues is only suggested and never made explicit. Nevertheless, the event has made its mark. The guests understand that if they fail to speak out, they will be contributing to the perpetuation of old problems. Grand political events will occur divorced from people who dare only to whisper among themselves. On the other hand, if they speak boldly and candidly, there may be reason for hope in the future of Poland. On this note, the theatrical event ended at about 4:00 A.M., December 10, 1973.

Retrospektywa was openly provocative in a society where open provocation was rare. This play was only one of the theatrical creations of 77, all of which exhibited boldness. And indeed, Theater 77 was only one of a half dozen leading theaters in the student theater movement in Poland, a movement that innovatively confronted the situation in Poland with a sincerity and openness that made it important both for cultural and sociopolitical reasons. The theater groups dealt in their works with some of the most essential problems facing Poland, such as the role of Catholicism, the role of Marxism, the role of political and cultural traditions in Polish life, national myths and complexes, and recent social and political developments.

Yet these theaters clearly were not anti-Communist, and

their members were not Polish dissidents. Rather, they were a group of artists (playwrights, actors, directors, musicians), some of whom were Party members, who through a legal channel offered alternative views of Polish life—cultural, political, artistic, and social. All their works were censored, yet they pushed and challenged, always attempting to expand the possibilities of expression. Through innovative methods of expression, they often circumvented the barriers created by official censorship.

The works of these theaters were not unusual in the Soviet bloc. Cabaret theater in Czechoslovakia in the mid-sixties, some of the works produced in the Taganka Theater in Moscow in the late sixties, and student theater in Hungary in the seventies were generically related to this Polish movement.

In other art forms, some of the finest critical works in film in Hungary and Poland, and some challenging literature in the Soviet Union, are officially tolerated and sometimes promoted by the highest authorities. The works themselves are their primary importance. Their open existence is a fundamental sociopolitical, as well as cultural, fact. Though the works of student theater, and other such works, are accomplishments in themselves because they reach a public, they achieve a wider significance—they change society. Critical imagination and cultural traditions not part of the official imagination become part of the official order. The society is then constituted not only by the totalitarian project but by a project of cultural freedom. In nascent form, the seeds for the struggle between the public and the totalitarian authorities (described in the conclusion of chapter 1) are planted. Now we analyze the sociological structure of the cultural tension within today's totalitarianism.

Totalitarian Culture versus Cultural Freedom

Artistic and scientific work such as socialist realism and Lysenkoism, which extend totalitarian culture, are not in the full modern sense cultural works. As we have already discussed, a fundamental characteristic of modernity is the differentiation of institutional spheres—politics, economics, the arts and sciences from religion, economics from politics, the arts and sciences from politics, and so forth. Socialist realism and Lysenkoism do not only reverse differentiation, they attack it. They embody dedifferentiation in that they exist primarily as political propaganda and only marginally as art and science. They use the cultural form as a mere vessel for extracultural purpose. On the other hand, critical culture such as Polish theater defends and extends cultural freedom and the project of modernity.

When not under attack, a work of autonomous science, to take the clearer case, addresses traditional problems left unanswered by work of the past. Contemporaries argue over the adequacy of contemporary answers without regard to religious or political dogmas. Ideally, contemporary exchanges are freely conducted, and contemporary differences of opinion and judgment are decided by scientific adequacy and not extrascientific motivations. Most often, inherited theories are elaborated upon (what Thomas Kuhn calls normal science).[2] Sometimes these theories are radically revised. Such is the everyday life situation of modern science.

I am not arguing that science can, or ought to be, uninfluenced by extrascientific factors, nor that it must be free in the liberal sense from state interference. Obviously, the imagination of the scientist is related to the collective imagination of his or her times. A prime example is the Darwinian notion of the survival of the fittest and the prevailing laissez-faire capitalist ethos of his world. Just as clearly, scientists face extrascientific economic and political constraints. They commonly must achieve economic and state support for their scientific megaprojects, and gaining such support does not always derive from purely scientific merit. In the United States, it often has to do with entrepreneurial grantsmanship. This has a parallel with the political reliability often required in the Soviet bloc (though with important differences).[3]

But even though science is shaped and constrained by extrascientific factors, scientific findings must nave independence from the shaping and the constraining. If the notion of the survival of the fittest had no scientific cogency, even though evolution theory fit well with the prevailing ideals of individual initiative and European dominance, it would not have become a cornerstone of modern biology. Even if a great deal of nonmilitary scientific inquiry was supported through the so-called War on Cancer during the last of the Nixon years, and this may have led to the proliferation of certain types of research rather than others, the research still had to be built on existing scientific theories of knowledge, and its saliency was still judged according to existing scientific canons. Thus the path of scientific development certainly shifted as a result of changing social practices and political pressures, but the structure of science itself was not challenged in the process.

Lysenkoism, as we have seen, does engage in such an attack. Lysenko gained support and defined a significant realm of the Soviet scientific enterprise by citing sacred texts and attacking the purported class background of scientists and their theories. Under such conditions, the very existence of science as an autonomous cultural process, a major fruit of modernity, is in question. Cultural repression, instead of freedom, becomes the norm. What purports to be science is not.

The same is true in the arts, though it is harder to demonstrate. The artist also engages in a conversation with his or her predecessors. In comparison with science, received knowledge is not systematized. What constitutes beauty and the culturally profound is most often not a matter of consensus (as in science), but is open to question and nondefinitive deliberation. Nonetheless, as T. S. Eliot argued, through the creation of works artists engage in a conversation with their predecessors and contemporaries.[4] Art does not merely manifest the psychological predispositions of the artist and the social conditions of its times, it develops cultural forms—poetics, symbolic structures, dramatic techniques and theory, color fields and usages of line, etc. The impressionists attempted to answer the questions posed by academic painting. The postimpressionists challenged the impressionists, as the whole array of twentieth-century painting engaged in a huge discourse on color and line. At stake was not the definition of true art, but the continuation of art as an autonomous cultural process, as an ongoing contentious conversation. Socialist realism, with its ideologically defined focus and themes, is outside this process, an extension of Party dictates, in fact dreamed up by the Party ideologist Zhdanov. Again, what purports to be culture is not.

The great significance of an embedded culture like the theater described here is that it uses official structures to strongly assert cultural autonomy. Though official cultural policy, based on the Soviet model, attempts to promote the goals of the Party, it also carries with it important, unintentional support for a resisting, autonomously defined culture. Primary among the supports are the availability of cultural traditions, the ambiguities of official ideology, and the everyday social tensions in official cultural institutions.[5]

Cultural Traditions and Independent Expression

Frequently, in attacks on dissent by Party dogmatists, unconventional literary, artistic, and scholarly expressions are described as being vestiges of the prerevolutionary order or under the influence of reactionary tendencies from abroad. Since according to official dogma the state of socialism exists, dissent, like crime, cannot be explained with reference to the structure and processes of the official order. Instead, it is attributed to factors outside the official system. Such is the case presented in Andrei Zhdanov's address to the Moscow Writers Union on September 17, 1946, which set the stage for the repression of the arts and sciences in the postwar period. Zhdanov blamed undesirable aspects of Soviet literature, its elements of irony, lyricism, and individualism and its apolitical character, on Western influences. He declared:

> Some of our literary people have begun to regard themselves not as teachers but as pupils of bourgeois and petit-bourgeois foreign literature. Is such kowtowing fitting for us, Soviet patriots, for us who have

built the Soviet order which is a hundred times loftier
and better than any bourgeois order? Is kow-towing
before the narrow-minded petit-bourgeois literature
of the West fitting for our progressive Soviet literature, the most revolutionary literature of the world?[6]

Because much of the public expression in societies such as
the Soviet Union is created with reference to cultural spheres
that reach beyond their immediate contemporary social situations, there is some truth in these attacks. Distortion begins
when Party officials imply in their attacks that these cultural
spheres are extrinsic to the official system.

A primary source of the development of independent public expression lies in the Party's support of prerevolutionary
cultural traditions. The literature, theater, art, and scholarly
achievements of prerevolutionary times have been lavishly
supported by the Party. The Party leadership strives to demonstrate that the present system is the fulfillment of the promise
of the national and international cultural heritage. Even during periods of the severest Zhdanovist policies, the support for
the traditional culture of the nation has provided an alternative for creator and audience to the sterile formula culture
developed by politicians. At the height of Stalinization, national and international traditions of cultural expression were
not only available as an alternative to Party-prescribed contemporary culture, but more popular than contemporary
socialist-realistic creations. (Thus in 1952, prerevolutionary
literature and theater were substantially more popular among
the Russian people than Party formula works.)[7]

The availability of traditional works has helped to transform contemporary creative expression. The obvious mediocrity of the bulk of socialist realism, when compared with
the works of Tolstoy and Kandinsky, Mickiewicz and Wys-
pianski, Kafka and Mann, pushes the artist in the direction of
the ideals of traditional art manifested in the models of the art
works themselves and in the model of the creative process
involved.

The works of the postrevolutionary artists are frequently elaborations in terms of present realities of the styles and creative impulses of the earlier works. The cultural heritage respected and supported by the official regime serves as a basis for public expression outside the narrow bounds set by Party formulas. Religious sentiment and the peasants' love of the land (*The Quiet Don*) and judgments of the fallibility of political leaders (*The First Circle*) and of the ambiguity of righteousness (*Dr. Zhivago*) are explicitly based on traditional literary culture, especially as it was developed by Tolstoy. In *Tango*, the Polish dramatist Mrozek portrayed the moral dilemma of the successful revolutionaries, the same revolutionaries whose ascendancy ends Witkiewicz's interwar play, *The Shoemakers*. In youth theater, the names and works of nineteenth-century nationalist poets and young revolutionaries are used as material for contemporary national expression.

The student theater group of Szeged, Hungary, recited songs and danced to the poetry and name of Petöfi in an unconventional production entitled *Petöfi Rock*, which, while appearing to be little more than a succession of marching-band formations, was more significantly a contemporary ritual celebration of the sacred value of national independence and a youthful search for meaning in the national culture. The theater STU of Cracow, Poland, in a modern musical, *Polish Dreambook*, considers the very problem of Polishness as it has been treated in traditional Polish literature. Through the images of the great romantic poets, this theater brings to the surface the primordial national myths and imaginatively calls for a national rebirth—drawing upon national traditions but transcending them, accepting the official order but calling for an overturning of its most repressive aspects.

Traditional culture supports independent expression not simply as artifacts to be studied and developed. Cultural traditions present artists with a model of creation that is markedly richer than the Party notion of *partinost* (Party spirit). Narrow formulas, artificially imposed as the basis of creation,

and politically imposed component parts of creative form
(e.g., the necessity to portray a "positive hero") may be overcome when the creative inspiration of the past, with all its
richness, is used as an alternative to the purported inspiration
of partinost. Notions of creative autonomy, criticism of authority, and moral independence are clearly seen to be part of
the creative process in traditional culture and are chosen instead of partinost by contemporary creators. Creators who
make such a choice often find themselves at odds with the
state cultural apparatus. Their works, subjected to censorship,
often do not legally find a public in their own country. And
even when they do, literary works are often difficult to obtain,
drama is presented at the margins of the theatrical world
(e.g., Polish youth theater), and sculpture and painting often
must be exhibited privately, unbeknownst to the general public. Nevertheless, the transmission of traditional norms of
creative autonomy supports the development of independent
public expression.

Marxism and Independent Expression

The very cultural symbols on which Party rule is based—
Marxist ideology, the ideals of socialism, and the promise
of a Communist utopia—also support independent public
expression.

Marxism is propagated to all members of Communist
societies as the most advanced world view. In the schools
and youth clubs, at work and at the workers' clubs, in newspapers and on radio and television, the virtues of Marxism—
its method, its insights and achievements, its promise and
strength—are loudly proclaimed. This intensive teaching and
praising of Marxism clearly have been intended to instill in the
masses a positive attitude toward the accomplishments of the
Party as the vanguard movement building a socialist society
and working for the Communist utopia. Party propaganda at
all points identifies true Marxism with the official Party position; the Party is always pictured as the leading agent of social
change along Marxist lines. There is a totalitarian culture.

Yet the official version of the proper role of the Party, the meaning of Marxism, and the nature of socialism and Communism have not simply been passively received and accepted or rejected by the population. Central values may have been internalized, but the accomplishments of the ruling elite have been critically evaluated. This pattern has been continuously evident in the cultural expression by intellectuals in the Party-dominated societies.

An important part of being an intellectual is to reflect upon the problems of the social milieu, using a specific expertise or talent and a personal world view. By dictating forms and themes and by inculcating the population with the Party's views, the official regime has attempted to direct and control such reflection upon the social milieu. While an immediate consequence of this has been the Party's apparent success—creation of socialist realism in the arts and the transformation of journalism and the social sciences into fields of propaganda—simultaneously the seeds have been sown for the birth of critical expression based on Party ideals, or at least utilizing these ideals as a justification. Though in periods of severe repression critical judgment is closely controlled, the use of key Marxist ideals is strongly encouraged, and these ideals, because not in and of themselves supportive of Party policies, may promote critical as well as supportive cultural creativity. Marxist ideology functions not only in Mannheim's sense as a symbolic system supportive of the status quo, but also in the sense specified by Geertz—as a symbolic system that "makes an autonomous politics possible by providing the authoritative concepts that render it meaningful, the suasive images by means of which it can be sensibly grasped."[8]

Marxism has provided for some of the most outspoken critics of the order the framework for their appraisals. Djilas's analysis of the emergence of self-interested bureaucrats as a new ruling class was based explicitly on a Marxist orientation.[9] Similarly, the critique of the practices of the Polish United Workers Party in the early sixties by Jacek Kuron and Karol Modzelewski was a Marxist assessment of the subordination of workers' interests to the interests of the ruling party elite, as Kolakowski's and Schaff's Marxist humanistic explorations were attempts to find a place for the individual in a socialist system.[10] The Medvedevs, in their anti-Stalinist writings, were involved in a similar quest.[11] Each of these writers, among them past Party members, apparently believed in the future of socialism and agreed fundamentally with the central values of the Party but evaluated critically the methods the Party used to achieve these central values. While the critical appraisals were quite different in each case, and even conflicted, the basic pattern of appraisal was the same; the performance of the Party was measured against its ideological promise.

There are obviously problems with such approaches, especially when they are contrasted with the more radically post-totalitarian works analyzed below. Before we systematically make such contrasts and clarify the problems with the approaches, a clear analysis of the daily life of cultural institutions is in order. The difference between the officially accepted critic and the post-totalitarian one is very much linked with the culture of daily life.

Official Cultural Institutions and Autonomous Culture

There are two fundamental types of cultural institutions in totalitarian societies. Each can serve as a support for independent expression, while it is supposed to serve the powers. On the one hand, there are cultural institutions which are manned by professionals addressing the general public under the direct control of cultural and educational ministries. Scientific academies, most professional theaters, universities, and literary publishing houses are prominent examples of these. On the other hand, there are cultural institutions not as clearly oriented to the primary goal of the creation and dissemination of culture as such. These institutions are formally attached to some political or social group or practical activity, and not under the direct control of cultural or educational ministries. The newspapers and publishing houses of various profes-

sional organizations, the research institutes of various industries, and the cultural houses of specific localities are examples
of this type. The cultural life in the first type tends to be more
professional and more involved in basic culture. The cultural
life in the second type tends to be more amateurish and more
involved in culture of specific interests. Yet, labeling the former professional and the latter amateur, or the former basic
cultural institutions and the latter applied cultural institutions, would be a mistake. Sometimes the finest professional
work is done in the second type of institution, and cultural
products of general interest to the whole society are produced
in this type of cultural institution. These institutions often af-
ford the intellectual the greatest degree of creative freedom
and thus have definite attractions for cultural innovators, both
professional and amateur.

Keeping this situation in mind, we may refer to the first type
as *primary cultural institutions* because of their direct ties
with central Party departments and governmental cultural
ministries, and because theirs is the primary function of cultural production for the whole of society, and to the second
type as *ancillary cultural institutions* because of their indirect
relationship with central departments and ministries and direct dependence upon other organizations which do not have
the production of culture as their primary task for economic
and political support, and because theirs is the ancillary function of cultural production for specific sectors of society. In
both the primary and the ancillary cultural institutions, the
ideologically inspired cultural directions and controls meet resistance, but the type of resistance is different. Thus the distinction between the two types is important for an analysis of
the social supports of independent cultural expression.

The chief function of primary cultural institutions is the
creation and dissemination of culture. Directives are received
from higher-level cultural departments and ministries, and the
main instrumental tasks of these cultural institutions—creation of new art, presentation of performing arts, conducting
of scientific research, and dissemination of knowledge—must

be performed in compliance with these directives. Yet, despite the official attempt to subordinate cultural values to political goals, the association in these institutions is still based on cultural activity, not compliance with political directives. These institutions, though formed or reformed to put into practice Party cultural policies as part of the overall practice of dedifferentiation, serve as potential institutional bases for differentiated cultural tendencies that may undermine Party cultural policies.

While some kinds of cultural work must be done in compliance with Party policies, the orientations involved in such work often conflict with Party policies. Unless partinost becomes the sole basis of culture (which is an impossibility), norms of cultural activity reaching beyond the boundaries of Party policy and the ideals fostered by central Party propaganda come into conflict with central directives.

The interaction of artists, scientists, and leaders in unions, institutes, and academies is based upon their professional competence, not politics. Here, political policies are evaluated in terms of professional criteria and may be judged as being in conflict with cultural work. Thus, Party-formed and -controlled writers' unions in the Soviet Union and Poland have served as platforms for denouncing restrictive cultural policies. Beyond such extraordinary occurrences, the conflict between cultural work and cultural policy is an underlying aspect of life in differentiated cultural institutions. A common attitude of the cultural intelligentsia is to consider Party cultural directives and censorship as obstacles to be circumvented, obstacles antithetical to their main creative task. Observers of culture in the Soviet Union and Eastern Europe note such attitudes as part of the institutional life of the social sciences, theater, literature, and the arts.[12] These attitudes may be suppressed, yet in primary cultural institutions they cause an underlying tension which may potentially support expressions other than Party-prescribed ones.

The situation in ancillary cultural institutions is more complex. Support does not come directly from high-level government ministries and Party departments of culture, but from organizations based on locality, social class, and industry. The ancillary institutions are controlled by and must serve the interest of these organizations, just as the primary cultural institutions must comply with high-level cultural directives. The result is not complete avoidance of party control, but instead a five-way crosscurrent of potentially conflicting sociocultural orientations within these institutions. There are the same conflicts that exist within primary cultural institutions, conflicts between (1) the values and requisites of cultural work and (2) the values and cultural policies of the Party and government ministries, in addition to conflicts among (3) perceptions and demands of high-level governmental and Party directives concerning the function of the supporting organization or social group, (4) the orientations of those within the sponsoring organization concerning its function and its relationship with the cultural institution it supports, and (5) the orientations of those within the ancillary cultural institution concerning their special role in society. The actual working out of these potentially conflicting orientations depends on the nature of Party policy, the supporting organization, and the cultural institution being supported.

Ancillary cultural institutions generally have not been studied in the West. Some consequences of organizing cultural institutions in this fashion have been noted; for example, in the Soviet Union, scientific research which is closely aligned with industrial enterprises, as in the West, is more technically oriented than in basic research institutes, and theater connected with cultural houses and factories is freer to experiment.[13] Yet, the analysis of the potentially conflicting sociocultural orientations outlined above has not been systematically studied. This is probably because of the paucity of data available concerning the functioning of these institutions.

In the case of Polish youth theater, up until the mid-seventies, the interaction of the five sociocultural orientations mentioned above was favorable. Party control and direction of the supporting organization and of the ancillary cultural

group were favorable and not too tight, and the sociopolitical
orientations of the supporting organization and ancillary cultural institutions were parallel.

If this is not the case, restrictions may be even more confining. When Party supervision is too tight, as it was during the
Stalinist period in the Soviet Union and Eastern Europe, ancillary cultural institutions become the propaganda institutions they were intended to be, for the transmission of Party
values to every sector of the society. When the orientations of
those in the supporting organization and the ancillary cultural
group are not parallel, the cultural group may be then subjected to harsh restrictions from the supporting organization
as well as from the Party.

The Accomplishments

Significant alternatives to totalitarian culture have been produced through both primary cultural institutions and ancillary
cultural institutions. Cultural traditions have been extended.
A critical creativity which resists systematic constraints has
been kept alive, and autonomous publics have been formed.
Thus cultural freedom, sociologically understood, emerges
from the totalitarian order. The totalitarian project of the dedifferentiation of the autonomous cultural sphere is limited.

Let us consider the case of *Retrospektywa* more closely. In
that theatrical work, the members of Theater 77 used openly
available cultural resources to present a theatrical piece which
was both formally innovative and politically critical. After the
Stalinist period, in the era of the "small stabilization," as the
peaceful years of Gomulka's time were called, the authorities
made available to the Polish public previously banned components of the national tradition, as a sign indicating that the
Polish road to socialism was distinctively Polish. 77 attempted
to use important components of the national tradition for the
purpose of criticism, not legitimation. The public singing of
a song commemorating the exploits of the Polish army in
Italy allows the authorities to claim the support of all patriotic elements for its program. By juxtaposing versions of the

song as a way of answering the political-cultural project of Gombrowicz, 77 subverted the official purpose of broadening the patriotic front and turned the song into a provocation of independent public discourse.

The discussion in the third part of the play was not about constituting and fortifying the official political order. Rather, it was about the link between national traditions and independent social action. The critical writings of the political exile Gombrowicz, also selectively made available as part of the official project of legitimating the distinctively *Polish* road to socialism, moved the discussion in this direction. 77, by bringing together two different artifacts of the national tradition—one superpatriotic and sentimental, the other highly cosmopolitan and skeptical—detached the political-cultural debate from official discourse. By dramatizing the distance between official politics and the problems of everyday life in the second part of the play, they showed the necessity for this detachment. In the third part of the "art opening," the discussion was an open provocation for free public discourse. But given the prevailing political conditions, even though the evening's events seemed to be critical with official approval, such discourse did not occur. The embedded public domain had reached its limits.

The three supports for independent critical culture were all used in this work. The art displayed, depicting famous historical paintings of Aleksander Matejko and others, clearly used national cultural traditions critically, setting the stage for linking "Red Poppies on Monte Cassino" with Gombrowicz. The second part of the evening's events, the depiction of postwar official politics juxtaposed with everyday problems, used the official ideology against itself, showing how little the discussion about the popular masses and the people's revolution had to do with the people's problems. And 77 used its ancillary status as a Polish student theater to say much more than was possible anywhere else in Polish society at that time. Starting in 1954, for a twenty-five-year period, student theaters were ancillary cultural institutions supported by the Polish Student

Organization (PSO). As the patron of student theater, the PSO provided the institutional basis for the independence of student theater.

The PSO was founded in 1950 as an explicitly apolitical student organization. The Party created this type of organization in order to reach and control a wider range of students than they could through the extremely politicized Union of Polish Youth. This was necessary because of students' adherence to orientations based on prerevolutionary cultural traditions, which were negatively disposed toward the new socialist order. The goal of the Party was to involve students in a Party-backed organization and thus gain their sympathies. Yet the consequence of establishing such an organization was to provide an institutional base of support for an apolitical, and even politically critical, public mode of expression. Even from 1954 through 1956, when the regime was still essentially Stalinist, student theater provided a unique stage for critical expression, reaching students and broader audiences. The basis for this expression lay primarily in the unanticipated consequences of the regime's propaganda and in the institutional structure established by the regime.

Until 1956 there was a great deal of repression of any kind of independent expression in Poland. After 1956 this repression loosened considerably but did not disappear. The central point here is that the drive to express independent ideals publicly was constantly reinforced even during the most repressive years. Thus, when intensive repression was lifted, a new generation of Polish artists and intellectuals, who had been subjected to constant propaganda during their formative years, was able to develop an important forum for critical political discussion.

The importance of the analytic scheme presented in this chapter becomes even clearer when we try to understand how the social bases of independent expression enabled such expression to reach the public in Poland in the early seventies, when *Retrospektywa* was produced, even though the direction of the general political situation seemed to make this un-

likely. At that time the situation for intellectuals and artists
had improved only slightly with the major political changes
introduced by Edward Gierek, who was able to keep independent intellectuals and artists quiet by exercising fairly repressive cultural policies while improving the economic lot of
the masses of Poles. The decrease in the number of books published, plays produced, and major research projects initiated
supports this observation.[14] It was precisely at that time, however, that student theater again produced highly critical works
for the first time since the late fifties.

The Limits

Yet even though cultural traditions, official ideology, and cultural institutions do significantly support cultural freedom,
they also significantly limit that freedom. While it is true that
a lot more can be said than "Big Brother is good" or "Big
Brother is ungood," Big Brother still has a say in the matter.

Hejduk, the director of Theater 77, did not seek to produce
a play directly about Gombrowicz, the problems of daily life,
or contemporary politics. In *Retrospektywa*, he developed a
work in which it was possible to consider these elements. He
was an expert in expanding the possible. His cultural task was
to gauge the prevailing political atmosphere and say as much
as he could. But significantly, the atmosphere defined what
he said.

In the late seventies, the ancillary support of student theater
became quite restrictive. The Polish Student Organization had
become the Polish *Socialist* Student Organization. It took on
more of the character of a Party front and began primarily to
control, rather than politically support, autonomous cultural
activity. When Hedjuk then retreated from the provocative,
other theaters began to produce works without regard to the
shifting political winds. Their works, most outstandingly
those of Theater of the Eighth Day, defined excellence and cultural and political innovations. 77 was still mired in official
ideology. There was a striking contrast between theater creators, writers, and other artists who began to consider the

premise that they should create their works as if they lived in a free society (the starting premise of the opposition culture), and those theater creators, writers, and other artists who continued to follow official directives and censorship.

The distortions of such considerations became evident when other artists, writers, and political activists essentially seceded from totalitarian culture. Even innovative and critical works like *Retrospektywa* began to show their limitations. The selections from Gombrowicz's diary read and referred to started to seem quite limited. The assertion that people were responsible for mistakes of the past because of apathy and lack of involvement left unacknowledged the repressive political conditions that blocked free political involvement. The discussion of politics within the existing order apparently did not allow for discussions which rejected the order as a whole. Censors, the secret police, and general rules of the social game in a totalitarian order (one doesn't speak unless others do and unless one knows to whom one is speaking) combined to limit the work. Real liberation from Newspeak and the totalitarian project was not clearly articulated, and if not in an avant-garde theater at the margins of society, then where? In this way the work sent a message of support of the existing order.

This was obviously a subtle kind of support, at first much less important than the innovative and critical thrust of this and other works of Theater 77 in the early seventies. But with the appearance in 1976 of an autonomous culture, completely free of the Party, totalitarian culture, and Newspeak, the supportive and apologetic elements of the theater began to take on greater importance. By 1978 Hejduk was condemning those who completely freed themselves of the official order. His logic was relatively simple and not completely self-interested. He did not believe that the opposition culture would persist, and felt that its only significant consequence would be to heighten official repression. Therefore, he was a steadfast opponent of those in theater who turned off the internal censor and freed themselves of Newspeak.

Such speculations, judgments, and conflicts characterize the post-totalitarian terrain. Before we analyze this in detail in chapter 6, we must turn to an analysis of the more fundamental cultural and political alternatives to Newspeak and totalitarian culture.

II

Post-Totalitarianism

F O U R

Truth, Politics, and Autonomous Culture

FOR CRITICAL CULTURE, changes in the severity of ideological enforcement are generally more significant than change in the Party's ideological line. It is the use of coercion that counts most, not its substantive rationalization. Since force defines reason, it hardly matters whether socialist internationalism or nationalist assertion is the present party line. As long as the basic totalitarian formula equating force and reason is in place, the arbitrary ideological content shapes the context of cultural expression and its justification.

Leniency on the part of Party officials allows for a struggle against totalitarian culture. As we have seen, cultural activists can work from the independent bases of public expression and achieve some degree of cultural freedom. Cultural traditions can be kept alive. Cultural form can develop independently of Party doctrine. Around developing traditions and forms, publics are constituted. Much can be accomplished in this: great works of art and science have been produced; important cultural pursuits have been kept alive, some with an excellence unsurpassed internationally—e.g., Soviet physics, Hungarian films and Polish theater. Yet, when a completely independent unofficial culture develops (as happened in Poland in the late seventies and to a lesser extent in Hungary in the early eighties), not only are the authorities with their cultural edicts challenged, but the officially accepted critical culture is threatened as well. A culture develops that has a very different relationship with force and the controlling powers, a culture which is potentially freed from the demands of Newspeak. Since the officially accepted critical culture achieves its significance in part through an interaction with the demands of officialdom, unofficial uncensored culture challenges such culture.

Official culture takes its cues from officialdom. Specific degrees of leniency allow for specific degrees of cultural innovation and critique other than the serving of some official purpose. Ideological formulations necessarily stupefy, because force, not reason, defines reason. Newspeak distorts communication to varying degrees.

Independent unofficial culture can be free from all of this. In the Soviet Union as well as Poland, unofficial culture began with the publication of previously censored texts. But the real cultural break emerges when imagination defines culture without considering censorship, when the permissible and the impermissible are no longer significant categories, and when insight and intelligence are more important than political daring. Then the real alternatives to Newspeak appear.

Such alternatives are reactions to totalitarian culture and official social structure. Culturally, the totalitarian relationships among truth, political force, and the ethics of art and science are frontally deconstructed. Sociologically, new and completely free cultural institutions are constituted. Such constitution is based on the cultural deconstruction and is the major project of independent politics. Post-totalitarian culture precedes post-totalitarian politics.

First we consider the culture and its politics of deconstruction, then in the next chapter the politics of cultural construction; both are embedded in and emerge from the interaction between official truth and the politics of everyday life. We start with a close examination of the emergence of post-totalitarian autonomous culture from the totalitarian political cultural context.

Truth, Legitimated Force, and the Development of Alternative Culture

In Solzhenitsyn's *The First Circle,* a *zek* (political prisoner), named Rubin, modeled after Lev Kopelev (now along with Solzhenitsyn in exile), has a pet project, the creation of Civic

Temples. The *zek* understands the quasi-religious role of Party ideology and wants to establish a more formalized setting for Party ritual. The need for such an institution is clear to Rubin. As he puts it, "at present it was more important for the Soviet Union to improve public morality than to build the Volga-Don Canal or Angarastroi."[1] This *zek* is presented by Solzhenitsyn as a comic figure, a true believer in the camps. Why comic and not tragic? For Solzhenitsyn the reason is obvious—it is patently absurd for a political prisoner to be devising schemes to strengthen the political forces oppressing him.

Yet the absurdity is even more profound. Belief has little to do with the effectiveness of official ideology, even though the ideology is ubiquitous. Public morality is most undesirable from the point of view of the authorities. This is the ground for analyzing systematically the substantial relationships among truth, politics and autonomous culture in the totalitarian order.

Truth

In the Soviet bloc, the enlightened scientific project of seeking objective truth has been transformed into the political project of acting according to the truth in history as it is understood by an empowered elite. The "truth" has become a powerful ideological support for social oppression. Though the tyrannical potential of the philosopher king has been known since the time of Plato, more is involved here. A specific method, official Marxism, is identified with the discovery of historical laws and movement. This method indicates that one specific class in society, the proletariat, has in its power the ability to grasp the movement toward the humane future. This has led to the identification of one agency, the Communist party, specifically that of the Soviet Union, as possessing the power to lead the movement.

Thus Trotsky could declare, "we can only be right with and by the Party, for history has provided no other way of being in the right."[2] Having gone this far, the Party can tolerate no other views. Human life itself becomes expendable. Since the future is known, and is wonderful, all sorts of barbarisms in the present are acceptable.

These features of official Marxism and Soviet Communism have been explored by such diverse figures as Arthur Koestler, Maurice Merleau-Ponty, Herbert Marcuse, along with Hannah Arendt.[3] I re-emphasize that it is with the discovery of an absolute, politically enforced "truth" in history that barbarism is legitimated. Gradually truth itself disappears. The crusader for truth, the Party, oversees the correct social life, but correctness is maintained through the absence of belief in an exploration of truth. This absence of belief creates the unique form of political legitimation of totalitarianism without terror—totalitarianism legitimated through disbelief.

Politics

It is a general sociological rule, explored in great detail by Max Weber, that when legitimation leads from power to authority, the success of domination greatly increases.[4] But there is no general rule concerning how legitimation as the justification for social power is achieved. The experience of Soviet-type societies under totalitarianism without terror suggests that power may be legitimated not only on the grounds of belief, as is commonly assumed and analyzed in contemporary sociology, but on the grounds of disbelief as well.

Traveling through Eastern Europe, one is struck by the ubiquitous presence of propaganda posters, billboards with revolutionary slogans, and public monuments commemorating the heroic acts of revolutionary workers, peasants, and soldiers. One is also struck by the ideological fervor of such publicity, which is marked and reinforced by the rhetoric of newspapers, magazines, and the most readily available books. Yet if one stays a while and listens to people, a tremendous incongruity appears. The official language of publicity and rhetoric is rarely used in interpersonal communications. Though official language is used during official transactions and as a source of humor and irony among friends, it is not used, as we have already observed, in nonofficial discussions about prices, economy, culture, and family life, even when people want to argue for officially promoted positions.

The official language is both ever-present and strikingly absent. When people want to communicate in an authentic interpersonal manner, they do not use the official language. When they desire ambiguity and obfuscation, they use it. This is similar to the use of "bureaucratese" by government and corporate bureaucrats in the West, an extreme example being the public statements of former secretary of state and NATO commander, General Alexander Haig.

But the mixture of politics and language goes significantly beyond that with which we are familiar. Not only are elegance and clarity sacrificed, as Orwell pointed out,[5] but linguistic obfuscation becomes a central element of political control, legitimating systematic domination. In the West, bureaucratic language may be used to assure domination in governmental, corporate, and even academic life. It expands the range of actions open to a bureaucrat. It provides a means to avoid moral responsibility. Systematic domination, nonetheless, is not involved. The language is not coordinated from a societal center and its use assured through a system of censorship, as in totalitarian orders. In short, in the West, bureaucratic language makes possible specific acts of domination and sets of such acts. In totalitarian orders, the functioning of the whole system is involved. In the case of our young social scientist, we saw how people related to each other through Newspeak. Now we must examine how, in the social hierarchy, subordinate and dominant relate to each other dualistically through Newspeak and nonofficial language.

Officially, the Party is the vanguard of the working class, and Party members relate to their non-Party colleagues from the position of enlightened leaders, drawing upon the experience of their colleagues and leading them in the building of a better world. Nonofficially, the relationship is a simple one of ruler over ruled. Officially, the creators of literature are promoted or discouraged because of their partinost (party spirit) and commitment. Nonofficially, the creators and portions of their work face a censor looking for explicitly forbidden topics, ideological positions, and names or even words (such as *freedom*). Officially, trips abroad, vacation leave, scholarships, work bonuses, and so forth are granted on the basis of explicit formal regulations; nonofficially, these privileges are based on such criteria as Party membership and service, nonobstructive public behavior, and family background.

Both the official and nonofficial justifications operate to legitimate action. Subordinate and dominant are conscious of both. In official interactions, when speaking explicitly to one another they are not only referring to official justification but are seeking to convey and interpret the nonofficial, real justifications. In private, apart from official interactions, the explicit statements and interpretations will be reconsidered, compared, and judged among friends. In such settings, it is even not unusual for the dominant to make explicit to the subordinate the nonofficial justifications for decisions and commands. Completing this crooked circle of explicit statements, implicit consequences, and interpretations is the fact that nonofficial private life is subjected to official public scrutiny.

Applications for Passports

Consider the case of two students, citizens of a socialist people's republic who sought to travel in the West. Quite often in their society a passport for such travel is difficult to obtain. The degree of difficulty may vary, but even when such passports are relatively freely given, the process is not easy; a great deal of paperwork has to be completed well in advance. The process can take the form of a bad melodrama. Days before excursions to the West are scheduled to begin, passports may not yet be received.

In the case under consideration, train and plane tickets were bought, tentative goodbyes were said to friends, relatives, and colleagues, arrangements were made for the care of pets, apartments, work, and so forth; yet in this state of preparation and anticipation, one citizen received his passport, while the other did not. Both citizens had received the same invitation from abroad, with the required promise of financial support for room and board and medical care. Both had filled out the same forms, in the same manner, and sent them to equivalent bureaucratic officials. Yet one citizen was told by a local official that there was an irregularity in the forms, while the other, in another locality, encountered no such problem. While the lucky citizen was abroad on his extended stay, the unlucky one, in defeat, informed friends, relatives, and colleagues of his fate and rearranged his financial and academic affairs for the coming year.

Such bureaucratic snags are not unknown in the West, but the range of factors which bring them about, the resultant uncertainty of the affected parties, and, most significantly for our purposes, the desperate search for understanding so that these snags might be avoided in the future, are all dramatically intensified in the East.

A simple administrative mistake may have been made in the case of the passports. But it is just as likely that the snag was due to some hidden factor related to the applicant: a father with a questionable political past, an unpolitic rejection of participation in Party-sponsored social activity, a friendship with a disgraced Party activist, close proximity to some social disturbance, or unorthodox statements made in a classroom, during official extracurricular activity, or even among friends, some of whom might have special "scholarships" from a security department. Or the snag could be related to the work of the local official evaluating the application, who could be having a clash with a colleague, leading to a super-cautious approach to all passport applications. A clash between the locality and a regional or national office could lead to the same result. Numerous factors might be involved in such official politics. Local leniency in the past might have resulted in official embarrassment (defections or undesirable activity abroad), leading to unusual caution and stringency. Or stringency might be enforced to produce an exceptionally clean record (from the point of view of central officialdom) to be used by a local official as a political base for upward mobility in the political apparatus.

In this case the local official who rejected the application did not refer directly to any of these reasons. He assured the passport applicant that official passport policy sought to encourage scientific, artistic, and cultural exchange between East and West, but said that in the student's case unfortunate irregularities presented problems. He encouraged the student to reapply in a year.

The student tried to clarify the irregularities but could not obtain unambiguous satisfaction. During the subsequent year he pondered the possible reasons for the decision and considered what had to be done to get a passport. In nonofficial conversations with friends and colleagues he planned unofficial meetings with officials, seeking both a clear and concrete explanation for the rejection and suggestions for avoiding it in the future.

The results of such efforts generally vary from continued uncertainty and ignorance to satisfaction contingent on bribery or cooperation with the internal or external security apparatus. This sort of meeting of official and unofficial worlds is a subtle substitute for brutal terror, but it yields the effective social disorientation and control which strengthen political authority. Officially passports are granted to all loyal citizens committed to the Party program of peace and international understanding, but nonofficially the program is a gloss covering a subtle system of political direction and control, to be not believed but interpreted.

The nature of the interaction between official and nonofficial language distinguishes liberal periods from hard times. In the hardest of times, nonofficial language and thoughts are severely restricted in public. They may never be privatized in complete individual isolation, as Orwell imagined in the case of Winston Smith in *1984*. Even in Stalin's Russia, official language and thought did not effectively penetrate intimate and small circles of friendship and kinship. The intensity and lifelong nature of Russian friendship is a manifestation of the vitality and persistence of nonofficial language and thought. But in hard times, spontaneity of thought and language without regard to calculation and overarching historical script may not go much beyond such circles. Liberal times, then, are defined by the expanded publicity for nonofficial language. Indeed, open dissidence, opposition, and cultural excellence can and do break down the official/nonofficial divide.

Alternative Culture

The sociological study of art and culture as alternatives to Newspeak is the study of that dense labyrinth of politicized poses and interpretations in which culture is created, distributed, and received in today's totalitarianism. This is most clearly the case when a cultural product challenges the labyrinthian character of official culture directly.

The simplest way is through satire. The most primitive form of this is the ironic use of official language. Official rhetoric of newspapers and propaganda texts may be turned into its opposite when placed within the cultural form and institution of cabaret theater or popular music. All official statements on the surface of the cultural product (that which is available for censorship) have a nonofficial and opposing subtext arising from both the context and the audience's expectation of satire. As we have observed, the critical potential of such satire is limited by its dependence on official language.

The most radical cultural critique occurs when official language is disposed of, when this language system is explicitly rejected. In George Konrad's *The Case Worker*, a novel which passed Hungarian censorship, this is artfully accomplished. The sterility and emptiness of the official life of the social worker is juxtaposed with the human tragedy experienced by his clients. Official control and its flat language, pointed to in the text but not articulated, are juxtaposed with concrete human experience. Human experience itself portrays the tension between (official) controlled life and (nonofficial) disordered life. The caseworker observes:

> On the sidewalk I am sometimes inclined to think that I can go where I please, cut across here, turn in there, or loop eccentrically around the block, but I fight off this paranoid temptation and submit to the

regulations that confine me to the common stream.
The street commands the pedestrian. The doorway
the oncomer, the stair the upgoer, the table and chair,
glass and knife the homecomer. And if, somewhere in
this conveyor belt of obedience, there is a breakdown
and the body disagrees from the appropriate order of
things, the policeman is there—and so am I—to put
it right with a few swift and well tried strategems.[6]

In poetic form, Konrad has embedded a universal dialectic
between spontaneity and control in the experiences of everyday life, supporting the novel's appeal outside of Hungary. But
in the Soviet bloc the universal becomes specifically political. The very concreteness of the mode of expression and its
truthfulness without recourse to official cliches (repeatedly
questioned and denounced in the text) represent a profound
political challenge.

The challenge itself has been forged in actual opposition
politics, spectacularly in the practice of Solidarity in Poland.
But where do such politics come from? Or for that matter,
where does the independent culture which represents this
politics come from?

Now we are approaching the most remarkable irony of
truth, politics, and culture in totalitarian orders. (Though
ironies abound, some are more surprising than others.) Perhaps it is not unexpected that an official historical truth embedded in institutionalized practice, not open to criticism and
reformed at the will of high-level officialdom, is disbelieved by
the populace and becomes a nontruth. If such nontruth becomes the basis of political legitimacy, yielding a unique political system replacing the violence but not the uncertainty of
totalitarianism based on terror, that phenomenon needs exploration, particularly with regard to the relationship between
the official and nonofficial worlds. Still, since the everyday life
of totalitarianism without terror is known, the irony here is
also not so unexpected. It is even somewhat familiar to us
through our experiences of bureaucratic life. But that the
literature, culture, and autonomous politics of the world of

untruth and its legitimation take simple truth as their starting point has remarkably ironic consequences.

Truth, Autonomous Culture and Politics

It is puzzling and disturbing to literary critics and observers that among the most accomplished literary figures of the twentieth century are the dissident writers of the Soviet Union and Eastern Europe. Solzhenitsyn, Milan Kundera, George Konrad, and Stanislaw Baranczak are among the famous cultural figures of both East and West. The Polish August and the life of Solidarity are stellar historical moments. How is it that such literary excellence and political accomplishment seem to appear disproportionately from the context of repression? Do we have to be willing to accept the old idea that the greatest creative achievements are only born out of suffering? Is there a basic conflict between the cultural good and the political good? Such is our apparent moral quandary.

Such cultural and political examples of excellence among creative artists and political activists have in common a search for simple truth. Too often the excellence is understood through a sentimental romanticism, and the unique historical event is obscured by the views of convention—political, ideological, and social-scientific. The supposition is that the culturally profound is a direct consequence of repression. The authorities have power in their hands; not only do they determine the course of history through their command of economies, cultural revolutions, and international politics, they even make dissenting literature and the arts serious because they deem them important enough to be censored. The creative artist then is the hero, locked in a battle with the forces of darkness. The work then has interest and appeal through a sentimental appreciation of the dimensions of the battle, i.e., the idea that life itself can be and has been on the line.

Such imagery accounts for the superficial appeal of the dissident in the West. No doubt it helps the emigre to market his or her work here. Further, and more importantly for our purposes, it establishes an authority for dissident cultural politics.

The Western and Eastern consequences of romantic sentiment are related. The Western media's concentrated concern and reports about the fate of dissident artists and intellectuals, and the political elevation of such concern as a central subject for discussion in an East-West forum such as the Helsinki Conference, turn isolated artists and intellectuals into potential spokesmen for every sort of discontent experienced by the citizenry of the Soviet bloc, spokesmen heard not only in the West but, through Western broadcasts, in their home countries.

Though at times dissidents have a broader audience in the West than in the East, when they reach their compatriots their stances are readily understandable and meaningful. As isolated romantic heroes they are twentieth-century versions of nineteenth-century visions. When Solzhenitsyn fought for truth and was denounced and deported, in a work called *Pushkin Lives* the Tanganka Theater of Moscow, a satirical establishment at the leading edge of acceptability, reminded the well-connected but daring establishment of Pushkin's heroic battles with repression.[7] An individual's bravery and talent, Western media attention, and officially promoted Soviet culture joined to make Solzhenitsyn a dissident celebrity.

Yet celebrity has its limits. As in the West, celebrity is manufactured, more the product of the manipulative forces surrounding an individual than a product of the individual's qualities. When there are qualities worth appreciating, celebrity becomes confining. Note how world statesmen, scientists, and movie stars are almost indistinguishable in publications like *People* magazine.

But socialist celebrity poses even more serious problems. Solzhenitsyn's prose was washed out by the glare of his dissident-celebrity persona. Such a persona, however bright, is a negative reflection of the official culture of politics and politics of culture, and is therefore limited in the same way as is satire. All the qualities of Solzhenitsyn's prose, most readily discernible in his early works—his linguistic innovations, his empathetic psychology, his power to see the universal in the particular—become reduced to one dimension: opposition to the Soviet order and culture through the medium of world-wide celebrity. Solzhenitsyn himself seems to have succumbed to this reduction.

The problem of celebrity status is a further obstacle for autonomous politics. The celebrity of the cultural dissident leads to a politics of despair, grand moral gestures within the context of social isolation. By itself the stellar quality of the dissident makes social opposition difficult, because opposition becomes a realm beyond the reach of mere mortals. A famous individual like Andrei Sakharov can lend support and even protection to lesser-known dissidents. But the absence of a free public life makes such individual patronage politically inconsequential, existing outside the view of the great bulk of the population.

Thus the sentimental romantic image of the dissident artist or intellectual as hero places a serious constraint on cultural excellence and political action. When the alternative culture of the East is viewed through such sentiment, it becomes its opposite, unidimensional ideology set against the totalitarian order.

But as we have seen, this is not the whole of opposition culture. A great irony lies in the fact that in a political world where absolute disbelief is the source of political legitimation, where the official language lacks clear meaning, where Newspeak is the mode of officially accepted public discourse, a powerful concern for conveying simple features of everyday life in precise poetic form animates much of the arts and opposition politics. This animation is translatable, so much so that the literature is among the best in the world today; importantly, *despite,* not *because of,* censorship. Consider this verse by the Polish poet Stanislaw Baranczak:

These Words

These words from reviewing stands and those in
    parlors,
these, sewn by the thick thread of a voice
into the official-blue bag of a suit, and

those, stripped naked of their denim
in the probing search of revision;
these, known from having been heard too often, and
        those,
scarcely remembered from having been seen
so rarely; these words, which easily
let themselves slip through the strainer of a
        microphone,
and those, which must work themselves through a
        grating
with immense effort; these,
delivered with unflinching audacity, and those,
whispered softly from shame and anxiety into the
        ears
of a guard; these, spoken staightforward
into the dry eye of a camera, and those, which at
        being spoken
one's eyes lower, for it is hard to bear a woman's
        tears;
these words, which are broken in conference rooms
by stormy, long, unceasing applause,
and those, in visiting rooms broken

by the intervention of a watchful clock; these words,
these words of speeches too long and conversations
        too short

are—I know it's inconceivable—words
of one and the same tongue.[8]

Here the major repressive agency of official language is addressed unambiguously. The limitations of human experience
are identified not primarily by making reference to overt repression and the censor but by language itself. The limitation
is overcome by the clearly understood poetic expression. The
poetry is formed as a straightforward negation of the repressive agency, but through a distinctive poetic voice. The
cultural and political goal of this political poem is the poem
itself. It is invigorated by the political struggles of the Polish
people, the emergence of the democratic opposition and the
struggles of Solidarity, but is not reducible to them.

Baranczak's personal quest for an independent voice, his attempt to tell simple truths, and his political goals are all immanent in his work.

If Porcelain, Then Only the Kind
If porcelain, then only the kind
you won't miss under the shoe of a mover, or the
          tread of a tank;
if a chair, then one not too comfortable, lest
there be regret in getting up and leaving;
if clothing, then just so much as can fit in a suitcase,
if books, then those which can be taken in the
          memory,
if plans, then those which can be overlooked
when the time comes for the next move
to another street, continent, historical period
or world;

who told you that you were permitted to settle in?
who told you that this or that would last forever?
did no one ever tell you that you will never
in the world
feel at home here?[9]

A world of total mobility, of constant movement, without personal past or future, without a home, is the world of totalitarianism. The official (enforced) truth is the whole truth—except for the voice of the individual. Beyond the totalitarian bleakness is the full voice of the poet.

Up to now we have observed how the bleakness has been confronted through institutional intrigue and the subtle use of publicly available cultural artifacts and models. Now we consider the direct confrontation between autonomous imagination and totalitarianism.

Imagination versus Totalitarianism

The dark quality of Hannah Arendt's vision of totalitarianism is unsurpassed. *Eichmann in Jerusalem* is *Everyman* in (bureaucratic) modernity. *The Origins of Totalitarianism* is a history of the West. Yet, she concludes her classic chap-

ter on totalitarian force and truth, "Ideology and Terror,"
optimistically.

> There remains also the truth that every end in history
> necessarily contains a new beginning. This beginning
> is the promise, the only "message" which the end can
> ever produce. Beginning, before it becomes a histori-
> cal event, is the supreme capacity of man. *Initium ut
> esset homo creatus est*—"that a beginning be made,
> man was created," said Augustine. This beginning is
> guaranteed by each new birth; it is indeed every man.[10]

The individual subjected to totalitarian control remains a
new beginning capable of new ends, capable of autonomous
culture and politics. The social bases of independent critical expression make available to the individual the means to
ends other than totalitarian ones. Yet as we have seen, in
officially accepted and even promoted critical culture, the
work includes the censor's mark of acceptance or rejection or
modification.

Miklos Haraszti, the Hungarian oppositionist, suggests
that such critical culture is "neo-Stalinist," "soft," "civilian
socialist culture"—not really an alternative. "In other words,
the artist, a soldier armed with paintbrush or pen under
Stalinism, is, after de-Stalinization, demobilized and returned
to civilian life. He remains, however, very much on active
duty; in the reserves, as it were, always aware that his status
might change the moment war is declared."[11]

There are, though, draft resisters, even deserters, and the
first steps toward desertion can easily be taken, even if they
may have very grave and dramatic consequences. In a 1983
interview conducted in Cambridge, Massachusetts, Baranczak
explained this.

Remembering Solidarity

In the late seventies Baranczak's reputation as a poet and
scholar had spread beyond Polish borders. As a political activist he was a founding member of KOR. As a cultural activist

he was an editor of *Zapis* (*Censored*), the first completely independent literary journal to be published in postwar Poland.
As an academic expelled from Poznan University, he was invited to visit Harvard for a year. His unofficial cultural and
political activities led to an official rejection of his passport
application. Despite international protests, he remained in
Poznan. When Solidarity emerged, the invitation remained
open, and the passport was given. In 1981 Baranczak went
to Harvard for a year. When the Polish state declared war
against Polish society, Baranczak was on a list of those who
were to be interned. His one-year stay became an apparently
permanent emigration.

In his Cambridge apartment, he was interviewed for Richard
Adams's film *Citizens*.[12] There he explained his activities as a
founding member of KOR and editor of *Zapis*. He described
meetings between workers and intellectuals during the Solidarity period. He emphasized the broad Polish desire to understand the workings of censorship and do away with it. He
talked about the sadness of exile. Then he explained how he
became an opposition poet.

It began almost as a private act, a simple intellectual exercise. In 1973 Baranczak wrote a long poem for himself about
everyday life in People's Poland. For the first time as a mature
poet, he wrote a piece without thinking about censorship. He
was not considering publication. No alternative publication
system, or *samizdat* network, then existed in Poland. He just
wanted to know what his poetry would be like if he did not
worry about the censor. When he completed the work, Baranczak typed extra copies with carbons and passed them on
to friends. They offered him encouragement, and at first he
thought that this was the end of the matter.

Months later, visiting Wroclaw (hundreds of kilometers
from his home in Poznan), Baranczak discovered that the
poem was circulating all around Poland. Someone he met
there showed him a copy of a retyped version of the poem
with some minor changes (in the retyping, some words were
dropped and others added, as in the children's game, "tele-

phone"). Without intending to, Baranczak had become an autonomous poet. His poem created a latent network of oppositional culture.

The political struggles of the seventies and eighties transformed this quiet dissident network into a full-fledged independent cultural world, in competition with official cultural institutions and arguably of greater intellectual and political significance. The emergence of such a world will be considered in the next chapter. Here we need to observe how an individual, along with other individuals, started anew and helped create an entirely independent culture, freed from the "velvet prison" (as Miklos Haraszti puts it) of censorship and official tolerance of mild criticism and innovation. The dark side of the story, of course, is that it was told in Cambridge and not in Poznan, Cracow, or Warsaw.

The starting point of autonomous culture is not in a polemic against officialdom, but in turning away from totalitarian culture and seeking to constitute an alternative, independent culture. Poets and novelists, painters and filmmakers, dramatists and political theorists attempt to go beyond the aesthetics of the censored. They neither assert that Big Brother is good nor put forward sophisticated or simpleminded critical versions of "Big Brother is ungood."

Living in Truth

Baranczak's personal decision to write a poem without the censor in mind is an instance of living in truth, as Vaclav Havel would put it.[13] In "The Power of the Powerless," written in the late seventies, Havel articulates the very principles which were being acted upon in Poland to constitute the first fully developed opposition movement in the Soviet bloc. Havel explores the importance of the official truth, which is an actual lie, for the maintenance of totalitarian control. He further analyzes the subversiveness of truth in its broader sense.

Havel tells us the story of a manager of a fruit and vegetable store who places in his window the slogan, "Workers of the World, Unite!" By analyzing why the greengrocer puts the slo-

gan in his window among the onions and carrots and what it
would mean if he did not, Havel phenomenologically reveals
the complex basis of today's totalitarian control. He observes:

> Individuals need not believe all these mystifications,
> but they must behave as though they did, or they
> must at least tolerate them in silence, or get along
> well with those who work with them. For this reason,
> however, they must *live within a lie*. They need not
> accept the lie. It is enough for them to have accepted
> their life with it and in it. For by this very fact, indi-
> viduals confirm the system, fulfill the system, make
> the system, *are* the system.[14]

For Havel, the most effective way of resisting the system is to
secede from it—to live in truth, as Baranczak did. Havel continues his tale of the grocer:

> Let us now imagine that one day something in our
> greengrocer snaps and he stops putting up slogans
> merely to ingratiate himself. He stops voting in elec-
> tions he knows are a farce. He begins to say what he
> really thinks at political meetings. And he even finds
> the strength in himself to express solidarity with
> those whom his conscience commands him to sup-
> port. He rejects the ritual and breaks the rules of
> the game. He discovers once more his suppressed
> identity and dignity. He gives his freedom a concrete
> significance. His revolt is an attempt to *live within
> the truth*.
>   The bill is not long in coming. He will be relieved
> of his post as manager of the shop and and trans-
> ferred to the warehouse. His pay will be reduced. His
> hopes for a holiday in Bulgaria will evaporate. His
> children's access to higher education will be threat-
> ened. His superiors will harrass him and his fel-
> low workers will wonder about him. Most of those
> who apply these sanctions, however, will not do so
> from an authentic inner conviction but simply under
> pressure from conditions, the same conditions that

once pressured the greengrocer to display the official slogan.[15]

The isolated grocer will suffer from his decision, as will
those who are close to him. But when the decision is cultural
or political, when the issue is not just negative, that is, refusing to put up a propaganda sign, when it involves positive political and cultural actions, totalitarian culture is challenged
with possibly enduring effect. The success of political challenges such as those of KOR in Poland and Charter 77 in
Czechoslovakia depends upon concerted and persistent action and the broadness of their appeal. They are highly vulnerable, though they can potentially overturn the system of living
the lie.

Cultural challenges in the arts and sciences can ironically be
both more fundamental and more enduring. They show the
official truth as the lie, and in their very form constitute living
in truth. Baranczak's poetry juxtaposes truth with lies, Newspeak with the poetry of everyday life, and the search for
enduring values with nihilistic relativity. George Konrad contrasts the coarseness and poetry of real human feelings with
the cleanliness and banality of social control.[16] Havel poetically
invents his own Newspeak in his play *The Memorandum* to
free himself and his audience from the "really existing Newspeak."[17] These and many other works culturally constitute the
power of the powerless. They depict totalitarian culture and
create alternatives. They embody the post-totalitarian terrain.

Havel describes the parameters of post-totalitarianism:

> Between the aims of the post-totalitarian system and
> the aims of life there is a yawning abyss: while life, in
> its essence, moves towards plurality, diversity, in-
> dependent self-constitution and self-organization, in
> short, towards the fulfillment of its own freedom,
> the post-totalitarian system demands conformity,
> uniformity, and discipline. While life ever strives to
> create new and "improbable" structures, the post-
> totalitarian system contrives to force life into its most

probable states. The aims of the system reveal its most essential characteristic to be introversion, a movement towards being ever more completely and unreservedly *itself,* which means that the radius of its influence is continually widening as well. This system serves people only to the extent necessary to ensure that people will serve it. Anything beyond this, that is to say, anything which leads people to overstep their predetermined roles, is regarded by the system as an attack upon itself.[18]

Havel uses the term *post-totalitarian system* somewhat differently than I do. He is referring to what I have called today's totalitarianism and totalitarianism without terror. He wants to indicate changes in horrors without changes in principles. Because the term seems to suggest movement beyond totalitarian principles, I have not followed his usage.

Because of this very ambiguity, Havel himself has stopped using the term *post-totalitarian.*[19] This seems premature. Post-totalitarianism, as used here, refers to the whole complex of totalitarian culture and the distinctive critical post-totalitarian voices and actions of resistance. Milan Kundera presents in a remarkably antisentimental fashion an elegant mapping of this post-totalitarian terrain, the words in the reviewing stands and those in parlors, the velvet prison and KOR, Newspeak and its alternatives.

In the Shadows

The politics and culture of the true believer and his opponents are within the shadows of twentieth-century horrors. In an exchange in Kundera's *The Farewell Party,* Olga, who is the daughter of a Communist enthusiast who was executed in a purge, asks Jakub, an older man who has protected her and is planning emigration, what her father was like, whether he perpetrated the same horrors as those who prosecuted him.

At first Jakub evades the question, but he finally concedes that it is a possibility, because "there isn't a person on this planet who is not capable of sending a fellow human being to death without any great pangs of conscience." [20] Olga objects: Jakub cannot explain away a specific inhumanity by claiming that inhumanity is universal. Jakub's response encapsulates the basic starting point of a post-totalitarian sensibility:

> "The majority of people lead their existence within a small, idyllic circle bounded by their family, their home, and their work," replied Jakub. "They live in a secure realm somewhere between good and evil. They are sincerely horrified at the sight of a killer. And yet all you have to do is remove them from this peaceful circle and they, too, turn into murderers, without quite knowing how it happened. Every now and again history exposes humans to certain pressures and traps which nobody can resist. But what's the use of talking about it? It makes no difference to you what your father was theoretically capable of doing, and there is no way of proving it anyway. The only thing you need to concern yourself about is what he actually did or did not do. And in that respect his conscience was clear." [21]

Here we see that critical post-totalitarian culture takes place within the shadows of totalitarianism. The relatively benign official politics of the Soviet bloc have their particular meaning because they are filially connected with the politics of terror and because they use the same language of politics. The independent culture emerging from the interstices of command has its special quality because it is created after the terror. In the cited passage, we observe the tendency to express awareness of terror's lingering presence and a marked preference for a concrete and particular culture rather than a theoretical one. The two are linked. Terror is the practical enactment of the extremist rationality of totalitarian culture. The single universal truth about class struggle on the geopolitical plane leads to the deduction that there is an inevitable battle between the capitalist and socialist blocs, which then helps the Party activist deduce that all who oppose present Party policy, or even obstruct it unintentionally, are foreign agents. This justifies the terror. Inside the theoretical framework, the terror is the continuation of the geopolitical struggle. It is a human necessity. Viewed concretely, it is murder.

Olga is haunted by her father's past, which she cannot know objectively. He is remembered by his friends and hers as a victim, as an ethical Communist persecuted by fanatics. But, as Olga says,

> "I was wondering whether he hadn't done to other people exactly the same thing as was done to him. After all, the people who drove him to the gallows were his kind; they had the same beliefs, they were the same fanatics. They were convinced that every opinion that dissented—no matter how slightly—was a deadly threat to the revolution. They were morbidly mistrustful. They sent him to his death in the name of a holy dogma which he professed himself. Why then are you so sure he was innocent of having done the same thing to others?"[22]

Jakub does not only remind Olga how banal the terror can be.[23] He further speaks about a particular person's specific actions. The terrors of the theoretical possibility of what might have been done are denied through the remembrance of individual action of what was done.

On Remembering

The theoretically overdetermined world leads to barbarism and to the political struggles of everyday life, as we have observed throughout this inquiry. It also leads to systematic forgetting. Kundera concretely depicts this in the opening of *A Book on Laughter and Forgetting*.

> In February 1948, Communist leader Klement Gottwald stepped out on the balcony of a Baroque palace in Prague to address the hundreds of thousands of his fellow citizens packed into Old Town Square. It was a crucial moment in Czech history—a fateful moment of the kind that occurs once or twice in a millennium.

Gottwald was flanked by his comrades, with Clementis standing next to him. There were snow flurries, it was cold, and Gottwald was bareheaded. The solicitous Clementis took off his own fur cap and set it on Gottwald's head.

The Party propaganda section put out hundreds of thousands of copies of a photograph of that balcony with Gottwald, a fur cap on his head and comrades at his side, speaking to the nation. On that balcony the history of Communist Czechoslovakia was born. Every child knew the photograph from posters, schoolbooks, and museums.

Four years later Clementis was charged with treason and hanged. The propaganda section immediately airbrushed him out of history, and obviously, out of all the photographs as well. Ever since, Gottwald has stood on that balcony alone. Where Clementis once stood, there is only bare palace wall. All that remains of Clementis is the cap on Gottwald's head.[24]

The chief problem of living in the world of Newspeak is not that one is forced to express support for an unbelieved politics in a language which is meaningless apart from itself. It is rather that the individual no longer knows what exists beyond official language and no longer knows what exists apart from the official lie. When celebrating the great achievements of the Party in February 1948, the Czech population may know that all is not well with the official account. They may even be of the conviction that the victory of Communism represents the defeat of the nation. But they cannot know about Clementis, about his Communist conviction, and about the details of the totalitarian culture that devours its own children. When the culture is blemished, it is simply airbrushed.

By opening his *Book on Laughter and Forgetting* on this note, Kundera is emphasizing the importance of remembrance. The world of official truths and official histories is absurd. But despair, at least at first, is not the answer to absurdity; rather, memory is. Kundera tells us tales of private loves and public frustrations to show us the tricks that memory plays on us and the tricks we play with memory. Nonetheless, he emphasizes that "the struggle of man against power is the struggle of memory against forgetting."[25]

If alternatives to the present are to be found, they will not lie in the future. Kundera sadly observes:

> The future is an apathetic void of no interest to anyone. The past is full of life, eager to irritate us, provoke and insult us, tempt us to destroy or repaint it. The only reason people want to be masters of the future is to change the past. They are fighting for access to the laboratories where photographs are retouched and biographies and histories rewritten.[26]

Does this mean that Kundera is at best a conservative, and probably a reactionary, unfeeling about human suffering and unwilling to dedicate himself to a better tomorrow? Is he but the latest fashionable anti-Communist, distant relative of the White Russian aristocracy, kissing cousin of Solzhenitsyn? Not at all. It means that he is deeply aware of the weaknesses of revolutionary redemption, a radical critic of totalitarian kitsch, what he has called the Grand March.

Totalitarian Kitsch

Kundera objects to the shouting about the future, which cannot be known, and the privileged understanding of the present, which obliterates real human experience. In telling the story of Sabina in *The Unbearable Lightness of Being*, Kundera observes:

> In the realm of totalitarian kitsch, all answers are given in advance and preclude any questions. It follows, then, that the true opponent of totalitarian kitsch is the person who asks questions. A question is like a knife that slices through the stage backdrop and gives us a look at what lies hidden behind it.
>
> But the people who struggle against what we call totalitarian regimes cannot function with queries and

doubts. They, too, need certainties and simple truths to make the multitudes understand, to provoke collective tears.

Sabina had once had an exhibit that was organized by a political organization in Germany. When she picked up a catalogue, the first thing she saw was a picture of herself with a drawing of barbed wire superimposed on it. Inside she found a biography that read like the life of a saint or martyr; she had suffered, struggled against injustice, been forced to abandon her bleeding homeland, yet was carrying on the struggle. "Her paintings are a struggle for happiness," was the final sentence.

She protested, but they did not understand her.

Do you mean that modern art isn't persecuted under Communism?

"My enemy is kitsch, not Communism!" she replied, infuriated.[27]

Kundera can write this, however, because he is a true post-totalitarian. He knows that "kitsch is the stopover between being and oblivion."[28] It wipes out real human endeavor, as the phenomenon of celebrity status previously discussed reduces real dissident struggle to a new form of radical chic. It avoids the difficult questions and substitutes easy answers. Kundera is beyond the political culture of pretotalitarian and prototalitarian times. He observes the simplicities of modern political dreams in light of modern (totalitarian) political experience. He portrays the politics of Franz, a good-willed Western European man of the Left:

The fantasy of the Grand March that Franz was so intoxicated by is the political kitsch joining leftists of all times and tendencies. The Grand March is the splendid march on the road to brotherhood, justice, happiness; it goes on and on, obstacles notwithstanding, for obstacles there must be if the march is to be the Grand March.

The dictatorship of the proletariat or democracy? Rejection of the consumer society or demands for in-

creased productivity? The guillotine or an end to the
death penalty? It is all beside the point. What makes
a leftist a leftist is not this or that theory but his ability to integrate any theory into the kitsch called the
Grand March.[29]

Beyond Left and Right

Kundera concludes that we must go beyond conventional political categories:

> Since the days of the French Revolution, one half of
> Europe has been referred to as the left, the other half
> as the right. Yet to define one or the other by means of
> the theoretical principles it professes is all but impos-
> sible. And no wonder: political movements rest not
> so much on rational attitudes as on the fantasies, im-
> ages, words, and archetypes that come together to
> make up this or that *political kitsch*.[30]

The love affair of Franz and Sabina is central to the plot of
The Unbearable Lightness of Being. Theirs is an affair of misunderstandings in which a participant in the Grand March
engages a post-totalitarian spirit. The engagement is revealed
in their contrasting attitudes towards music.

Kundera writes: "For Franz, music is a source of intoxica-
tion and release from rationality and responsibility, it opened
the door of his body and allowed his soul to step out into the
world to make friends." For Sabina, "people are going deaf
because music is played louder and louder. But because they're
going deaf, it has to be played louder, still. Noise masked as
music [is] total ugliness."[31]

Though these contrasting views of music are presented reasonably by Kundera in a section entitled "A Short Dictionary
of Misunderstood Words," it is clear where his prejudices lie.
He wants to show how the search for absolute lyrical happiness in music, as in politics[32] (and love),[33] leads to horror.
For Sabina (and Kundera), the Communist ideal of complete
human harmony is much worse than the Communist reality.
Absolute cheerfulness is a horror. A society without conflict is

a society without humanity. In the West, such propositions
are theoretically intriguing. In the Soviet bloc, they are the
experienced ironies of history. Aesthetic, erotic, and political goals all must be *self-limiting* (to use the self-descriptive
phrase of Solidarity). Logical conclusion is a horror. For the
post-totalitarian, the fanaticisms of the Communist and the
anti-Communist are equally unacceptable. Kundera presents
his general observation on this point:

> World domination, as everyone knows, is divided be-
> tween demons and angels. But the good of the world
> does not require the latter to gain precedence over the
> former (as I thought when I was young); all it needs is
> a certain equilibrium of power. If there is too much
> uncontested meaning on earth (the reign of the an-
> gels), man collapses under the burden; if the world
> loses all its meaning (the reign of the demons), life is
> every bit as impossible.[34]

Throughout his writings, Kundera plays with this theme,
leading to significant misunderstandings and ironies.

Ironies of Sex and Politics

Kundera's attitudes towards sex and politics are filled with
ironic ambiguities and ambivalences. Irony is a type of self-
limitation. It is the cultural form of post-totalitarian resistance. Throughout his writings Kundera on the one hand
seems to be an antifeminist, depicting man as predator,
woman as prey,[35] and a rape as a joke,[36] and identifying sex
with violence. On the other hand his female characters often
display independence and distinction, from Tamina in *A Book
on Laughter and Forgetting* to Sabina. He often insists, in in-
troductory remarks to his novels and in the novels themselves,
that his are romances, farces about sexual, not political, adventures. But the works are filled with political observations,
theories, and speculations, and the sexual relations depicted
appear not erotically but politically. Indeed, the confusion of
the public with the private is one of his major themes. The

stories in *Laughable Loves* are his most explicitly nonpolitical. Yet they are about the ironies of domination and subjugation. It is in the political tales where Kundera's ambivalences are most significant. Clearly he knows that politics are important. Having had his life so fundamentally transformed by political events, from the Czech Communist takeover to the Prague Spring to the Soviet invasion, he could not see things otherwise. But he doubts the wisdom of political commitments, both Communist and anti-Communist. This has led to some superficial commentary from critics like Norman Podhoretz[37]—Kundera is not sufficiently vigilant, he is naive, even an apologist. But beyond such simplicities are Kundera's very serious reflections on the simultaneous need for political action, and political action's limitations. The ambivalence is the message. Knowing where political certainty linked with force leads, he proceeds cautiously.

He tells us the story of Tomas, a Prague doctor. Most deeply committed to his professional life as a surgeon and to his erotic adventures, Tomas in the spring of 1968 understood the political liberation as Kundera did. Kundera tells us:

> Anyone who thinks that the Communist regimes of Central Europe are exclusively the work of criminals is overlooking a basic truth: the criminal regimes were made not by criminals but by enthusiasts convinced that they had discovered the only road to paradise. They defended that road so valiantly that they were forced to execute many people. Later it became clear that there was no paradise, that the enthusiasts were therefore murderers.[38]

When the fact of murder became clear, the question of responsibility arose. Former true believers maintained their innocence on the grounds that they did not know of the horrors of terror. Tomas saw this (and clearly Kundera sees it) as being beside the point. He asked, "Is a fool on the throne relieved of all responsibility merely because he is a fool?"[39] The tale of Oedipus was brought to Tomas's mind. Not knowing was not an excuse for Oedipus; when he discovered he had slept with his mother, he blinded and exiled himself.[40]

Tomas writes an essay around this theme, and his fate revolves around the essay. It is shortened, simplified and published. After the Soviet invasion, Tomas loses his job and profession, emigrates, returns, loses friends, and becomes a dissident hero in the eyes of others (particularly his estranged son), all because of his comparison between the behaviors of ex-Stalinists and the hero of a classical tragedy of ethics. In the end he finds himself on the margins of society, first a window washer and finally a worker on a collective farm.

As a dissident (in the eyes of others), Tomas is approached to sign an open letter of protest to the Party. Kundera logically shows us that a politics of ultimate ends (Tomas's son asks him, "Aren't you on the side of the persecuted?") comes into conflict with a politics of responsibility:

> Is it right to raise one's voice when others are being silenced? Yes.
>
> On the other hand, why did the papers devote so much space to the petition? After all, the press (totally manipulated by the state) could have kept it quiet and no one would have been the wiser. If they publicized the petition, then the petition played into the rulers' hands! It was manna from heaven, the perfect start and justification for a new wave of persecution.
>
> What then should he have done? Sign or not?[41]

Tomas does not sign. His inaction is depicted with sympathy. His son and a dissident editor who approached him, on the other hand, are portrayed as naive and fanatical, misunderstanding Tomas's reflections on the Oedipal myth as a call for making strong distinctions between good and evil and for justice, when in fact Tomas's intent was to criticize the subjective feelings of innocence and lack of responsibility of true believers.

Just when this leads the reader to believe that Kundera is

counseling the reader to a stoic ethic of private resistance as opposed to political action, Kundera breaks the narrative and distances us from that conclusion:

> Staring impotently across a courtyard, at a loss for what to do; hearing the pertinacious rumbling of one's own stomach during a moment of love; betraying, yet lacking the will to abandon the glamorous path of betrayal; raising one's fist with the crowds in the Grand March; displaying one's wit before hidden microphones—I have known all these situations, I have experienced them myself, yet none of them has given rise to the person my curriculum vitae and I represent. The characters in my novels are my own unrealized possibilities. That is why I am equally fond of them all and equally horrified by them. Each one has crossed a border that I myself have circumvented. It is that crossed border (the border beyond which my own "I" ends) which attracts me most. For beyond that border begins the secret the novel asks about. The novel is not the author's confession; it is an investigation of human life in the trap the world has become.[42]

Indeed, the whole fragmentary tone of Kundera's novel distances the reader from drawing clear conclusions. Novels pose questions, in Kundera's judgment, they do not offer answers. He clearly is cautious about political commitments, especially about ones to which he is most sympathetic. He knows too well where politics can lead, but he knows as well that to withdraw from politics is not possible. It means choosing a slow rather than a quick death. Such is the trap the world has become.

From Culture to Politics

To understand the emergence of autonomous culture, we saw how this culture had to deconstruct the relationships between official truth, political force, and the ethics of the arts and sciences. In Kundera's work, we observe a post-totalitarian re-construction of the relationships between truth, politics and culture. The reconstruction takes place in the shadows of to-talitarian terror. Remembrance is a key cognitive function of the reconstitution. Totalitarian kitsch must be avoided at all costs, and the political culture needs to move beyond the truisms of the Left and the Right. Irony and self-limitation are key formal and normative commitments. The particular way Kundera works out his reconstruction is the work of an indi-vidual. Facing the problems of political exile, Kundera and his fellow Czech exile Josef Skvorecky have chosen alternative politics. While Kundera distances himself from the emigre population, Skvorecky as the publisher of an emigre press, helps to inform it.

Others do things differently. Though George Konrad, Vac-lav Havel, and Adam Michnik are three post-totalitarian po-litical writers, they approach political-geopolitical problems in significantly different ways.[43] Indeed, the political strategies and commitments of political dissidents and oppositionists vary tremendously. However, the differences take place in the same post-totalitarian universe of discourse.

In the next chapter we analyze the political thoughts and actions that have constituted this universe. The following chapters consider the world of post-totalitarianism and its challenge to those of us who have had the good fortune not to experience totalitarianism directly.

FIVE

Autonomous Politics

THE POST-TOTALITARIAN universe of discourse is a free public domain.[1] The primary post-totalitarian political commitments are necessarily the constitution and defense of this domain. Though Kundera in a fundamental sense is antipolitical, revealed for instance by the story of Tomas, his novels formally represent these commitments. Here I attempt to come to terms with post-totalitarian politics, first by identifying the difficulties of understanding post-totalitarian political events, especially the politics of Solidarność, with social theories that have not confronted totalitarian conditions; second, by outlining the emergence of an autonomous political domain in Poland, using the political theory of Hannah Arendt as a guide; and third, by showing how Adam Michnik as political theorist and activist has struggled to establish a democratic and liberal post-totalitarian politics and culture.

Theoretical Inadequacies

A major problem with contemporary political theory is that it does not confront totalitarianism head on. Without such confrontation the political alternatives to totalitarianism are misunderstood. This is most strikingly apparent within the Marxist tradition.

Marxism, both as theory and as praxis, casts a broad and long nineteenth-century shadow on twentieth-century thought and action. In Poland, it is most often understood as the theoretical root of the society's most recent sufferings. This presents a remarkable challenge to Western Marxism. Many avoid the challenge through simple theoretical denial. On the one hand, Soviet Marxism is not Marxism, Soviet socialism not socialism. On the other hand, Solidarity, given the pro-

Western, religious, and nationalist orientation of its members, is not a genuine workers' movement. Beyond such theoretical pathology only the brave dare tread.

Daniel Singer does so with a confidence he confuses with clairvoyance. He began his well-known study *The Road to Gdansk* before the Polish August. He sought to develop a Marxist critique of Soviet socialism by analyzing in separate essays (1) Solzhenitsyn as a witness of existing Soviet reality but a false prophet, (2) the transition from Stalin to Khrushchev and Brezhnev, and (3) the social composition of the Soviet elite, intelligentsia, and working classes. He then turned to the Polish case, "not . . . as a model . . . [but] as an example, an illustration of how the workers can suddenly enter the political stage all over Eastern Europe."[2]

Singer's developmental scenario of actually existing socialism is a relatively simple one. Stalinist terror, horrific as it was, served primitive accumulation. Khrushchev's rule of reform from above was illusory. The uninspired restoration of the Brezhnev period, an era of artificially preserved political stability in which diehard apparatchiks had as their main purpose preventing any initiative from below, brought economic crisis. Singer postulated that this would lead to a political crisis.

The rising cost of the infrastructure and the steep decline in labor supply are at the roots of crisis. These two factors set the stage for a genuine socialist opposition; not just a dissident civil rights movement, but an alternative political program with socialist content. The workers, not the intellectuals, are to be the primary subjects ushering in the socialist alternative. The Polish workers, according to Singer, initiated the process, first in the early seventies by establishing a veto power over elite decision making, and then in 1980 by establishing an independent working-class organization. The process is not yet complete, in Singer's view, because it has not been taken "to its logical conclusion, the seizure of power."[3]

In such a way, Singer explains the specific significance of the Polish developments. But he does this by avoiding the most interesting and pressing sociological and political questions. He seems to predict Solidarność, but he takes for granted the processes by which the Polish workers were mobilized and casts doubt on the importance of their specific normative commitments and collective identities, i.e., freedom, human rights, and Catholicism. The major weakness of his work is its tendency to substitute a rather stale polemic for political and cultural analysis. The polemic is for socialism, against not only the new philosophers and other varieties of Western anti-Marxists, but also against the "irrational," "regressive," and "nationalistic" views in Solidarity, the Polish opposition, and the Soviet dissident movement. Scattered throughout the text are denunciations of "latter-day Christopher Columbuses 'discovering' the Gulag in the 1970s" and diagnoses of "the latest French flu, the fashionable reduction of all conflicts to the ahistorical confrontation between human rights and the totalitarian state."[4] More serious is a refusal to understand the Polish events on their own terms. Singer repeatedly attempts to belittle the role of the church and does not even try to understand the unique political character of Poland in the eighties.

Thus, rather than attempting to understand the relationship between the Polish Catholic church and Solidarity within existing socialism, he curtly dismisses the church's activities of the seventies. He cynically declares, "Deprived of its prewar allies, it [the church] adroitly switched its slogans from the rights of property to the rights of man."[5] Rather than trying to understand how Solidarity by its very existence has transformed the Polish social order, he bemoans the fact that "the Polish labor movement has not yet found its bearings. It is still groping towards a project and searching for an ideology."[6]

Singer is stuck in outdated theoretical polarities: capitalism versus socialism, liberal democracy versus social democracy, formal freedom versus substantive freedom. One must choose which side of the barricade one is on, and one must explain the choice with a complete theoretical system, he seems to be counseling the Polish workers. Thus, as with Marxists gen-

erally, along with many other social scientists, he does not
take totalitarianism seriously, and as a consequence he cannot understand the specific qualities of its alternatives. He
views the alternative culture of Solzhenitsyn as simply an ideology. He condemns the distinctive accomplishments of post-
totalitarian politics.

Within Solidarity and in its wake, other critically inclined
theorists and scholars have sought to avoid such theoretical
inadequacies. Here we consider the theoretical activism of
Jadwiga Staniszkis and the theoretical political pilgrimage of
Alain Touraine. These authors represent a sample of a vast
literature written in response to Solidarity. They are distinguished in that they seriously attempt to confront Solidarity
directly, even its inconvenient and therefore most interesting
uniqueness, and that they use sophisticated theoretical tools in
this confrontation.

The Polish sociologist Staniszkis analyzes the issues of collective identity and mobilization from the perspective of a theoretically inclined social activist. Her central focus is on the
relationship between workers and intellectuals and on the
machinations of the Communist Party factions and their effects on the dynamics of Polish society. She writes from within
the Polish democratic social movement, but her basis for
analysis and critique is the distance provided by her highly sophisticated theoretical perspective.

While Singer's analysis is draped around a conventional
Marxist narrative (social contradictions lead to class consciousness and class action), Staniszkis presents a series of
parallel but interrelated narratives based upon five analytical
problems: the evolution of working class protests;[7] the evolution of the political system from a totalitarian to an authori-
tarian-bureaucratic regime;[8] the development of post–World
War II geopolitics;[9] the dynamics of economic and political
cycles;[10] and the Polish ritualization of political conflict.[11]
These parallel narratives were written on different occasions
and are somewhat repetitive and sometimes contradictory,
but taken together they present a powerful interpretation of
Polish political and social change.

Geopolitics restricts the field of action in the Soviet bloc. The facts of geopolitics change, allowing more or less severe Soviet domination within the field, but these facts function as the ultimate control of social change. Ultimate control is not the deciding factor at every moment. Out of geopolitical necessity came a political culture of an elite and of the masses drawing upon older Polish traditions of symbolic politics and reacting to economic and political systemic crises, which also resulted from the geopolitical facts.

Staniszkis has an ironic (almost demonic) sensibility. Throughout her text she observes tremendous incapacities among the Polish workers and remarkable political savvy within the Polish elite. Both observations should be taken seriously, but clearly both must be approached with caution. Even the most casual observer of the Polish scene must be astonished by the wisdom of the Polish workers and the foolishness of the Polish political elite, and even though the working class may not be the natural revolutionary subject portrayed by Singer, its centrality, which he highlights, cannot be ignored.

Staniszkis presents a different picture. As an invited expert in the Lenin Shipyards and as a participant and close observer throughout the Solidarity experience, she consistently underscored the hidden weakness of the social movement and strengths of the regime. Hers is the position of an activist, but an activist of a special sort. Bringing to bear her sophisticated theoretical understanding of political discourse (drawing from Basil Bernstein), Staniszkis shows that the workers' poor linguistic and mental skills are of critical importance, resulting in an unclear comprehension of the subtleties of the Gdansk negotiations and consequently a dependent relationship with intellectual experts, a lack of appreciation of democratic norms, authoritarianism within the union, and the development of irrational symbolic politics. Their distrust of intellectuals, institutionalized economic and political structures, and political manipulations by the elite are all shown to exacerbate the workers' problems.

The Party elite is significantly stronger in Staniszkis's ac-

count than in Singer's or just about any other. From the point
of view of ordinary Polish people with little or no access to the
information about machinations of the factional intrigues
within the ruling party, the food price increases in 1970,
1976, and 1980, which instigated worker protests, were poorly
formulated and presented; the anti-Zionist campaign of 1968
resulted from a protest by students and intellectuals; and anti-
Semitism was a component of Polish de-Stalinization. Yet
Staniszkis interprets all of this as subtle intra-Party intrigue
and purposive societal manipulation. Official corruption becomes East European "corporatism," the Party incapacity to
repress the intellectual democratic opposition (KOR) is a
Marxist "repression tolerance," and even de-Stalinization
becomes a Soviet version of "artificial negativity." [12] Specific
versions of Warsaw gossip are presented as facts and incorporated into Western-generated critical sociological theories,
leading to superior wisdom.

In that there are different versions of the gossip, her theory is
seriously flawed. Even Staniszkis admits that she may be overly
preoccupied with Party elite intrigue. Because notions of linguistic competence, repressive tolerance, neo-corporation,
artificial negativity, and even breakdown theories of social
movements are controversial within the Western social orders
they attempt to explain, the flaw is intensified. Staniszkis, like
Singer, claims a superior theoretical wisdom over the activist
in the social movement. Though Singer draws from one social
theory, while Staniszkis is an eclectic, a similar problem remains: their knowledge is based primarily on a priori theory
that does not take into account the distinctiveness of the totalitarian experience. While Singer, with his use of key concepts and superior knowledge, is a practitioner of totalitarian
reasoning, Staniszkis seems to be a victim of it. Searching for
powerful alternatives to totalitarian culture, she does not find
them among her compatriots but looks to the superior wisdom of Western critical theories. In the process, she explains
away the accomplishments of post-totalitarian culture and
politics, referring to the underlying truths revealed through

Western theory. She thus strangely echoes totalitarian cultural reasoning.

In Alain Touraine's work, we find a theorist seeking alternatives to such theoretical traps. In his theory and research on social movements, Touraine has attempted to address the intellectual hubris of previous theorists of social movements. His works draw from a critical Marxist tradition, but he attempts to emancipate himself from it. In *Post Industrial Society* and the *Self-Production of Society,* works that have France as their primary referent, Touraine seems to replace one scheme of development and progress (Marxist) with another (grounded in information and technology). In *The Voice and the Eye,* he develops an explicit method of sociological intervention as a means to avoid such schemes, using the point of view of participants in social movements.[13] This method is most successful when applied to Solidarity, in comparison both with his application of it to French and Western social movements and with other approaches to Solidarity.[14]

The method is a relatively straightforward form of participant observation applied to social movements. Research is conducted with an understanding that theoretical wisdom is not superior to social activists' knowledge. In *Solidarity: Poland 1980–81,* the researchers tried to help militants gain a more adequate self-understanding. The militants accepted, rejected, or modified the theorists' hypotheses. Hypotheses were considered valid if they facilitated further discourse and self-understanding and if they led to a more informed future course of social action. They were considered invalid if they created "noise."

Interesting discourse resulted, though not without considerable theoretically-inspired noise. Touraine and his colleagues met with union activists in major cities of Poland during the Solidarity period. They found considerable variation over time and space in the activists' commitments and understandings. The movement was not studied as a consequence of major structural factors (interpretations based on national struggles and societal modernization are explicitly rejected);

rather it was studied from the point of view of its participants' normative commitments.

Solidarity was thus hypothesized to be a (1) working-class struggle of (2) national protest and (3) a democratic movement.[15] The three normative points of this characterization were drawn from a number of narrative accounts of social movements in Eastern Europe in the postwar period. All components of the movement, Touraine maintains, lead to a struggle over "winning back the social space from a regime weakened by the failure of its economic policies."[16] For Singer, this failure is less significant than the crisis of the political system. For the French and Polish authors of *Solidarity*, the failure presented the possibility for social action.

They found a moral movement, open to a diversity of social forces, neither pseudoscientific nor dogmatically egalitarian in its orientation. Some activists, like Walesa, had the social movement as their primary commitment; others, like his chief advisors Geremek and Mazowiecki, sought primarily a liberation of society. Both radicals and moderates were committed to self-limitation of the movement, but in strategically different ways. The workers in the studied groups had strikingly different conceptions of Solidarity's construction and development: e.g., Jerzy's theory of social movement, Grzegorz's theory of societal liberation, and Jozef's theory of national independence. These theories shed light on and ultimately confirmed the hypotheses of a three-component normative structure of the movement. Different groups in the movement placed varying degrees of emphasis on democracy, class struggle, and national independence. The diversity of views within Solidarity was thus made understandable. The development of the movement, from the victory in Gdansk to the declaration of the state of war, led to a weakening of the democratic commitment. Touraine and his colleagues in this fashion revealed the internal life of this unique social movement.

But there is a profound, unacknowledged contradiction between Touraine's previous theoretical analysis of social movements and *Solidarity*. Further, the theory blinds the researchers to their most important finding. The theory is developmental, based on a purported transition from industrial to postindustrial society. The fact that domination in the latter is based on control of information and knowledge means that opposition social movements must be self-reflective. Thus the method of sociological intervention is understood to be both a scientific method and a political strategy of postindustrialization. Ironically, Solidarity, with its commitments to traditional nineteenth-century norms of class struggle, national independence, and democracy, is most self-reflective and open to Touraine's method. Apparently, the developmental theory should be cast into doubt because of the methodological success. This, though, is not openly considered; instead, the findings are still presented as developmental phases: Solidarity I, the trade union movement seeking societal compromise; Solidarity II, the social movement seeking societal self-organization; and Solidarity III, the political movement in search of national independence.

While the phases and changes in primary normative commitments are not seen as being inevitable, they are the central focus of the authors' forecast for Solidarity's future as an underground movement during martial law. But by staging social experiments with workers' study groups, Touraine and his colleagues actually discovered something much more interesting: the social interactive constitution of Solidarity's distinctiveness, directly related to the totalitarian order which the union is up against.

When a group of workers discuss their attitudes toward the Party, they seem to compete with each other in voicing their hostility. No compromise seems possible. Any sign of Party liberalism, they agree, is a product of centralized manipulation. But when the group is introduced to a lower-level Party official, something else emerges. Antagonism is present, but an understanding of limitations serves as a basis for a search for resolution of societal conflict. Individual attitudes, in fact, do not change, but the interactive grounds of the union's social practice become apparent. Individual autonomy, group soli-

darity, and open discourse are clearly interactive norms. Recognition of conflicting interests and an attempt to overcome
them, or at least to seek a workable compromise between
them, become more important goals than the realization of
absolute principles.[17] This is the other side of Singer's observations that Solidarity lacks ideology, i.e., its post-totalitarian
commitment.

The historical source of such norms, unfortunately is not
systematically investigated by Touraine et al., but another social experiment does highlight an instance of the norms' identification. The occasion was the introduction of Adam Michnik
to a Gdansk workers' group. Michnik, as we will see in detail
below, was a central figure in the democratic opposition of the
seventies. As a leading figure in KOR (the Committee to Defend Workers), he was the object of a systematic campaign of
vilification in the official media. The workers certainly did not
believe the official propaganda, but they did have their suspicions. They were proud of the achievements of their activism
and highly critical of the purported superior wisdom of intellectuals. They were against anything that smacked of Leninism. Traditional contempt for intellectuals, coupled with
Michnik's leftist past, his Stalinist father and brother, and
more, led to their suspicions. When the group met Michnik,
the suspicions were suspended—at least for the time of their
meeting. A Polish worker identified as Zbigniew summarized
the transformation: "Some of us, including me, had our doubts
about the intentions, the means, and the origins of KOR. Now
I know that Solidarity came out of KOR. They said it before,
now it's us who are saying it!"[18] Workers learned that their
opposition to elitism, dogmatism, and tendentiousness was
the basis of the social compromises, welfare functions, and activism of KOR. They learned of and identified with the similar
experiences of taking part in autonomous public action as a
fundamental end in itself.

Modern social science and its theories have focused upon
capitalism and socialism—their histories, structures, and con-
stitutions. The theories reviewed here, like the theorists and

activists first confronting totalitarianism in the interwar period, are groping to explain the world beyond. Singer's application of Marxism to Soviet and Polish realities is strained by the awareness that his authors of socialist transformation (the Polish workers) are decidedly not socialists. Staniszkis's superior wisdom comes in various and sometimes contradictory forms. The tension between Touraine's social theory and his empirical findings is not always acknowledged, but is accurately presented.

Hannah Arendt—Our Guide to Post-Totalitarian Politics

Hannah Arendt's political theory not only provides a means for understanding totalitarianism, it theoretically illuminates as well the free political alternatives to totalitarianism. In pitting herself against a philosophical tradition that she feels had distorted the notion of freedom by "transposing it from its original field, the realm of politics and human affairs in general, to an inward domain, the will, where it would be open to self inspection,"[19] Arendt reformulates the issue of political freedom in a nonpartisan post-totalitarian fashion. For Arendt, freedom takes place between people. It exists in activity that calls something into being that did not exist before. Freedom is the condition in which the individual in a community—i.e., the citizen—may, if it is within her or his capabilities, make a significant mark in the presence of others. Free public life exists to observe the new action and to preserve the conditions for such action. Freedom is constituted by politics. Freedom is not located in the region of the individual life unconstrained by political interference, as the liberals believe, nor is it realized in the act of collective liberation and achievement, as Marxists believe. Rather, Arendt finds it situated in the defense of and actions in an autonomous public realm, in which individuals can live and act in their plurality, according to their own principles, but essentially in interaction with others.

Arendt's writings have a romantic element, a tendency to substitute a poetic of politics for systematic analysis. Nonetheless, her examination of the free public domain, which, for her, is totalitarianism's opposite, clarifies the dimensions of post-totalitarian politics.

Action, politics, and the public domain are the central positive normative concepts of Arendt's political philosophy.[20] She identifies three fundamental types of human activity: labor, work, and action. Politics, as opposed to violence, is concerted free human activity, and it is located in the public domain, not the private one.

Paul Ricoeur has observed that, at the outset, one must judge this theory of Arendt's as a phenomenological philosophical anthropology, not as a sociology.[21] Human beings *labor,* actively satisfying their basic biological needs; from craftsman to artist to industrial worker and capitalist, they *work,* fabricating the human artifice; and they distinctively *act* with word and deed to create a world of meaning and significance and to insert themselves as ends in themselves in this world.

From labor to action, a hierarchy of human distinctiveness exists. Labor and work deal with the necessity of human survival; action deals with the very definition of humanity. We see the former as private activities, the latter as demanding publicity. At this point the normative element of Arendt's theory becomes most apparent. By proposing the aforementioned typology of human activity, she holds to the ancient distinction between the realm of necessity and the realm of freedom and insists upon the profound differentiation between private and public life. Thus, politics and freedom are found in the public domain and set apart from the economic and the administrative domains. In the public domain, action—in the Arendtian sense—occurs and is an end in itself. *Freedom of action in the public domain, therefore, is the most fundamental of citizen rights.* The private domain must be protected against public incursions. The confusion of public and private issues is a major negative legacy of modernity and a necessary condition for the origins of totalitarianism. As we have seen, Kundera provides us with literary explorations of such a political philosophy.

Solidarność and the political theories associated with it start from the same sensibility. In Solidarity's political action and Adam Michnik's political theory, we can observe the political problematics of such a theory. Kundera can claim that his aim as a novelist is to raise theoretical questions; those who act politically must attempt to answer questions. Here we analyze the tentative answers of Solidarity and one of its major theorists.

The Events Leading to Solidarity

There is a striking convergence of Arendt's political philosophy and the actions of Polish citizens in the late seventies and the eighties. This convergence provides a strategic means to understand post-totalitarian politics and its challenge to modern political thought and action. To appreciate this, we consider an outline of recent Polish history.[22]

In 1976, the Polish authorities attempted to forestall an economic crisis by drastically increasing the price of food. As in 1956 and 1970, worker protests were the immediate response, but this time the regime did not fall. Instead, the authorities rescinded the price increases the day after "consultation with the nation" and arrested and repressed the "consultants"—that is, the worker protestors. At this point, an unprecedented series of developments occurred. A group of the most prominent critical intellectuals founded the Committee to Defend Workers (KOR). Deciding to live in truth, they openly publicized a campaign for the legal defense of the workers who were being repressed by the authorities and the financial support of their families. The links among intellectuals formed in 1975 to protest constitutional changes were expanded in 1976 to include working-class activists. First, they published a bulletin of information with the names, addresses, and telephone numbers of its contributors. Then, a whole series of independent activities came into being—publishing houses, libraries, schools, nascent independent newspapers and journals—to accompany collective protests. In Arendt's terms, a realm of freedom, a public domain, was emerging. The primary end of all opposition activity—or,

more precisely, opposition action—was to engage in such action and attempt to protect its domain as an independent
arena, free of official language and control, but with no pretense that it would overthrow officialdom. The understanding
of the opposition activists, from the most prominent cultural
figures to the printers and truckers who invisibly and most he-
roically supported the opposition alternatives, was that the
Communist system could not be reformed from above. Instead,
they hoped to establish and defend pockets of independence
from within which they could protect themselves, minimize
oppression by officialdom, and enjoy fundamental human
rights of self-definition, expression, and self-determination.
Not until 1980 did this strategy of reform become visible to
all Poles and, in fact, to the whole world.

In the summer of 1980, strikes were called and settled
throughout Poland. Wages were at issue, and compromise
settlements were reached. In August, in the shipyards of
Gdansk, something unique occurred, by now well known: the
linkage of economic and political demands. On the basis
of this linkage, strikers from various factories—first from
Gdansk, Gdynia, and Szczecin, then from all over Poland—
engaged in united action. Because of this united action, a
broad political, social and cultural—but not economic—
transformation of Polish life occurred.

The politicization of the Gdansk strike was unique. It involved the politics of free discourse and collective action, not
a politics directed against the Party and the state. The workers
demanded economic redress based upon a common perception of their daily needs. They also demanded collective self-
defense—including the reinstatement of workers harassed
and fired for previous activities, release of political prisoners, and most important, the right to engage in self-defense
and the right to unionize and strike. Though they understood
that a fundamental reordering of society would result, they
took great care to avoid a direct attack upon the ruling party.
They aimed to achieve independence from Party control, not
to attack it directly or initiate an alternative party. Thus,

we repeatedly heard union spokesmen claim that they were simple trade unionists, uninterested in partisan politics, ideological disputes, and political labels. When pressed by foreign correspondents and political observers, the most the unionists would concede was a commitment to democracy—a concern that primarily involved self-determination.

The self-determination at stake in 1980 was an aspect of the political action Hannah Arendt describes. The strike began with such activity; Solidarity has institutionalized it. Delegates and advisers to Solidarity were chosen according to the merits of their actions of this sort. Indeed, Solidarity extended its functions by providing an increasingly comprehensive domain for such free political action.

Because of the fleeting appearance of such political life in the modern world, Arendt views it as a lost revolutionary tradition. In Poland, we can observe that a rather well-advanced institutionalization of this tradition has slowly emerged over the last three decades and become fully developed since August 1980. The Catholic church has provided its most prominent structural support. It also has been supported by official cultural life, emerging in the form of critical and autonomous theater, literature, and social and political thought. For more than twenty-five years, both in the case of officially accepted critical culture and in the case of the Catholic church, a relatively autonomous public domain existed.

Given the primary end of the church as religious practice, life within the church and its auxiliary institutions provided a significant public alternative, not only for belief but for journalism, art, theater, and literature. These alternatives appeared in the form of Catholic newspapers, journals, theaters, publishing houses, and even an independent Catholic university. Such activities were not directed, explicitly at least, against the prevailing official order. This was most dramatically demonstrated during the Pope's visit to Poland in 1979. Millions turned out to see the Pope and pray with him—in a totalitarian order in which all publicity was controlled by officialdom. As a result, they began to grasp their potential politi-

cal power. But this was not the political power of a Western
interest group or the politics of an existing socialist official
party. On the contrary, it was power accumulated by citizens
acting in concert. Arendt observes that "such power corre-
sponds to the human ability not to just act but to act in concert; it belongs to a group and remains in existence as long as
the group keeps together." [23] Such power was truly manifested
in the Polish August and its aftermath.

The Polish government commission signed an agreement
with the representatives of the striking workers in Gdansk on
August 30, 1980. [24] Because the workers demanded direct
broadcasts from the Lenin shipyards, on that Sunday afternoon the entire Polish nation watched the momentous event.
The collective participation in Gdansk had immense significance for later events. For the first time, the authorities had to
acknowledge worker rights publicly. For the bulk of the public, the shock was tremendous, for the official mass media had
kept its audience in the dark about what was happening in
Gdansk and in Silesia. Even after telephone connections with
Gdansk were opened, and after small paragraphs in the central
press appeared, the regional newspapers completely avoided
the topic. Official television, then, played the peculiar role of
broadcasting the good news. This good news, proclaimed by
Lech Walesa, announced the coming birth of the independent
and self-governing unions. To the disoriented public, the authorities appeared shockingly compromised, for they had
feared open discourse, always attempting to reserve public expression for themselves.

On Monday, August 31, workers returned to their factories
and mines, and the government commission returned to the
ministries, but life in the country could not return to the old
order. The old order of the week before already seemed completely anachronistic to the Polish populace. The government
signed agreements but did not know what to do. It did man-
age to send appropriate directions and policies to lower-level
officialdom. For the first time in postwar Poland, space was
unambiguously created for spontaneous citizen action—for

self-organization, for the discussion of principal values that would shape future actions.

The Poland of early September 1980 was a Poland of meetings. People met in their work places and talked about the same things the strikers in the shipyard spoke about during the two weeks of the strike—equality of opportunity, equality before the law, and what to do to protect the society against the pathology of official corruption. At the September meetings, various unions were established that had in common an independence from the government's company unions. Warsaw scholars—those who managed to return from summer vacation—met on the second of September in a private apartment. One hundred people were present from about twenty scientific institutions. The second meeting, held in the officially rented hall of the Institute of Basic Technical Issues, drew five hundred people. Two weeks later, the First Congress of the Independent and Self-Governing Union of Scientific, Technical, and Educational Employees was held. It was primarily a union for Warsaw residents, yet it already had fifteen thousand members. This union, like most created at the time, soon joined Solidarity, which was not actually formed until the middle of September.

Most Poles saw the conclusion of the Gdansk strikes. But in the first days of September, little was known about what had happened during the strikes. The first formal written reports were delayed by one month. In the meantime, handwritten and typed copies of the original strike bulletins, entitled *Solidarność*, circulated throughout Poland. In the Warsaw chapter of the Polish Sociological Association, and in the club of the Catholic intelligentsia, intellectuals who had been in the shipyards during the last three days of the strike discussed the event. They had gone to Gdansk with a letter signed by leading intellectuals supporting the strike. They were asked for concrete help, and they gave it as advisors.

The hunger for information was intense. People ran from meeting to meeting, from conference to conference. Private life seemed to disappear. A crowd of people surrounded the

Catholic intelligentsia's club during a meeting between the advisors and the workers. Thanks to a large open window in the club and a public address system, the crowd could listen to the discussion inside. Cars passing on Copernicus Street stopped, people rolled their windows down, and in that position they remained and listened.

The picture of what happened in Gdansk was presented by a remarkable documentary film, *Workers Eighty*. This ascetic film, shot during the strike, depicted the final phase of negotiations between the government representatives and representatives of the Interfactory Strike Committee. It showed government subterfuge and the firm resolve and intelligence of the workers. It showed the authorities being pushed to negotiate for the first time. It also showed workers who somehow knew how to negotiate.

Following protests by workers and artistic groups, the censor permitted the film to be shown at closed screenings. People bought tickets in their work places, and they and their whole families attended the show. The film was not only the first lesson, the beginning of a compelling educational experience in political culture, it was also an important element in Polish cultural life during the early months of Solidarity. It showed Solidarity at its birth. Widespread demands for showing the truth about Gdansk led to the film's existence and circulation throughout Poland. *Workers Eighty* recorded the historical agreements; it also taught people that it is worthwhile to think the unthinkable. People urgently sought to make up for the lost thirty-six years of the postwar period. Because they had a lot to say, their meetings lasted for long periods. Most Poles were not afraid to speak.

The people urgently wanted to know things, not only to multiply their bank of knowledge or to know about facts previously forbidden to them, but also to know how to understand their world. From October onward, numerous open lectures and conferences took place. The Learned Society for Independent Knowledge, the initiator of the oppositional Flying University that existed in the late seventies, organized lectures on recent Polish history, literature, and social and economic problems. The largest auditorium at Warsaw University, which seats two thousand people, could not accommodate all those who wanted to attend. The society had to transmit the lectures to nearby halls. The collective, open, public participation in events that earlier would have been forbidden reinforced a belief in the possibility of changes for the better.

A new kind of university public emerged. Together with students, workers from the Ursus Tractor Factory, the Warsaw Steel Mills, and the Rosa Luxemburg Bulb Factory listened to Professor Edward Lipinski, the distinguished socialist economist and a founding member of KOR (the Committee to Defend Workers).

Because of the public's new presence in open lectures, the character of the university changed. Formerly, the generations and the social classes had been separated and seldom overlapped. In general, students under thirty years of age studied during the day. Their nonstudent peers and their elders who wished to study had a separate educational program.

The new public lectures organized at Warsaw University by the university's Solidarity unit, or by the new Independent Student Association, invalidated these old customs and cancelled the old divisions between young workers and students. Students and senior citizens, artists and clerks, scholars and workers filled the auditorium. With these new lectures, Warsaw citizens grew accustomed to dropping into the university. Stalls with independent and union publications were set up on the university grounds. Here one could buy historical books about World War II and about the events of March 1968. Here one could buy Baranczak's and Milosz's poetry, the Communist Party *samizdat* (unofficial independent publishing), and pictures of the Pope's visit to Poland. Here various buttons and T-shirts mimicking official propaganda—such as those reading AE (anti-socialist element) or CC (creeping counter-revolutionary)—were sold. Here, on a long wall with bulletin boards previously used for official announcements, people could read the latest news, statements of Solidarity leadership, announcements of lectures and meetings, and satirical cartoons.

The university grounds, in this way, stopped functioning as a place reserved only for the university community and became a new and lively place for open public life. When, on March 13, 1981, a worker gave a speech on the university grounds to commemorate the events of March 1968, it was not unusual. When a twenty-seven-year-old worker from the Ursus Tractor Factory, Zbigniew Bujak—who was the leader of Warsaw's Solidarity regional chapter and later a principal leader of underground Solidarity—said, "Workers came here in order to guard this terrain and to protect the creation of culture and scholarship," that sounded quite natural.

Thirteen years earlier, in March 1968, the authorities sent workers on buses to the university grounds and used them against protesting students. Now the workers of the Warsaw steelworks made a plaque commemorating those events. The workers and scholars placed on the wall of the university a text engraved in bronze, shaped like a strike leaflet. This plaque read:

> In this courtyard, on 8 March 1968, a student rally was dispersed. The events of March stand as a brutal sign of the persecution of independent thought, of the devastation of national culture, and the unity of Polish society. Today, in Solidarity, recognizing the justness of the wronged, we put this plaque into stone, for future generations.

The text was signed by "students, the employees of Warsaw University, and the workers of Warsaw."

After August, the wise could no longer give guidance to the less than wise by using ready-made prescriptions. No one had the experience of action in independent unions, and activity in the old official unions was of no help. The experience of Western unions also was of little use, for those unions function in completely different political and economic contexts.

The experience of Solidarity had to be grounded in self-education.

Sociologists in Warsaw, understanding well how wrong it would be to instruct workers how to act, organized workshops for interested union activists, including "Some Problems of the Thirty-Five Years of Contemporary Poland," "The Conditions for Union Democracy," "Experience of and Chances for Employee Self-governance in Poland," "Basic Problems of Self-management in Yugoslavia," and "Practical Problems for Internal Union Democracy."

Such activities—which involved the broad mass of Polish people, not just union activists and leaders—created a new culture, which had dialogue as its first principle. This culture of dialogue is not only a culture of mutual help, it is a culture of plurality and the free public domain, a post-totalitarian culture.

Union bulletins testify to the power of the culture of dialogue, to its creativity and accomplishment, and to its ability to enliven previously isolated and silent individuals, social groups, and regions. The first bulletin, *Solidarność*, was published in the striking shipyards on a single page. The name presented the hope and expectation of the strikers that others would join them.

In the striking shipyards, thirteen issues of *Solidarność* appeared. After sixteen months of Solidarity activity in various regions, factories, and social groups, scores of issues of two hundred different bulletins were published. Some of these appeared in the tens of thousands. These bulletins complemented the general demand for the 500,000 copies of the Warsaw *Tygodnik Solidarność* and the 250,000 copies of the Szczecin *Jedność*. The authorities refused to grant the union even one hour of access to television each week, so it spontaneously formed its own localized and uncensored system of societal communication.

In May 1981, in the Ursus Tractor Factory, the first Congress of the Union Presses took place. The participants tried to list all the bulletins in the nation. Because all cultural life was previously centrally controlled in People's Poland, the necessity of such an accounting was novel. Most of the publications included in their titles the word *solidarity;* the second element of the titles usually indicated the name of the region, city, or work place: *Lower Silesian Solidarity, Slupsk Solidarity,* and *Solidarity of the Warsaw Polytechnic.* The titles of many other bulletins appealed to values absent from the social life that preceded Solidarity's birth. These titles used a fundamental language invigorated with meaning restored by the Gdansk agreements. The Warsaw region published *Independence* and *Legality,* Walbrzych published the *Independent Word.* Siedlice published *Independent Voice.* Lodz published *Defense.* Titles such as *Free Unionist, New Road, New Word,* and *Renewal* indicated categories distinct from official everyday newspapers and from the abused language of official life. Such titles as *Aspirations, Concretely, Directly, Resonance, Views* and *Connections* articulated a strong need to participate and communicate.

The bulletins fulfilled various functions, but they primarily served to inform their readers. Credible, uncensored, quick information was essential for organizing the social movement when it was being formed. If information had been received only through officially censored sources, the unionists could not possibly have acted together. The bulletins generally were published in small provincial centers far from large-scale industry. In such places, local authorities were well-established and secure. The changes there occurred quite slowly and met with considerable official resistance. In these settings, the independent union press became an important instrument for the union position. It informed readers of the abuses of authority. Conflicts became public knowledge, and stronger Solidarity chapters came to the aid of the weaker ones.

A truly autonomous public domain had developed in Poland. Limited to local political problems and most accomplished in its encouragement of free speech, this public domain was stifled by martial law. Underground Solidarity and an extensive underground press continued, but they lacked the most essential characteristic of Solidarity and the press of its day: open publicity. This points to the essential tragedy of post-totalitarian politics: given unfavorable geopolitics and the simultaneous existence of totalitarian culture and post-totalitarian culture, the identification of reason with force will prevail.

Could such public life as that described above have co-existed indefinitely with the Party and state apparatus? Can one separate the public and the private as neatly as Arendt suggests? Answering such questions with assurance is fool-hardy. Solidarity and the Polish authorities were both caught in a tragic dilemma. The free public domain of Solidarity could flourish only with the acceptance and the cooperation of the Polish authorities. Yet the strategy of the independent public domain was based upon a complete suspicion of the Party and state apparatus and of Marxism. The leaders and members of Solidarity, therefore, never really attempted to nurture a more favorable Party leadership and attitude. Poles mainly viewed liberalization of the Party, whether at a special congress or in the so-called horizontal movement, with ridicule or disinterest. Before evaluating these events, one should re-call that the Poles believed that any concerted attempt by Soli-darity to win over the Party leadership would have been an open invitation to a replay of the "Czechoslovak follies of 1968," when the Soviets invaded that nation because of the unreliable nature of its Communist Party leadership. Nonethe-less, to resolve the economic crisis and the breakdown in the legitimacy of the Communist regime, the authorities needed the cooperation of the Polish people in increasing productiv-ity through harder work and resolving numerous localized bottlenecks and breakdowns in the system of production. That is, Polish officialdom could overcome its problems only through the functioning of an organization much like Soli-darity, yet doing so would undermine the backbone of the Communist bureaucracy and the patronage system of the no-menklatura and possibly raise the wrath of the Soviets.

Thus, after August 1980, both before and after the state of

war of December 1981, Polish society has been caught in a
stalemate. In 1980 and 1981, a time of great opportunity, the
grounds for compromise were never found. In a time of repressive politics, after 1981, the politics of the free public domain could not match the might of coercive control. Moreover,
coercive control could not be absolute, both because the per-
sonnel for enacting a reign of terror seemed to be in short supply and because such a reign of terror would not resolve, but
would only compound, the economic crisis.

This Polish tragedy provides the context for the post-
totalitarian struggle in Poland. The totalitarian regime apparently cannot make compromises with the Polish nation, and it
is well aware that the autonomous public life presents the
most fundamental challenge to its authority. Nonetheless, the
remembrance of free public life is alive in the Polish people
and is periodically and widely commemorated in monthly
protests marking the strivings for Polish independence. The
only hope is that at some point a new regime, along with the
Soviets, will understand that it must make a compromise with
the aspirations of the population, not only for reasons of human rights but also for the sake of the long-term viability of
the political order. The authorities maintain the order through
a continuation of military might, public despair, political
stalemate, and economic collapse. Any alternative must include the freedom of the public domain as it emerged in the
Solidarity period, for it has become an integral part of Polish
political culture.

Adam Michnik—Theorist of Post-Totalitarian Democracy

The writings of Adam Michnik have contributed greatly to
that culture. In them, he seeks to ensure that Poland's post-
totalitarian political world will be a democratic one. We have
seen that the struggle for a free public domain, where citizens
in their plurality as equals speak and act in the presence of
others, is a fundamental component of the struggle for human
dignity and rights in the twentieth century. Without citizens'
rights, people have become nonentities. Arendt has cogently

illuminated the origins of totalitarianism as a development of depoliticization: as a destruction of citizenship rights and responsibilities. Her hope for the future, the postscript of totalitarianism, was for citizens to begin anew. Adam Michnik is an author of this postscript.

Michnik began early. In a Warsaw high school where he was subjected to disciplinary action, he organized an informal discussion group among his fellow pupils. From there his political career began in earnest. As a university student in 1968, he was a leader of demonstrations demanding more freedom in Polish universities. For his activities, he was arrested and imprisoned. Since that time he has been periodically in prison, serving a total of eight years.

Out of prison, he has been one of the leading figures in the Polish democratic movement. Through his writings and political activity he has helped shape the character of that movement. In the sixties, as a student activist, he was a neo-Marxist of sorts: the child of Communist parents and a student of the renowned critical philosopher Leszek Kolakowski, among others. His political work was directed to making the existing socialist system more humane. In the seventies his understanding of politics and ethics shifted in significant ways. He turned from the existing socialist order and explored in his writing means for fundamental social transformation. He investigated Spanish labor unions as possible models for Poles in their search for independent political means to resist tyranny. He inventively researched Polish history to inform present-day action. As a Polish leftist, never abandoning the Polish socialist tradition, he challenged secular intellectuals to reconsider their attitude toward the Catholic church in *The Church, The Left: A Dialogue*.[25] And, most politically creative, in his essay "The New Evolutionism," he formulated the fundamental principles and strategy which animated the political action of KOR (the Committee to Defend Workers) and Solidarity.[26]

As an activist in the seventies Michnik was deeply engaged in the politics of the democratic opposition, but—more than his specific organizational and political actions—his pen was his most powerful political weapon. His writings outline a textured, democratic post-totalitarian political culture.

His letters from prison reveal this most directly.[27] He expresses strong political convictions, animated with tolerance for those who disagree. He maintains ethical values which guide his political actions and thoughts, but understands those who honorably hold different convictions based on divergent ethical judgments. He argues for his position by turning away from ideological cliches and combining poetic insight with dispassionate political reason.

On December 13, 1981, a state of war was declared by Polish authorities against the purportedly antisocialist elements in the Solidarity leadership. In fact, the Polish regime declared war against Polish society. All telephones were disconnected except those needed by the repressive force. Most of the official print and broadcast media were silenced. Public transportation and communication were severely limited. There was a real absence of free speech. Ten thousand people were arrested and interned, Adam Michnik included. In prison, he began to write. He offered his general view of the "Polish War." He critically appraised efforts by the regime to co-opt the opposition. He commented on recent events, cognizant of centuries of Polish history.

Michnik's starting point is active remembrance. "The entire body of experience of the nineteenth- and twentieth-century underground activities serves today as a book of knowledge about the values and methods of illegal resistance. This book must be reread, so that we can adapt old examples to new situations."[28] When he wrote letters to friends, counseling them on emigration and the signing of letters promising to desist from antistate activities, or when he wrote letters denouncing the Polish minister of the interior (the head of the secret police), he was actively engaged in such rereading, with poetic irony.[29] Here is his account of the imposition of martial law, written in February 1982:

The war was declared on the Poles without a moment's notice. In the future, the historian will appreciate the precision of the strike, the excellent timing, the efficiency of the action. The historian will appreciate the consistency with which the enemy's resistance was overcome, and the poet will certainly sing the praises of the brilliant military victories that took place in the streets of Gdansk and in the yards of Warsaw factories—in steelworks, mines, and shipyards. By capturing with an outflanking movement the Polish radio and television building, not to mention the telephone exchange, General Jaruzelski has covered the Polish armed forces with glory. Indeed, not since Jan Sobieski's siege of Vienna has any of our military leaders been able to claim such a success. Now musicians will compose symphonies, artists will design wreaths, and film directors will make patriotic films—all to honor the generals of that December night. The Council of State will certainly vote a new decoration for participation in the campaign of December, 1981.[30]

Michnik starts by clearly characterizing the irony of the Polish situation and goes on to analyze its tragedy. With a cool analytic blade he compares the events of 1956 in Poland and Hungary and those of the Prague Spring of 1968 with the Solidarity period, and sums it up poetically: "One can hardly speak of 'socialism with a human face;' rather, one must speak of 'communism whose teeth have been knocked out,' communism that could no longer bite and no longer could defend itself under attack from organized society."[31]

In his letters Michnik offers periodic appraisals of the recent and distant past as guides for future action. He counsels an understanding of mistakes and a reappraisal of past strategies without recrimination. He reviews a dark situation with optimism and tolerance: "In this struggle there are no final victories, but neither are there—and here is a slight reason for optimism—any final defeats. . . . So I wish my good friends, especially those who are being pursued and who are fighting, much strength to allow them to cross the empty darkness that stretches between despair and hope. And much patience to allow them to learn the difficult art of forgiveness." [32]

Michnik analyzes history and social structure like a highly professional social scientist. As a political writer, he has counseled deliberation and reconciliation, using humor to cool hot heads and metaphor to suggest rational action. Ethics, reason, deliberation, and reconciliation are his themes and are all necessary for the rule of the people to be attractive—in the words of our founding fathers, to be other than the rule of the rabble. Given the depth and longevity of political repression in Poland and the absence of successful modern democratic experience, the fact that Michnik's writing style and explicit message embody these central democratic-republican virtues is of great import. But we should not forget that he is, as well, a passionate writer and citizen. His deepest commitment is to a rather old-fashioned notion of human dignity. He passionately criticizes those who attack it. Since the totalitarian system is predicated upon a daily compromise of dignity,[33] the reason for the Polish people's attraction to Michnik's subtle, ironic, and difficult moral message (to learn the difficult art of forgiveness) comes into view.

A Letter to a General

In late 1983 Michnik was imprisoned and charged with treason. General Czeslaw Kiszczak, the minister of internal affairs, gave him a choice. As reported by Michnik in an open letter to the general, "either I spend next Christmas on the Cote d'Azur or else I will be facing trial and many years in jail." Michnik interpreted the significance of the offer:

> I am writing this letter exclusively on my own behalf, but I have reason to believe thousands of people in Poland would agree with me.
> I have reached the conclusion that your proposal to me means that:
> 1. You admit that I have done nothing that would

entitle a law-abiding prosecutor's office to accuse me
of "preparing to overthrow the government by force"
or "weakening the defensive capacity of the state" or
that would entitle a law-abiding court to declare
me guilty.

I agree with this.

2. You admit that my sentence has been decided
long before the opening of my trial.

I agree with this.

3. You admit that the indictment written by a compliant prosecutor and the sentence pronounced by a
compliant jury will be so nonsensical that no one will
be fooled and that they will only bring honor to the
convicted and shame to the convictors.

I agree with this.

4. You admit that the purpose of the legal proceedings is not to implement justice but to rid the authorities of embarrassing political adversaries.

I agree with this.

From here on, however, we begin to differ. For I believe that:

1. To admit one's disregard for the law so openly,
one would have to be a fool.

2. To offer to a man, who has been held in prison
for two years, the Cote d'Azur in exchange for this
moral suicide, one would have to be a swine.

3. To believe that I could accept such a proposal is
to imagine that everyone is a police collaborator.[34]

Logical and ironic, working with common sense but break-
ing out of the political cliches of what Kundera calls the
Grand March, Michnik unmasks the implications of the general's offer of exile in his four agreements with Kiszczak. He
reveals the official lie. He shows what it means in truth. Everyone knew the charges of treason were trumped up. It took
Michnik to illuminate their moral implications, bringing honor
to the convicted and shame to the convictors. In his differences, Michnik's democratic irony is revealed. To call your
political opponent a fool and a swine is not particularly inno-

vative or persuasive. But what does one do when it is the case? Michnik has an answer, and represents the ethical blindness of his adversary. The mere epithet becomes a true description of character with his third disagreement. By putting himself imaginatively in the place of the jailer, he fully portrays the deficiencies of the jailer's viewpoint.

Having a sufficiently dark view of human prospects, Michnik remains optimistic. Thus he writes in prison, with hope and brilliance, not only the letters but full-scale historical and literary studies. While he was writing to Kiszczak, he was also working on *From the History of Honor in Poland*,[35] a companion volume to Milosz's *Captive Mind*. Whereas Milosz, in exile in the fifties, sought to explain how and why specific intellectuals became enthusiastic supporters of Marxist-Leninism and Communism, Michnik, in prison in the eighties, sought to explain how others maintained their cultural and ethical independence. Michnik's underlying intellectual theme is the search for hope, dignity, and reason in the darkest of circumstances. He writes with the full awareness of the totalitarian condition.

Michnik's other political essays, written during the Solidarity period, during the period of the democratic opposition (the late seventies), and even earlier, present a clear picture of a post-totalitarian democrat. Though the essays are part of the social change emanating from the twists and turns of Polish history and determining that history, they nonetheless present a consistent set of ethical and political positions and a creative approach to interpreting history.

Michnik Remembers

The visit of John Paul II to Poland was a key factor in the emergence of Solidarity. In the postwar period up to that time there had been three major uprisings of Polish workers, in 1956, 1970, and 1976; one separate intellectual revolt, in 1968; a persistent and pervasive distrust and even hatred of the political, social, and economic system by the population throughout the period; and, after 1976, the beginnings of the constitution of alternative social and cultural institutions (social welfare, publishing houses, alternative educational enterprises, newspapers, etc.). The development of the democratic opposition, as all these alternative activities were labelled, epitomized national attitudes towards the existing order and the meaning of Polish resistance. Yet the experience and practice of totalitarian rule kept the opposition within relatively confined social circles.

John Paul's visit changed this; Michnik explains, first as a simple social observer:

> It will be a long time before anyone fully comprehends the ramifications of his nine-day visit. The phrase of the writer Julian Stryjkowski—"Poland's second baptism"—keeps coming to mind. Indeed, something odd did happen. Those very people who are ordinarily frustrated and aggressive in the shop lines were metamorphosed into a cheerful and happy collectivity, a people filled with dignity. The police vanished from the main streets of Warsaw and exemplary order reigned everywhere. The people who had been repressed for so long suddenly regained an ability to determine their own fate.

Then, as a moral analyst:

> The democratic opposition fully respected the religious character of the Pope's visit and did not try to take advantage of it to further any political goals. This is not to say that the visit/pilgrimage did not also have a political dimension. For some time before the arrival, the Western European press occasionally compared the Pope's upcoming pilgrimage to the Khomeini's return to Iran and his struggle with the Shah. This analogy was intended to suggest a parallel sense of the conflict between a dictatorial power, with its modernizing tendencies, and a social movement of protest which articulated itself through anachronistic ideas and retrospective utopias. But one can hardly imagine a greater misconception. The body of values and attitudes represented by the papal homilies and

speeches had nothing to do with the spirit of in-
tegrality, or a desire to return to an era when the
Church had "means of wealth" at its disposal and
used those more than anything else. The Pope said
clearly, "There is no imperialism in the Church. There
is only public service." It was also clearly stated that
the Church wants to pursue its goals through nonpolitical means. In the popular perception, the Pope's
pilgrimage gave Poles the opportunity to express their
true aspirations and aims; it was a national plebiscite.
But it was not simply a question of choosing between
Catholicism and atheism. I saw Catholics grinding
their teeth as they listened to the Pope. I saw atheists,
meanwhile, deeply touched by the Pope's words.
"What are you in favor of?" we were all asked. "Of
conformist consent to totalitarian coercion or of the
inviolable right in God's and man's order of things for
human beings to live in freedom and dignity?" An
overwhelming majority of Poles chose the latter.[36]

Here Michnik highlights the emergence of a new national
democratic consensus for freedom of religion and human
rights. He goes on to cite particular Polish historical prece-
dents for this emerging autonomous (from the Party-state)
consensus: the heroic struggles of the nineteenth-century political rebels Jaroslaw Dabrowski and Romuald Traugott, the
martyrdom of Maksymilian Kolbe and Janusz Korczak, the
experience of the Holocaust and the Warsaw uprising.

Michnik concludes his reflections of the Pope's visit with
subtle questioning:

Am I allowed to reject . . . culture based on Christian
values, on faith, hope and love?
Anyone's reply to this most important question of
a man's life risks sounding a little false. Everyone
should answer it for himself and to himself. Because I
believe that this system of values is rejected not only
by those who continually violate human rights because of their positions, or by those who permit them
to do so by remaining silent and following in Pontius

Pilate's footsteps, but also by those who declare solidarity with these values, but defend them by way of dishonorable methods.

I will not here make a list of those methods. Let me just say that when I listened to John Paul's homily in Cracow, I had a strange feeling. When the Pope asked the faithful Catholics "never to forsake Him," he was also addressing me: a pagan.

He was urging me to avoid those dishonorable methods.[37]

Here Michnik is not only the talented writer, but a practical philosopher and political strategist. He responds strongly as a private person to the idea of Poland's second baptism, but as a moral, thinking, acting agent, he wants to draw the most fully humane conclusions. He knows from personal experience (remember, his parents were committed Communists) how destructive social utopias can be; how dreams of absolute good can yield absolute evil. So he affirms his commitment to Christian values of human rights with his fellow citizens, but then cautions them that this is not enough. He did not invent the nonviolent, tolerant, pragmatic character of Solidarity, but in this passage he is bringing it into view.

Michnik identifies himself with Christian values, but calls himself a pagan. More is involved than a writer's ironic conceit. The dignity of the human individual is not only the end of his politics. The search for dignity is as well the method of his thought and action. He seeks to maintain his autonomy and dignity. As a man of the Left, he has contributed immeasurably to Polish political culture by helping to forge an alliance between "enlightened," Western-oriented intellectuals and the church (indeed, a conservative church). In doing this, though, he did not give up his independent position. He warns against the sacralization of politics even when he observes that this is not the significance of the Pope's visit and the position of the Polish church. Individual independence, dignity, and judgment may in theory be inalienable rights, but as a practical matter, they must be constituted and defended in concerted action.

We can observe this in Poland as results of the grand political events of 1956, 1968, 1970, 1976, and 1980–81. Slowly an autonomous public life emerged, opposed to repressive authority. Human rights became a human accomplishment. But human rights and democracy are also products of political imagination. Michnik's appreciation of the church argues for an alliance between the church and secular intellectuals as a practical matter, but it does more. It demands religious and political freedom as means and ends. It challenges secularists to consider seriously the contribution of the religious to the quest for social justice. It cautions the religious against dogmatism. Michnik surveys Polish history and contemporary politics in a similar normatively critical frame of mind.

In the early seventies, in "In Shadows of Ancestors," Michnik used his remembrance of Jozef Pilsudski as a means to address the problems of Polish political culture. Pilsudski tends to be remembered as a hero or as a villain, as a cryptofascist or as a great nationalist. For Adam Michnik he is a man who accomplished a great deal during certain moments of his life, whose ideas about the Polish nation have much to say to the present generation even if he ultimately succumbed to authoritarianism. Michnik remembers that at the beginning of the century Pilsudski was the great national hero of the socialists, who were accused of being "Russian seeds" and "Jewish tools" by the supernationalists of the day. Michnik forthrightly changes his own position on the Polish-Russian War and appreciates the interwar sovereignty which sustained an independent political culture, albeit in flawed circumstances. He contrasts Pilsudski's struggles for an independent Poland, as a confederation of nations, with the national chauvinism ascendant today both within official circles and in the opposition.

In the late seventies there was a reborn cult of Pilsudski, nurtured by the supernationalists in opposition. Before this fact, in the conclusion of his essay on Pilsudski, Michnik warned against it:

> I did not write, and did not intend to write a congratulatory scroll for Jozef Pilsudski. For my generation,

which has heard so many lies, truth is of the utmost
importance. I have tried to write the truth about the
events that took place at the beginning of this century
because I consider them to be of the utmost importance. It is from those experiences that independence
rose. But I am writing my own, rather personal view
of Pilsudski and his role, and I would not like to forget the dark side as well. . . .

Pilsudski died in 1935. In his last years many former comrades distanced themselves from him, while
an unsavory mob of "adulators and rascals" grew to
surround him. And yet the leaders of the Polish Socialist Party, perhaps even recent prisoners of Brzesc
marched in his funeral procession. Why did they take
part in this farewell? No doubt they were saying
goodbye to their youth, to a segment of their lives.
But surely it was not this alone. They were bidding
farewell to a man who had given Poland and the Poles
a sense of dignity, which is as essential to the health of
a nation as oxygen is to the human body.[38]

In this essay, Michnik takes a generally popular Polish political figure, vilified by the Communists and overly glorified
by their opponents, and illuminates his accomplishments
without overlooking his significant flaws. For the development of an independent political culture, the piece facilitated
the reinvigoration of the Polish Left. It distanced the Left from
political cliches: the necessity of choosing between workers'
rights and national independence, the mythology of the good
Lenin and the bad Stalin, and automatic anti- and philo-
Semitism. Michnik suggested that national independence and
democracy are the primary political projects when ideological
cant and irrationalisms are identified and rejected. These are
themes he developed even more forthrightly in subsequent
writings.

Ten years after Michnik wrote his essay on Pilsudski and
the Polish socialist tradition, he wrote one of his most controversial essays, "Conversation in the Citadel." It is very much
the political companion to "Shadows of Forgotten Ancestors."
In "Conversation in the Citadel," he brings his political com-

mitments to their democratic conclusion. This essay is a lesson in post-totalitarian reasoning, most strikingly apparent when opposed to the official totalitarian truth.

In the essay, Michnik presents an appreciative assessment of the politics of Roman Dmowski and the political movement of National Democracy. This movement, strongly implicated in a variety of national chauvinisms and protofascism, was the alternative current to Pilsudski's socialism at the turn of the century. Michnik is aware of Dmowski's faults but wants to analyze his strengths as well. Here is his overall assessment:

> Roman Dmowski was an excellent analyst, but he was a prisoner of his phobias. He was the co-founder of Polish pro-independence thought and the co-culprit of Polish narrowness. He sowed the seeds of rationality in political thinking, yet carried the germs of xenophobia which caused gangrene in wide areas of intellectual life. He shaped Polish minds and depraved Polish consciences. He shaped them by developing the idea of a politics of activism, teaching about geopolitics, injecting harsh realism; he degraded them by formulating a concept of the nation and an idea of Polishness that led straight to totalitarian solutions.[39]

The essay was controversial because Michnik seems to emphasize Dmowski's astute geopolitical observations, his understanding that in politics there is a radical difference between an ethic of ultimate ends and the ethics of responsibility, and his conviction that the struggle for national sovereignty requires both the independent Polish institutions of everyday life (in education, social welfare, economic life, etc.), and clear though distant goals of national independence.

In an epilogue to his critics, Michnik explains his intentions:

> The intention behind "Conversation in the Citadel" was somewhat perverse: I wanted to interpret anew—through the eyes of one who had been formed by leftist tradition—the content in the political concepts of the National Democrats and to uncover the values

hidden beneath the thick layers of insult, resentment and falsehood. I naturally concentrated on those motifs that characterize the wisdom and shrewdness of the National Democrats' political thought. Ideological polemics—the logic of political disputes—always make people exaggerate their adversaries' flaws and whitewash their own mistakes. This may be why I applied the opposite method in this article: I saw my own tradition in the crooked mirror of its dangers and deformations, and the National Democratic tradition in the brightness of its virtues. But I also pointed out the shadows in the thinking of the National Democrats, although admittedly I tried to understand their origins instead of unmasking their symptoms.[40]

Michnik recognizes virtue in his political adversary. This is not only an historical problem. Many members of the opposition today identify with the tradition of National Democracy. Their supreme value is not democracy and political independence, but nationalism and sovereignty. They, like their predecessors, sometimes flirt with national chauvinism and anti-Semitism. By emphasizing their political virtues, Michnik attempts to civilize Polish political culture. When one views one's opponent as having integrity, not only are political liberty and tolerance possible, but so is a pluralistic search for the common good.

When officialdom faces opposition, disagreement or even the unconventional, it naturally condemns, censors, represses. Since it claims a monopoly on truth and uses state power to enforce the truth, alternative views and ways of life are seen not only as different but as objectively false. Political discourse is constituted by a series of declarations, not by discussion. Different ways to socialism and new and more humane Marxisms may serve the powers and therefore flourish at some points, but they are always suspect. They are easily declared heretical in official Newspeak—antisocialist, counter-revolutionary, bourgeois liberal, etc.—and repressed. Socialist marketeers become capitalist inroaders; true internationalists, rootless cosmopolitans. Michnik opposes such certainty, not only as an anti-Communist or nationalist or leftist, but as a democrat committed to the deliberative reason that democracy requires. Operating in a political world strikingly lacking a democratic culture, he acts and writes as if one existed, and, ironically, by his doing so, it may be born. Here is a variation on an earlier opposition theme.

The Free Public Domain

The primary operative principle of the democratic opposition in the seventies and of Polish society during the Solidarity period was a relatively simple one: to act as if one lived in a free society. This led people to act freely and liberated Polish society, demonstrating the power of the powerless. In remarkable ways, the fruits of this liberation persist in the post-Solidarity period. People not only remember their experience of freedom, but, despite considerable risk, sustain alternative autonomous social, political, and cultural practices and institutions; from underground Solidarity to collective protests, independent publishing houses, and educational enterprises. Now, though, conspiracy is necessary. Openness, the primary asset of the democratic opposition of the seventies and of the Solidarity period, is dangerous. Conspiracy is the rule of the day, and undersides of the Polish political culture have revealed themselves: political moralism, blind anti-Communism, and new forms of ultranationalism.

In his historical and social investigations, Michnik addressed these problems.[41] In "Maggots and Angels," by reviewing the compromises of earlier Polish heroes he cautioned the opposition in the seventies against political moralism and hatred of those who compromise with the existing political order. In "A Year Has Passed," he analyzed the democratic strengths and weaknesses of Solidarity when political repression was on the horizon. And in "On Resistance," he explained the foolhardiness of ultranationalism and extreme anti-Communism seeking instant change. Rather, Michnik maintained, Poles must organize themselves for a long march, preparing alternative social, political, and cultural arrangements, so that when an opportunity arises for social change it will be effective and just.

In "The New Evolutionism," Michnik wrote what proved to be a kind of theoretical constitution of the Polish democratic opposition and Solidarity. He analyzed the strengths and weaknesses of postwar strategies of social reform. He revealed that the nineteenth-century choice between reform and revolution no longer exists. He realistically considered the complexity of Polish-Soviet relations and drew the neoevolutionist, post-totalitarian conclusion that a "program for evolution ought to be addressed to an independent public, not to totalitarian power." Acting as if they were free, Polish citizens freed themselves in line with Michnik's ideas.

The central democratic thrust of Michnik's actions and writings is a part of a broad Polish political transformation. Michnik is a passionate participant in the transformed Polish politics. Though he is viewed as a great political and moral symbol (in a sense the thinking person's Walesa), his specific stances on the pressing issues of the day are often received quite critically. Some believe his sense of moral purpose overwhelms his democratic commitment. Some view him as overly secular, others as overly religious. Some view him as too uncompromising, some as compromised. He is far from a symbol of unity. Rather, along with other intellectuals and activists, he represents a part of a plurality, while in the great bulk of his historical and literary writings he presents a commitment to plurality. Together with his compatriots in a broad range of political debates, then, he is attempting to write the political postscript to totalitarianism, a very difficult task embedded in the overall post-totalitarian situation.

III

The Post-Totalitarian Mind and the Neototalitarian State

SIX

The Post-Totalitarian Terrain

THE PRESENT-DAY post-totalitarian situation is a complex one. Though totalitarian culture still exists, as does officially accepted criticism, the challenge of free public culture has fundamentally transformed unofficial and official public life, giving rise to a post-totalitarian frame of mind. The post-totalitarian mind is shaped by the experience of totalitarianism and by the cultural and political liberation from this experience. It speaks both the language of Newspeak and its alternatives. The politics of the totalitarians and their opposition are in competition, but they are sometimes mutually supportive, as are the politics of totalitarian culture and the free public domain.

When totalitarianism first emerged, it overwhelmed the autonomous culture of Germany, Russia and its empire, and Central Europe. Thus, for example, the social science of Germany ceased. Its continued existence and excellence were found only in exile.[1] Russian theaters became empty shells, little more than caricatures of their former selves.[2] With a political elite holding the monopoly on force, and with force defining the truth, culture was severely undermined and independent politics were extinguished. Yet when some critical expression was officially accepted, cultural excellence and cogent independent expression again became a possibility. We observed this in the case of Polish theater. Numerous other examples abound, from Andrzej Wajda's *Ashes and Diamonds* to George Konrad's *The Case Worker* and, of course, Aleksander Solzhenitsyn's *A Day in the Life of Ivan Denisovitch*.

But as we have also observed, such critical expression, often highly metaphoric, is subjected to official manipulation and censorship and therefore is limited. Miklos Hareszti ironically imagines the likely fate of Solzhenitsyn if he were subjected to "soft totalitarianism": "If Solzhenitsyn had lived in Hungary, he would have been appointed president of the Writers Union. And then no one would have written *The Gulag Archipelago.* And if someone had, Solzhenitsyn would have voted for his expulsion."[3]

A clear and present danger of totalitarianism, in its soft and hard varieties, is cultural silencing and forgetting: Solzhenitsyn not writing or writing insignificantly, Poles not remembering the political actions and cultural works of their predecessors. This can happen through direct and brutal repression, but it can also occur through intentional obscurity. When writers try to trick the censor through metaphors and dense symbolism, cultural and political inheritance and aspiration can be lost. Grand heroic actions such as those of the Polish workers are directed against these dangers. Such heroics are built upon little private decisions—Baranczak writing a poem disregarding the censor; a greengrocer not putting "Workers of the World, Unite!" in a shop window; decisions to live in truth, as Havel puts it.

When a great number of people decide to live in truth, even in a totalitarian situation, they reveal (again in Havel's words) the power of the powerless. They deconstruct the totalitarian relationships between reason and power, and their reason empowers independent political action.

This is most evident to us in the career of Adam Michnik, but it can be, indeed has been, the experience of a broad spectrum of East Central European citizens, from the Czech Party reformers to Polish union activists, and perhaps even to Mikhail Gorbachev. More about this controversial point later. First we must appreciate the post-totalitarian configuration as a whole. It is constituted by the emergence of an independent public domain, then by the relationship between the independent domain and the domain of the officially tolerated critical discourse, and finally by the relationship between these domains of critical discourse with officialdom. The alternatives of Newspeak are shaped by Newspeak, but they may in the end destroy it.

The relationships analyzed here are not simply structural. They involve changing political cultures and changing relationships between force and reason. This is most apparent in the writings of the leading independent intellectuals of Central Europe.

Independent Public Life and a Post-Totalitarian Mind

The texts of Vaclav Havel and Milan Kundera, Adam Michnik and Stanislaw Baranczak, Miklos Haraszti and George Konrad combine modern and classical virtues. The same quality of mind and presentation is found in Hannah Arendt's work—not surprisingly, since her first major theoretical endeavor was *The Origins of Totalitarianism* and all her subsequent works assume the existence of modern tyranny. She was in this sense the first post-totalitarian theorist.

Such theorists are straightforward, though clearly not unsophisticated. They address a general public, though they draw upon a broad learning. They combine an appreciation for the authority of cultural traditions with an awareness that these have been challenged. They arise from quite specific circumstances, yet they are cosmopolitan and worldly. These combinations represent not only cultural continuity, the Central European intellectuals resurrected,[4] but also a reaction to totalitarian ideology, culture, and politics. Post-totalitarian culture represents a clear break from these three central components of the totalitarian world.

Ideology versus Public Philosophy

Totalitarian ideology starts with one simple idea, which unlocks the mysteries of the human world. The idea is understood as being the underlying reality behind the complicated world of human appearances. Appearances are explained by the simple idea or some deduction from it.

The post-totalitarian mind reacts against such notions. Appearances are taken seriously; the existence of underlying realities is doubted. "For us," writes Arendt, "appearance—something that is being seen and heard by others as well as by ourselves—constitutes reality."[5] She does not question the im-

portance of private life; "there are very relevant matters which
can survive only in the realm of the private. For instance,
love."⁶ But she does think that a primary problem with modernity is that it does not understand the centrality of human
appearance as public reality.

The present-day critical post-totalitarians seem to agree.
When Adam Michnik writes about the Catholic church, the
Polish socialists, and the Polish nationalists, he does not judge
them essentially as absolute forces for good or evil, nor does
he know the meaning of their activities by referring to their
class or racial bases. Rather, he judges their specific public activities. What they appear to have done is what they have
done. Dmowski may have been xenophobic, but he did appreciate the complexities of geopolitics. Pilsudski died a dictator,
but he contributed a great deal to a tolerant multinational
conception of Poland. The Catholic church is the most important support for liberty and pluralism in postwar Poland, but
when Cardinal Glemp and Father Tischner contribute to a
sacralization of politics, no matter how good their intentions,
they must be criticized.⁷

Though Kundera has made the confusion between public
and private a fundamental theme in his work, he too insists
that what we see is what is. He declares repeatedly that his
romances are erotic adventures, definitely not political ones.
He does not want his sexual farces to be understood as metaphors for political tragedies. Politics and sex should not be
confused. Though they intersect in his work, neither should
be understood as the underlying reality behind appearance.
Freud and the Freudians would have sex behind politics.
Marx and the Marxists would have politics (or at least political economics) behind sex (or at least patterns of courtship,
the family, etc.). Kundera presents dual story lines which
sometimes meet in revealing ways.⁸

Totalitarian Politics versus Democratic Politics

The epistemological decision to take appearances as reality,
specifically political appearances, has profound political ef-

fects. It leads to a new type of political practice, a negation of totalitarian political practice. The totalitarian model of politics posits an intimate relationship between Party practice and underlying truth. The totalitarian Party is not only a partisan organization on the model of nineteenth-century European class parties, organizing interests, people, and goods. It does not seek the common good through public deliberation, on the model of Anglo-American parties.[9] It delivers the truth and absolute liberation from historical exploitation. Because it purports to have knowledge of the truth, opposition can only mean support of retrogression and exploitation. State support of the underlying truth, i.e., ideology, justifies, indeed requires, terror.

The post-totalitarians see this for what it is—human barbarism. But unlike direct antifascists or anti-Communists, they draw a radical political conclusion. The absolute truth in politics is dangerous.

Simple-minded anti-Communists identify the Soviet Union as an evil empire and Communists as a force of darkness. The absolute certainty of such convictions justifies a broad range of questionable political policies. Since Communism is an absolute evil, the most brutal sorts of old-fashioned tyranny are not only tolerated but actively supported. Furthermore, anyone who questions such support is labelled as morally and politically suspect, again in absolute terms, and this is not only a product of McCarthyism and the McCarthy period. For example, a distinguished moderate Democratic senator from middle America was publically denounced in 1987 as a Communist sympathizer by the Republic Senate campaign committee.[10] Such absolute anti-totalitarian convictions require compromising democratic ideals, both in foreign policy and in domestic politics as well. At their political roots, the Watergate and Iran-Contra scandals had as their basis a disregard for democratic norms on the grounds of true belief in anti-totalitarian practice. Nixon disregarded the rights of dissent of the anti–Vietnam War social movement. Reagan and his subordinates undermined the role of the Congress in making

foreign policy. Both the Nixon and the Reagan administra-
tions knew the truth about the dangerous world, as Colonel
Oliver North put it, and this knowledge not only permitted
but required antidemocratic practice.[11]

The contrast with the post-totalitarian position is striking.
Milan Kundera's most telling political satire seems to be reserved for ridiculous anti-Communists, not totalitarians. He
repeatedly reminds his readers of the totalitarian's good intentions. Goodness and strong moral convictions made young
Stalinists monsters. Political certainty is the problem, not
one ideology or another. Such certainty and deep conviction
among anti-Communists are ridiculed. For Kundera, the slogan "the barbarity of Communism" belongs to the vocabulary
of American kitsch,[12] very much parallel to the kitsch of the
leftist Grand March and totalitarianism. His warnings against
kitsch simplicities may dismay American anti-Communists
such as Norman Podhoretz,[13] but they are central to the critical post-totalitarian point of view.

Almost all of Michnik's writings work against what Kundera has labelled political kitsch. Michnik never finds the
simple key to a problem which leads to logically deduced action. He almost always maps out a field of valuable, though
contradictory, political opinions and ingeniously shows how
they can be made compatible, or at least how those who hold
them can be brought together in a public forum where they
can honorably resolve their differences and act in concert. He
shows how the Left and the church,[14] leftists and rightists, National Democracy and Polish socialism, the need for romantic
revolt and the need for pragmatic reform of economic conditions, even Communists and anti-Communists,[15] can find a
common ground for peaceful political interaction. His moral
and political outrage is reserved for those who do obstruct
such honorable resolution.[16] He does not synthesize views and
try to unite people on the basis of a political and complete
resolution of differences. Rather, he presents an intellectual
and political framework within which people can come together to resolve their differences.

This is a primary democratic role of the post-totalitarian intellectual. Michnik, along with others, shows in his writings and his actions that autonomous political action is possible. The early days of KOR and Michnik's famous essay "The New Evolutionism" accomplished this. Furthermore, he helps provide the conditions under which political interactions can be democratic, showing how people of good will with honest differences can come together to resolve their differences, as long as their intentions are based upon mutual respect. Then he and his intellectual colleagues counsel political actors with expert knowledge and informed political judgments.

To bring about the emergence of a democratic transformation, which such activities engender, an empty space must be established for deliberative resolution of societal problems, as Claude Lefort has shown.[17] The role of the post-totalitarian intellectual with democratic commitments is not to provide definitive answers to political problems, but to help inform the just resolution in the open space—a free political arena. Here we have a most striking practical contrast between the totalitarians and the post-totalitarians.

The totalitarian intellectual, armed with the truth and the gun to enforce it, is a vanguardist. He acts in the name of the people or the masses, a class or a race, but he knows better than they what is in their interest and what is historically inevitable. He and his party lead society, whether society wants it or not. This is understood as being justified on the grounds that society eventually will want it, when the truth about which the intellectual dreams is realized, when the masses have matured, when the political project has borne its fruits.

The post-totalitarian intellectual not only is suspicious of such vanguardism, she or he as a matter of principle opposes it. Since political truth is denied, pluralism and democracy become practical ideals; differences of opinion become a positive goal to be nurtured. The role of the political intellectual is not leadership but service. He or she gives political actors advice, not the correct policy. Political actors of different views must resolve their differences in a public domain, for all to see and judge. Intellectuals, then, assist citizens in making judgments, rather than provide the correct interpretations.

Thus, for example, George Konrad, the Hungarian novelist and social thinker, writes judgments of the Central European Coalition in his essay *Anti-Politics*.[18] From Yalta to Gdansk, he considers the actions of political agents and draws conclusions. But these conclusions do not reveal the truth of the postwar period for those caught between Eastern and Western models. They just outline his view of the terms of social conflict. For a resolution of the problem, Konrad awaits the action of political agents. Along with Ivan Szelenyi, he has already suggested (in *Intellectuals on the Road to Class Power*) that to do otherwise is to initiate a new tyranny, a tyranny of the intellectuals.[19]

The proper role of the post-totalitarian intellectual is also not that of a policy analyst. The starting point is an understanding of the importance of indeterminacy in human affairs. Between past and future is the possibility of human action and democratic decision. As we have seen, totalitarians know the meaning of the past, and brutally coerce in the present in order to bring about the inevitable future.

Futurologists, or behavioral policy analysts, are not so brutal, but they too tend to disallow human volition and act in a fundamentally antidemocratic way. The future is not decided by human reasoning, choice, and deliberation, but is projected from the present. Generally the role of the policy analyst has been to discern trends and to develop the correct policy.[20] The job of the post-totalitarian is to ponder the meaning and choices of the present, reflecting upon experience and considering future possibilities. Of course there is no logical reason why policy studies cannot be developed democratically, but this requires that trends be considered much more skeptically than presently is the rule.

Post-totalitarian politics, then, are not the politics of the totalitarians or policy analysts. They are a democratic politics of rational deliberation (not choice) among equals. The political leaders of Solidarity were not intellectuals, socialists, or technological experts. They were citizens, i.e., members of a social movement. The Polish intellectual elite advised the leadership on political matters, but did not decide important issues on the grounds that they knew the truth of history (the claim of the vanguard), nor did they decide on the grounds of their expertise in the techniques of social planning (the claim of the policy analysts). The intellectuals were fellow citizens facing the political challenge of the totalitarian order in a democratic fashion. To do this they had to go to the root of the totalitarian order—totalitarian culture. They sought to substitute a democratic culture for a totalitarian order. This necessarily required a reformed relationship between reason and coercion.

Totalitarian Culture versus Democratic Culture

When force defines reason, there exists an official truth about everything. We have seen that force defines reason differently throughout the totalitarian order. Bases of autonomy in the social structure do develop sometimes, even with official intention. The thaw in the late fifties and early sixties in the Soviet Union was used by Khrushchev against his Stalinist opponents; the cultural liberalization of Deng Xiaoping in China in the eighties seems to be used by the economic modernizers against the economic isolationists. At times the zone of autonomy develops more or less by itself, e.g., the case of Polish youth theater. Sometimes it seems necessary—the loosening of the Stalinist grip during the war. But at other times, despite apparent necessity, it is repressed, e.g., the case of Lysenkoism.

Even with such differentiation through time and space, the cultural root of totalitarianism, force defining reason, remains the persistent characteristic of the totalitiarian order. In today's totalitarianism, once the official truth is disbelieved, it becomes generally recognized as the official lie. The totalitarian Party forms to realize an ideology. The ideology presents a closed system of meaning interpreted to be the whole truth. Referring only to itself, its meaning outside itself is defined by Party force. Therefore, whatever the Party says is true, is true in official public life. Newspeak, the special language of this

life, develops. Everyone knows the language is actually meaningless, or at least arbitrary, but all must use it. People struggle
to get on with their lives, trying to discern from the ambiguous discourse what official actions are likely to be and how
they will affect their daily life.

As with the young scholar described in chapter 2, a cloud of
official ambiguity and uncertainty surrounds all lives. When
terror recedes, Newspeak and legitimation through disbelief
become the rule, but the fog of an official unreality does not
lift. Nothing can be believed: history and contemporary politics, information about environmental safety and world events,
economic news and reports on educational reform. As Arendt
observed, the end result of the rule of the lie as official truth is
cynicism, "an absolute refusal to believe the truth of anything,
no matter how well this may be established." And "the result
of a consistent and total substitution of lies for factual truth is
not that the lies will now be accepted as truth, and the truth
disguised as lies, but that the sense by which we take our bearings in the real world is being destroyed."[21]

With the loss of this sense, Party domination is realized. On
the other hand, fighting for the truth and living in truth become important forms of resistance. For the poet this involves
the invention of a language that is clearly not Newspeak—as
Baranczak put it, not "those words which easily let themselves
slip through the strainer of a microphone," but "those which
must work themselves through a grating with immense effort."[22] The literature of the opposition is built upon those
words, from the political theory of a Michnik to the theater of
a Havel to the prose of a Kundera to the poetry of a Baranczak.

The words of this opposition are the words of a democratic
culture. Their meanings tend not to be hidden and obscure.
They favor straightforward vernacular language rather than
formalized literary discourse, and, most importantly, they
promote the formation of autonomous politics for democratic
deliberation. In Havel's words, by speaking the truth, they
make possible living in truth and demonstrate the power of
the powerless. Arendt explains why this power may prevail:

> Truth, though . . . always defeated in a head-on clash
> with the powers that be, possesses a strength of its
> own. Whatever those in power may contrive, they are
> unable to discover or invent a viable substitute for it.
> Persuasion and violence can destroy the truth, but
> they cannot replace it.[23]

The official truth readily reveals itself to be a collection of lies. A public appearance of the truth brings together those in opposition, creating alternative publics and empowering those publics. The most spectacular case of this is Solidarność.

Solidarity emerged as an escalation of speaking and living in truth, demonstrating the power of the powerless. It was a culmination of workers' struggles against the harsh realities of living in the workers' state and intellectuals' struggles to speak the truth. Workers protested price increases, tried to form unions, and demanded greater freedom. Intellectuals fought against censorship and established defense committees and alternative education and publishing. In fighting against the authorities, they came together to form an open, independent public life where speaking and acting upon the truth became a real possibility. The discourse was open to a wide variety of political stances and social classes.

As we have seen, Adam Michnik's writings are simultaneously a product of this openness and an important part of its constitution, pushing it in a pluralistic and democratic direction. His essay "The New Evolutionism" opened the post-totalitarian political era. It named already existing developments and brought them into clear public view, crystallizing them in the process. He combined a post–World War II, East Central European logic, i.e., a Soviet bloc logic, with a specifically Polish logic. Revolutionary change is not only not possible, he argued, it is undesirable, "given the absence of an authentic political culture or any standards of democratic collective life." As well, he had little hope for change intitiated by the Party: "Resistance was terminated by the [Polish] events of March 1968." Reform from above provides little hope, because in the final analysis those who wait for the day to serve democratic reforms in the Polish Party, when a Polish Dubcek will appear, only serve totalitarian power.[24] The fact that the Polish liberals instituted martial law in 1981 underscores the saliency of this point.

In place of reform from above and revolution from below, a strategy which combines Polish romantic and neopositivist impulses, Michnik proposed reform from below, "an unceasing struggle for reform and evolution that seeks an expansion of civil liberties and human rights."[25] For this to succeed, reformers and dissidents should address themselves not to authorities but to their fellow citizens. The authorities then will make changes under social pressures. "Nothing instructs the authorities better than pressures from below."[26] In this seminal paper, Michnik told the story of past attempts to bring about social change, pointing to the new way, which in the end became the strategy of Solidarity. The strategy surely became much more successful than Michnik had imagined.

Michnik, then, could not consider as a serious problem what specific effects a successful new evolutionism would have on official political, cultural, and social structures. But it has had effects which have deeply transformed the world of Newspeak and its alternatives. In this sense, there exists a developed post-totalitarian order. The post-totalitarian order is most fully developed politically in Poland, but culturally it exists throughout the Soviet bloc. It also, ominously, suggests the possibility of a new totalitarian state on the horizon.

Polish Specifics

Once fully autonomous cultural and political activities emerge and become a normal part of everyday life, as they did in Poland during the Solidarity period, activities within the totalitarian order are challenged and transformed. This is true in the domains of both officially accepted criticism and official policy. Those who have sustained themselves by saying and hearing variations on "Big Brother is ungood" must face the limitations of that theme. Those who have publicly identified official truth with truth become embarrassed by lies.

THE POST-TOTALITARIAN TERRAIN

The choices for the authorities are rather simple: accept and compete with the free public domain, as in the period of Solidarity's legalization; attempt to repress it, as in martial-law Poland; or engage in controlled competition, a combination of repression and competition, as in the post–martial law period.

The problems facing the realm of officially accepted criticism are significantly more complicated. It is caught between the strategies of officialdom and the successes and failures of those who have seceded from the totalitarian order. Viewing the official critic's predicament as a problem of everyday life, he or she must find a way to be something other than an official apologist. Viewing the predicament as a problem of social change, the official critic as political agent must reinvigorate revisionism or officially tolerated alternative viewpoints of pluralism. From both points of view, she or he is at the mercy of the authorities.

In "A New Evolutionism" Michnik tells of the successes and failures of revisionism and neopositivism. The Polish revisionists sought to democratize and humanize the Party and its system. The Polish neopositivists, as Catholic geopolitical realists (like the Polish positivists of the nineteenth century) and anti-Marxists, wanted to work for fundamental change of the totalitarian system from within. They cooperated with the authorities, waiting for the day when the Soviet bloc would disintegrate and they would lead the nation. Both the revisionists and neopositivists shared the belief that change would come from the Polish leadership. As Michnik colorfully puts it, "they both counted on rational thinking of the communist prince, not on independent institutions that would gain control of the power apparatus."[27] Though Michnik and Polish activists decisively questioned these beliefs in 1976, by the mid-eighties, in a post-totalitarian era, they have again become important.

Before the emergence of an autonomous public sphere, revisionism and neopositivism had an important symbiotic relationship. Revisionist intellectuals, with their central themes of "humanistic socialism," "Marxism with a human face," and

"Marxism and the human individual" kept alive "the ideas of truth and humanism which were under attack in the official propaganda."[28] Further, by engaging in political critiques and activism, they served as models of activism rather than of withdrawal and resignation. In this way, as Michnik states, "revisionism laid the basis for independent participation in public life."[29]

The neopositivists, on the other hand, during a long period of conciliation with the authorities, focused on one "specific political objective—to expand the domain of civil liberties."[30] The revisionists developed a series of neo-Marxisms and strategies for Party liberalization. The neopositivists as Catholic laymen published officially accepted (and censored) journals and took part in Polish political institutions, specifically the *Sejm* (the Polish parliament). They gave legitimacy to official pluralism but, by doing so, also kept alive the ideal of pluralism.

Thus, through the activities of the revisionists and neopositivists, the key norms of autonomous public life—public participation, civil liberties, and pluralism—were kept alive for most of the postwar period. In the late seventies and in 1980–81 this did not seem to be enough. The semblance of public participation, civil liberties, and pluralism provided by the revisionists and neopositivists was overshadowed by the real thing, i.e., the democratic opposition and Solidarity. Yet in the mid-eighties the officially accepted and promoted critics have a new role to play. The authorities and their opposition need a well-developed gray zone to deal with each other. The authorities need a way to achieve some popular support, at least active compliance. The opposition, given geopolitical realities after martial law, needs a means to exert influence upon official structures. In this situation, the authorities may be more open to popular initiatives, but popular initiatives must be addressed to the authorities. As Michnik's political mentor, Jacek Kuron, has observed:

> Today the authorities have reached the point where they are feverishly seeking the people's approval. There seem to be two reasons for this: keeping Po-

land relatively quiet for the sake of Gorbachev's peace offensive, and gaining the people's cooperation in the reconstruction of the economy.

In this situation, the range of concessions the authorities could be forced to make is quite broad. Of course, they must be forced. . . . The fact is that Polish society is outside the totalitarian system. Now we have to work to inject our independence into dependent state structures.[31]

The independent society must interject its character into the official system, but the problem remains how and where to send the message. During the Solidarity period, messages were sent through the Gdansk agreements and legal institutions. In the post—martial law period, present-day revisionism and neopositivism are necessary. Someone has to use official ideology and Newspeak to free officialdom from its confines. This role, of course, is quite different from the role of the official critics of an entrenched totalitarian order.

The real-life situation of the post-totalitarian order is proving to be even more surreal than that of totalitarianism without terror or belief. The force of Newspeak reaches its limits as the power of its alternatives expands. The authorities try to use Newspeak, and espouse it to the population, as a rhetoric of legitimation for their power and privileges. Having recognized and then disavowed contact with Solidarity, the voice of the independent public, the authorities pretend they have the support of the public. But since active opposition is a recent memory for the bulk of the population, and since the support structures of the opposition are in place (such as union organization and independent publishing and education), a pretense of popular support is hard to sustain. People play the game of legitimation through disbelief within much more narrow confines.

As the Party attempts to reassert its leadership role in (i.e., control over) official institutions and enterprises, from the universities to industrial plants, it cannot depend on people's compliance. Even in official interactions people are reluctant to use Newspeak, because they know that an independent public opinion will judge them negatively for doing so. Thus the heroic imagery of progressive struggle is giving way in official pronouncements to the rhetoric of geopolitical necessity and nationalism.

In everyday official interactions, the pretense of a nation united in building socialism is being replaced by very soft imperatives. For official consumption people must admit little more than that Solidarity made mistakes and the authorities are not completely corrupt. For example, it has been accepted by the authorities that the rector of Warsaw University supported Solidarity and would not purge the university of Solidarity supporters. The authorities may have wanted such a purge, but they knew that to demand more would require a cultural revolution, closing the university, a move they were not ready to make. Thus they fired the completely independent elected rector of the Solidarity period and turned down the rector the faculty chose in his place (a person with equally visible Solidarity credentials), but accepted an independent physics professor who was not too politically engaged but still had university autonomy as a primary goal.

To gain acceptance by the population, the official language is developing an external referent. It is no longer a closed, completely self-referential system. Professed official ideals are economic reconstruction, not world revolution; social reconciliation, not class conflict; amiable church-state relations, not atheism; national survival, not proletarian internationalism. The population surely has doubts about official sincerity and the possibility of Communist authorities achieving such ideals, but they do support the ideals, and through such support the authorities make their claim of legitimacy. Official critics—the present-day revisionists and neopositivists—are those who accept the explicit and implicit components of these claims and attempt to expand their veracity.

The Jaruzelski regime's claim of legitimacy has spoken and unspoken elements. It openly asserts that it declared martial law to prevent social chaos. Not so openly, it strongly implies that if it had not intervened, the Soviets would have intervened with much more dire consequences for the nation. Thus the state of war is represented as a nationalistic act. There is no reason, in my judgment, to doubt that Jaruzelski and his colleagues are sincere in making this representation.

But there are self-delusion and duplicity here along with tragedy. The regime's understanding of geopolitical necessity led it, on nationalistic grounds, to repress the only genuine and sustained mass social movement for national independence and self-determination to appear in the Soviet bloc in the last forty years. The regime's understanding of necessity was clearly not endorsed by the bulk of the Polish population. Such understanding serves the particular interest of the ruling group and furthers the subservience of the Polish nation to the Soviets. Perhaps martial law would have been worse with Soviet leadership, but martial law enacted by the Communist state against an independent public is still repression.

Nonetheless, there is now room for present-day neopositivists and revisionists to take the regime at its word in order to interject some greater independence, pluralism, and democracy into official structures, and this need not be a completely cynical maneuver. The starting point for such official critics is the conviction that Soviet domination and the existing system based upon totalitarian culture will persist for the foreseeable future—as one such neopositivist, Pawel Spiewak, put it, "for the next half century."[32]

From this proposition, which is far from preposterous, it follows that political effectiveness requires dealing with the system to make it more humane. Outright opposition seems to be naive, moralistic, and politically inconsequential, more a continuation of the nineteenth-century Polish tradition of romantic gestures than a twentieth-century confrontation with totalitarianism. Therefore, expanding the breadth of what it is possible to say with official acceptance is more important than speaking freely unofficially. Improving the quality of official cultural institutions such as high schools and universities is more important than establishing underground educational

institutions in churches and private apartments. Even accepting and actively participating in the regime's new structures of
social consultation and trade unionism—Jaruzelski's democratization and renewal program, which was clearly formulated to co-opt independent institutions—is more important
than supporting those independent institutions of the democratic opposition and Solidarity. This sort of logic, carried to
its extreme, suggests Party activism and reformulation of official ideology by the critically disposed.

People go along this "realistic" road to varying degrees. At
one extreme is absolute rejection—those who maintain that
any relationship with the authorities is politically compromising, an act of collaboration. At the other extreme is the regime
itself. Martial law was not the work of Party hardliners, in
fact, but of the liberal faction of the Party, of people whose
Party activism dates back to the revisionist hopes of 1956,
among whom were opponents of the anti-Semitic, anti-liberal
campaigns of 1968.

Between these two extremes is the realistic appraisal of
some Solidarity advisors and leaders. Jacek Kuron clearly
opposes blind anti-Communism, the mentality that "either
we win or the Reds win." He observes, "like all institutions,
we grew conservative and have not yet adjusted to the new
situation in which pressure on the authorities is possible but
requires some cooperation, some participation in official institutions."[33] Kuron, Michnik, and others understand that
there is a need for the official institutions to be less rigid, so
that the Polish autonomous public can exert its pressure on
them with success.[34] Therefore, they do not completely reject
participation in official cultural and political life, though in
their minds caution is clearly in order. As Czezlaw Bielecki
has noted, "reconciliation is not possible with a gun at your
head."[35]

Others not only recommend participation, but inventively
take part. One of the most controversial cases in point is that
of *Res Publica,* a self-styled neoconservative journal of politics and letters, originally published illegally but legalized

as of 1987. The relatively young contributors to this journal are culturally elitists, politically Christian Democrats of
sorts, and quite cosmopolitan in their worldview. They are re-
fined and consider themselves political realists but, unlike the
nineteenth-century positivists, are certainly not in any sense
fellow travelers. They do not accept Polish subordination
to the Russians as a good and in no way justify such subordination. They simply see it as inevitable and want to work
effectively within the system of this inevitability. They are
not Marxists, and, unlike the revisionists, they do not even
pretend to be. But they do fit into the Newspeak net of the
Jaruzelski regime. Their desire to be realistic, effective, and
both officially published and of independent mind serves the
regime's normalization plan.

A wide variety of opinions and subjects is to be found in
Res Publica. Yet despite the freewheeling nature of its con-
tents, the journal is now published on deceptive theoretical
grounds. Though the contributors are actually highly critical
of the existing order, no author will openly question the legitimacy of the regime and its totalitarian culture—in this case
the surreal cultural milieu of nationalist claims based upon the
Soviet threat combined with fealty to the Soviets and proletarian internationalism, and the legacy of the state of war. In
fact, the journal's strategy of being the only point of mediation
between church and state, state and autonomous public, and
autonomous public and church, with direct loyalty and obli-
gation to none, is implicitly based upon the view that the regime is illegitimate, or that the autonomous public is. For
recognizing the legitimacy of one implies the delegitimation of
the other.

The legitimacy of the autonomous public is based upon the
premise that the regime is illegitimate, in that it has declared
war against Polish society and has never negotiated a peace.
The regime is condemned not only for declaring this war on
self-serving grounds. It is further condemned for seeking reconciliation and normalization without serious consultations
and negotiations with Solidarity's leaders, the only demo-

cratically chosen representatives of Polish society, or without instituting new but real democratic procedures. The regime has made *normalization, reconciliation,* and *democratization* the Newspeak equivalents of *Party domination* and *social repression*—a variation of Orwell's "War is Peace."

The regime, on the other hand, bases its legitimacy on the grounds that Solidarity and the democratic opposition were led by antisocialist elements, forces of chaos. To give the opposition any legitimacy would undermine the regime's explanation for its very existence.

This is the dilemma of the gray zone, given the opposition's recognition that there is now room for political and cultural action. Inevitably some people will judge others as going too far or compromising too early. But movement towards compromise is apparent. The compromise is distinctively posttotalitarian in that the compromisers must continuously deal with both an active regime and an active independent public life. In order to be effective, they must situate themselves between the authorities and society—they must use the language of Newspeak and its alternatives.

SEVEN

The Withering Away of Totalitarianism?

POLAND IS in the most advanced post-totalitarian political situation in the Soviet bloc. But culturally, post-totalitarianism has become a general phenomenon. Throughout the region, creators have simply said no to the system and drawn upon surviving cultural artifacts to forge new cultural languages outside the bounds of Newspeak, and this has affected both official and unofficial politics.[1]

The power of imagination has also found concrete independent social supports. In Hungary, with a particularly liberal cultural policy, the development of alternative publishing has closely followed the Polish model. In Czechoslovakia, after the Prague Spring, creators have pushed beyond the "Big Brother is ungood" rhetoric of Newspeak criticism, sometimes using quite unlikely social supports. Most spectacularly, a group of leading scholars and cultural creators have formed the small alternative world of the Chartists, Charter 77. Most subtly, a group of jazz enthusiasts have turned an officially accepted newsletter on jazz into a major forum for the independent cultural discussion. Both groups face severe repression, but persist. And in Moscow, the post-totalitarian configuration escalates. Gorbachev may not be a democrat in the sense of Western democratic ideals, nor in the sense put forth by the post-totalitarian democratic critics, but clearly both a language outside of Newspeak and a political culture apart from totalitarian culture have infiltrated the walls of the Kremlin.

The spread of post-totalitarian politics is not an inevitable evolution. But it does represent a cumulative cultural challenge. Solidarity emerged, and the political culture of the Soviet bloc will never again be as it was before Solidarity. Though it may not be the case that workers from around the bloc will directly copy the actions of Polish workers, Polish actions do stand out as striking evidence both that collective resistance to the totalitarian order is possible and that the totalitarian leadership will not easily tolerate such resistance.

The way different people in different places at different times use such evidence has varied. When people emphasize immediate results, the Polish August and legal Solidarity are interpreted as straightforward failures, provoking the reaction that there is no use in doing anything. In 1956, changes in the Party apparatus in response to social uprisings led to disappointment in Poland and tragedy in Hungary. In Czechoslovakia in 1968, even Party reform proved to be impossible. In Poland in 1980 and 1981, grass-roots reforms ended in disaster. Each conceivable strategy of resistance can be interpreted as a failure: reform from above (Poland 1956 and Czechoslovakia), reform from below (Poland, 1980 and 1981), revolution from above and below (Hungary 1956). Yet this pessimism only makes sense if the totalitarian system is viewed as unchanging, and this clearly is not the case. It has changed over time and from place to place.

Totalitarian Phases

We have observed three fundamental phases in totalitarian development. In its first phase, in Hitler's Germany and Stalin's Soviet Union, terror was an integral part of totalitarianism. Its definitive institution was the concentration camp. It provided a new type of political culture. Whereas political reason and force are always intimately related, as Foucault has demonstrated, totalitarianism conflates the two absolutely. Jews and kulaks were defined ideologically as a dying race and class, respectively. Therefore, genocide and mass starvation were not simply political programs, but historical inevitabilities.

In the second phase of totalitarianism, so-called post-Stalinism, the terror subsided. Force and reason were still conflated. An official truth still prevailed, enforced by the powers of the state. The publicly spoken word and the published written word had a single official set of meanings. Political authority, though, came to be legitimated through disbelief.

The shift from totalitarianism in the era of Stalin to totalitarianism without terror involved both substantial change and continuity. The brutality and immense human suffering came to an end. But the political culture and its challenge to freedom, reason, and self-determination persisted. Legitimation through disbelief emerged. The leeway for officially accepted criticism broadened. The changed cultural configuration, one with more criticism and officially disbelieved discourse, presented the possibility for people to speak, experience, and live in truth. In the seventies, given some official reluctance to engage in frontal repression, an independent public realm emerged. Significant Party reform on the Czechoslovak scale has not been attempted in this circumstance, nor has revolution from above or below.

Further, it is crucial to remember that the social systems based on totalitarian culture vary significantly, and such variation presents changing opportunities for political action. Not only do the systems' economic circumstances, national histories, and specific political experiences differ tremendously (from the terms of their "liberation" to their geographic proximity to Moscow), but the more basic relationships (from the point of view of political culture) between official truth, tolerated criticism, and autonomous culture have varied over time and space. This has led to changing opportunities for a variety of political strategies. As we have seen in the case of post–martial law Poland, those who at first as a matter of principle and strategy avoided contact with official institutions later advocated such contact and official reform.

Changes in the political-cultural configuration have also led to widespread alternative activities and the development of a post-totalitarianism beyond Poland. In Hungary, official critics soberly "know" that the Hungarian negative experiences with concerted autonomous action, i.e., the Hungarian revolution of 1956, make the development of anything like Solidarity impossible. But such development is in fact on the map of possibilities, for both the critics and the officials. Further, an opposition with alternative publications flourishes on a small scale in Hungary. Such publications are tolerated, as were similar publications in Poland in the late seventies. Though they reach a relatively small audience, they are completely outside the fold of official culture. They provide a clear basis for understanding the limits of official criticism and, in a time of political and economic crisis, present a clear critique of the false promises of the liberal Communist economic reforms of Janos Kadar. Thus, a new, realistic consciousness of the Hungarian situation is available to the population in a straightforward language outside the limits of Newspeak. The language can speak directly to the experiences of the Hungarian population.

The false promises of Kadarism are felt deeply by the Hungarians. Two jobs per capita has become the rule rather than the exception, and supporting the increased consumption levels is becoming ever more difficult. In such a situation, it is not at all clear that the Hungarian population will continue to interpret the experience of the Polish August and Solidarity as further proof that independent collective action is doomed to failure. They may instead begin to consider it as evidence that such action is possible, and judge that it may succeed given very significant changes and uncertainties in official circles. As Hungarians contemplate the end of the Kadar period, and as with the rest of the world they try to figure out exactly what is going on in Gorbachev's Kremlin, more of them may very well decide to live, speak and act in truth and discover the power of the powerless. The wisdom of the official critic, who knows that the people fear radical change more than they dislike their present situation, may no longer stand.

It is not appropriate to predict which way Hungary, Czechoslovakia, Romania, and other nations of Eastern Europe and the Soviet Union will go. It suffices to emphasize that they are moving, to greater and lesser degrees, within a new *posttotalitarian* situation. Epitomized by Solidarity, this new situation is defined by a new language and autonomous public action. It involves changes in the relationships between force and reason and between official and unofficial life, an undermining of the legitimation through disbelief, and an unlocking of previously untapped cultural and political energies.

From the point of view of officialdom, the changed relationships are a problem, but the untapped energies are also a potential political and economic resource for the authorities. Thus Mikhail Gorbachev's policy of openness can be understood as an attempt to gain the support of intellectuals in a campaign for economic revitalization. He permits the publication of banned books, the viewing of shelved films, and the showing of avant-garde art works. In return he hopes to rally support from the most creative and critical for his plans for economic modernization against a significant part of the Party apparatus. But more is involved than such political and economic strategy.

Gorbachev's reforms utilize an alternative cultural discourse for official purposes. This makes the analysis of the relationship between officialdom and Newspeak alternatives not only an intriguing theoretical task, but a pressingly practical one. From the point of view of this inquiry, the central question is: to what extent is Gorbachev disengaging the totalitarian relationship between force and reason, and choosing the alternatives to Newspeak over official ideology? The way we answer this question has broad practical and theoretical implications. It can inform approaches to international politics and to the politics of the totalitarians and their opponents. It will tell us about the fate of twentieth-century barbarism: whether it is disappearing or emerging with a new face.

As we have closely analyzed, a key to this movement was and is the reinvigoration of language in the works of such writers as Milan Kundera, George Konrad, Stanislaw Baranczak, Vaclav Havel, and Adam Michnik. Such poets, novelists, dramatists, and political theorists have systematically deconstructed the totalitarian relationship between force and reason. They are political in the sense that they are anti-ideological. They are culturally significant beyond the Soviet bloc because they have dedicated their work to a reinvigoration, a valorization, of language as a means to communicate fundamental pluralisms and refutable truths. Their works reveal a new political culture which has extended throughout

the Soviet bloc and has had its effects on the highest Party officials and accepted official critics as well as oppositionists. This
post-totalitarian culture is a culture of openness, public debate, public appearance, and antidogmatism.

Now we will consider how Gorbachev's glasnost and perestroika can be viewed as official attempts to co-opt this culture for official (totalitarian) purposes. The official attempt at
co-opting oppositional culture and its programs constitutes
the third phase of totalitarianism, suggesting that totalitarianism may be withering away, or that a neototalitarianism may
be emerging.

The Withering Away of Totalitarianism?

The degree and genuineness of glasnost and its impact on Soviet domestic life and on foreign policy are hotly debated
topics. The issues are crucial. The postwar geopolitical map
lies in the balance. The whole postwar political culture might
have to be rethought. Ronald Reagan of "Let Reagan be
Reagan" needed the evil empire as much as Gustav Husak
needed his Big Brother. Much of Western politics has been defined by approaches to anti-Communism. Third-world politics has involved choosing between such anti-Communism
and anti-imperialism (i.e., vaguely pro-Sovietism), and Socialist bloc politics has been defined by degree and quality of
subservience to Moscow. If glasnost is real, all of this can become obsolete. The slogans of glasnost are the slogans of
Western enlightened public opinion—freedom, democracy,
efficiency, modernization. If Gorbachev is committed to these,
the cold war may very well be over, as New York's Governor
Mario Cuomo has declared.[2]

There are, of course, reasons for caution. The nature of
Gorbachev's commitment must be appraised, as must the obstacles he faces in realizing his reforms. While it may be clear
that the Soviet regime has no real intention to promote democracy (as understood in the West or by the democratic opposition in the Soviet bloc) the positive democratic, liberal,
and modern thrusts of changes in Soviet life should not be too
quickly dismissed, nor should the obstacles to these changes.

In such a situation, the reactions of foreign and domestic observers and activists engaged in the politics within and outside the Soviet bloc often say at least as much about the observers and the activists as about the changes in the Soviet Union. Optimists, generally on the moderate Left—Western liberals and social democrats—with their interest in emphasizing the centrality of domestic social problems and minimizing the Soviet threat, see something genuine in glasnost. The official publication of each previously banned work, the release of each political prisoner, is taken as proof of good Soviet intentions and fundamental social change.

Pessimists, generally on the Right, view this with deep suspicion. For them the persistence of official atheism is sure proof that the Soviets are a dark force—even darker now, because Gorbachev is shrewd.

For the more politically sophisticated pessimists, the issue is one of political balance and survival. If Gorbachev is for real (not at all a certainty), he will face the entrenched power of the status quo, especially from high-level bureaucrats in the *nomenklatura*, who derive their benefits from the inefficiencies of the present system, enforce their interests through totalitarian culture, and explain their interests as the common good, using Newspeak. Khrushchev was the last to challenge their interests, and he did not last long. Gorbachev will either succumb to the power of the bureaucrats and become a new Brezhnev, with slightly better public relations, or go the way of Khrushchev.

Realistic variants of this theme start with the distance between Gorbachev's rhetoric and reality. Political prisoners remain, even though many have been released. Previously banned books now published are usually those of the dead, sometimes of authors who still play cat and mouse with censors, but rarely, if ever, of authors forced into exile.[3] Criticism of waste and corruption tends to be directed at fairly low-level officials or high-level officials close to Gorbachev's opponents.

Then there is the issue of whether the economic reforms will or can be successful. Most observers agree that Gorbachev has as his end not the political goals of democracy and freedom, but the economic goals of modernization—delivering the goods and competing with Western capitalist economies. Communist aesceticism—the antivodka and anticorruption campaigns with their appeals to socialist morality—clearly will not work. Gorbachev started with such neo-Stalinist tactics, but then escalated the struggle to openness and restructuring, including significant decentralization and use of market mechanisms. It is not certain whether he can implement these more radical reforms to a point where they yield enough efficiency to overcome the economic hardships they will engender in people's lives. From the point of view of the economic output of the system, decentralization and the expansion of market mechanisms likely would be beneficial in the long run. But the political-economic question is whether short-term costs will prevail over long-term benefits.

On the front line of resistance to economic changes are the planners (and high-level party officials associated with them), who are now being told to plan themselves out of a job. On the second line are the millions of people in inefficient industries who will become unemployed in a society with relatively low job mobility and no unemployment insurance. Apart from the political problem here, the immediate economic downturn that such reforms may very well yield could easily lead to a reform that quickly self-destructs before it gets started. Thus, from purely political and economic perspectives, the realists have good reason to wonder whether Gorbachev is sincere and, if sincere, whether he has any chance for success.

On the other hand, they do not really ask the most fundamental questions. The Western realists, along with the hopeful optimists, are both too broad and too narrow in interpreting the significance of the Gorbachev reforms. They are too broad in the sense that they interpret small advances and resistances as systemic characteristics. The release of a political prisoner indicates reform for the optimist, i.e., the dismantling of a system that includes political prisoners. For the pessimist, the fact that other political prisoners remain reveals that the system remains; therefore, there is no reform. Simple political appearance reveals that an advance was made and other advances need to be made. Likewise, increases in economic performance should not be measured against the imagined benefits of complete economic reform, but against recent performance.

Viewed in this fashion, Gorbachev has done pretty well. There have been increases in economic performance. There have been prisoners released. Cultural life is significantly freer, and even some elements of democratic practice have been introduced into political life. If we follow the sensibility of the post-totalitarian mind, considering political appearance as political reality, we can appreciate what Gorbachev has accomplished. Something very important indeed is going on in Moscow.

But such a conclusion is tempered by the post-totalitarian critique of totalitarianism. A Newspeak of reform is being instituted, but it is still Newspeak. Glasnost, democratization, and perestroika, along with the other slogans of the Gorbachev policy, are still officially defined. The truth is still defined by force. When Sergei I. Grigoryants begins publishing a completely autonomous journal entitled *Glasnost*, he and his enterprise are denounced in the official press. *Democracy* in the new Newspeak clearly does not include the open examination of and unconstrained demonstrations for self-determination of the Soviet republics. And restructuring would not include the kinds of social activism that Solidarity inspired.

Adam Michnik, while explaining how seriously he took the changes in the Soviet Union, pointedly underscored that in Poland "we already have our method of perestroika."[4] This clearly would not be readily accepted by Gorbachev and his colleagues, including General Jaruzelski, who is from all reports the closest Eastern European leader to the Soviet leader.

From the point of view of the alternative political culture, Gorbachev's strategy is an extremely subtle one. His great innovation has been to use for official purposes alternative sensibilities like calls for openness, democracy, and restructuring, employing a cultivated informality without permitting the development of a personality cult. Not facing the threat of a self-constituting society such as in Poland, he seems to be trying to simulate its energy through official channels, in the hope of overcoming the stagnant societal inertia of the Brezhnev years.

Gorbachev's problems are almost the mirror of Jaruzelski's. The general came to power in a highly activated society moving in the direction of complete autonomy from the Polish Party-state, and therefore away from the Soviet bloc. The Polish Party-state itself was in eclipse. Its control over Polish life was diminishing. Educational institutions, factories, localities, trade unions, and the industrial working class were avoiding its control. The only thing that held the regime together was the conservative impulse to maintain the privileges of the existing order with force. In such a situation, Jaruzelski declared war against society and essentially dissolved the existing Party-state in hopes of slowing society down. In this repressive goal, and only this, he clearly succeeded, although the social problems which fostered the development of the trade union movement remain.

On the other hand, Gorbachev heads a well-entrenched and developed Party-state which deeply penetrates the social structure. The legal and economic systems are products of its creations and extensions of its policies, as are all other spheres of cultural, political, and social life, from education to daily newspapers to family practices. What distinguishes Soviet practices from Polish, Hungarian, and Czech imitations of those practices is that they are taken as being natural and necessary by Soviet citizens. After seventy years, they know little else. That means seventy years of revolutionary rhetoric, with ever more conservative political practice yielding a stagnated society. Newspeak has been an essential defining part of the scenery for nearly three-quarters of a century.

Apparently people no longer see what is in front of their eyes. For public consumption they pretend to see what the Party tells them to see. They have been taught to suspect individual initiatives and respect Party initiatives. They have learned that individual survival and comfort are directly linked with public adaptation to prevailing Party policy. In the name of social dynamism, people conservatively accommodate themselves to a conservative order. Apart from the military sphere, this purported revolutionary order is marked by widespread stagnation and personal cynicism. Its economic growth is grinding to a halt; its technology is ever more inferior to that of the (political) West; much of its literature, theater, and painting lacks the excitement and openness of the West's, of its own fellow-socialist nations', and of its own past's.

Gorbachev is responding to this crisis of cynicism and stagnation by attempting to incorporate the dynamism of the autonomous public sphere within the official order. His game is a complex one. For example, he takes the term *democracy,* one used previously in official discourse—workers' democracy, socialist democracy, people's democracy, democratic centralism—and he gives it some greater outside referent. Previously *democracy* was used for antidemocratic purposes—e.g., the *democratic* in *democratic centralism* justifies the authoritarianism of Party leadership; the *democracy* in *People's democracy* distinguishes it from polities that attempt to institutionalize real democratic practice, i.e., the "bourgeois democracies." From any political point of view, using any political criterion, these terms are devoid of meaning outside of the official ideology. The democracy of people's, workers', and socialist democracies and democratic socialism lacks the competing parties (of modern [liberal] democratic theory), the autonomous publics (of republican whiggery), and the breakdown of social hierarchy (of the radical democratic populist tradition). Now Gorbachev is investing the term with external referents and real meaning. Democratization, in Gorbachev's lexicon, means challenging the privileges of the Party hierarchy, some choice in local elections, more openness to local initiatives, and decentralization. But this meaning is still officially defined. There is democratic substance in Gorbachev's reforms, but they still have a totalitarian core.

The core need not be apparent. It can be a deep, hidden structure, because there is no broad public pressure for democratization except at the peripheries of political life in the Soviet Union and in Eastern Europe. To the citizens of the Baltic republics, to Armenians, Jews, and other ethnic and religious groups with mobilized identities other than that of the "new Soviet man," the limits of the reforms have become quickly evident. If they could, they would use democracy and openness for other than official purposes. From the official conservative point of view, and perhaps from the independent Russian nationalist point of view, such usage would indicate disorder. Gorbachev certainly knows this. His gamble is that the benefits of societal mobilization, increased economic output, greater cultural and technological activity, and more clearly defined and supported internal and external political policies will make such potential costs tolerable.

He possibly further hopes that the conservative society will assert social control where political control was previously used. Official limits on public protests may be replaced by social limits; a conservative citizenry without democratic traditions now free to express their disapproval of unrest may silence it as disorder, or at least popularly support the state in such silencing.[5] Thus, by using democratic culture and a political language with greater external reference, i.e., the alternative to Newspeak, official (repressive) politics may derive greater popular support.

From an official point of view, the danger in this is that such popular support will become, over a long period of time, a component of political life not easily controllable, and a social basis of independent political culture. For the time being, though, this is not the danger in the Soviet Union. What we observe there is an attempt to use national traditions, habits, and experiences to extend official politics. Gorbachev can bank on a deep tradition of Russian intolerance and twentieth-century inertia to allow for some greater official tolerance and dynamism.

Though the effects of this on the whole Soviet empire are

not certain, the overall impact on official politics will likely be to reinforce already existing tendencies of national differentiation. The Romanian regime will continue to resemble the fascist order of the interwar period.[6] Neo-Kadarism will follow the Hapsburgian model, so-called Goulash Communism. The East German state will follow its Prussian model. Neither indigenous nor Soviet official politics are likely to change these courses on their own. The content of the totalitarian culture will vary, but the enforced relationship between truth and force will not anywhere be dismantled through official action.

Here lies the great significance of the Polish experience and its potential relationship with Gorbachev's reform. The opportunity for systematically deconstructing the official truth is now a possibility. The means for developing an independent public life, for moving from a post-totalitarian culture to a post-totalitarian politics, have been demonstrated by the Poles. The Soviet reform tries to co-opt the new culture to strengthen the official order. In doing so, Gorbachev cynically acts on the assurance that an independent political culture has been extinguished by the building of socialism. The leaders of the democratic opposition in their political actions, and the creators of post-totalitarian culture in their works, suggest different societal, if not official, outcomes.

The Neototalitarian State and its Discontents

The changes occurring in the Soviet Union are probably as significant as the changes which followed Stalin's death. The move then was from a totalitarianism with terror to one which substituted cynicism (a legitimation through disbelief) and inertia. This led to an opening of cultural activity (the thaw), and a marked improvement in the daily life of average citizens (with the abatement of terror, a sharp decrease in fear). Yet, in totalitarianism both with and without terror, as we have seen, a special relationship between force and reason persisted, and Newspeak developed. An official truth, the actual lie, prevailed. A culture of systemic ignorance and cynicism was peacefully institutionalized.

Gorbachev adds a new twist, while attempting to sustain
the totalitarian theme. Alternatives to Newspeak are now
being incorporated into the official order. An attempt is being
made to use the power of the powerless for official purposes.
Gorbachev shows that the demonic tale of modern tyranny
may be an elastic, never-ending story, as is modern capitalism.
Marxists since Marx have been anxiously awaiting capitalism's final crisis. Similarly, observers of the Soviet scene
have shown how the conflict between the imperatives of economic and technological development and ideology *must* lead
to either a political-economic crisis or the "end of ideology."[7]
What Gorbachev shows is how the ideology can be made to
appear more elastic, probably without changing its fundamental character, in order to foster economic growth.

Capitalism now includes the welfare state, state economic
planning, industrial policy, and trade unions. It has accommodated its most severe critics while maintaining its fundamental economic character. Gorbachev is demonstrating a
not quite parallel process, totalitarian elasticity. He is attempting to improve economic output using the themes of the
post-totalitarian critics (democracy and liberty) without their
substance.

Democracy, in any significant sense of the term, cannot be
officially defined. It cannot simply be a gift of the rulers to the
ruled. Its reach must be actively defined by a free citizenry.
This the totalitarian ruler, be he a Polish general or a Russian
bureaucrat, does not tolerate. Gorbachev and Jaruzelski are
manipulating the ideals of their post-totalitarian opponents in
pursuit of a totalitarian order characterized by economic
growth and efficiency and continued ideological rule. If they
achieve their goals, the totalitarian order will be less pernicious. There will be fewer political prisoners, a more diverse
cultural life, and perhaps a less militaristic geopolitics. Perhaps it would be very much like the velvet prison Miklos
Haraszti describes with his tongue deeply embedded in his
cheek—with Staniszkis' "socialist repressive tolerance," "socialist artificial negativity," and "socialist false conscious-

ness."[8] But it would not be a democracy, nor would it have significant liberties.

For the ideals of democracy and liberty to become a real part of Soviet and Soviet-bloc life, the Havels and Michniks, Harasztis and Solzhenitsyns, Sakharovs and Kunderas would have to take part openly in legal politics and culture. Jaruzelski's normalization and Gorbachev's openness will not even approach that scenario without independent public action forcing the issue. Thus, Michnik's practical conclusion in "The New Evolutionism" stands: the source of fundamental change in the Soviet bloc is "an unceasing struggle for reform and evolution that seeks an expansion of civil liberties and human rights."[9]

The importance of Gorbachev from the point of view of democracy is that he has set the stage for an intensification of this struggle. Now the people in the Soviet Union and the Soviet bloc may fight over the meaning of democracy and attempt to give it real content—from the refuseniks to the Armenian nationalists, from the Polish workers to the Czech jazz enthusiasts. Soviet totalitarianism is not withering away; Gorbachev is seeking to give it a new life. In the process, though, he invites the post-totalitarian onto the political stage.

Epilogue: Them and Us

So WHAT DOES all this mean for us, in the West?[1] The immediate meanings are political. If we understand the post-totalitarian mind as a, if not the, dynamic force in official and unofficial political life in the Soviet bloc, foreign-policy makers must take this into account. It would help us understand how to listen when Mikhail Gorbachev talks, and how to judge his opponents. The way we would balance our human rights concerns with concerns about military balance clearly would be affected. We would have to take most seriously the judgments of independent post-totalitarian political actors and view much more skeptically official pronouncements, even in the era of glasnost, and we would have to learn to consider the range of opinion among oppositionists as a sign not of confusion but of normal political deliberation. By virtue of their situation in the existing order, they have unique insights into the meaning, or lack of meaning, of official pronouncements. We must utilize their insights when they are available to us. Policy makers must read not only Gorbachev's *Pravda* but Grigoryant's *Glasnost*.

Such practical imperatives derive from the starting point of our inquiry into totalitarianism. We have seen that the native oppositions to totalitarianism actually provide a most cogent understanding of the totalitarian phenomenon. They have understood the force of officialdom in opposition to the experiences of daily life. They have provided the possibility of understanding totalitarianism as a cultural form in opposition to a free public culture.

We find ourselves in a unique theoretical situation. By taking the post-totalitarian mind seriously, we gain insights into the neototalitarian state. We are looking at an erratic and

dangerous political structure through the eyes of its most experienced, insightful, and creative opponents. This presents a
stark contrast with usual Western views. As we have already
observed, Western views of totalitarianism and Gorbachev's
neototalitarian state are projections of Western politics as
much as analyses of the very significant political other. There
is a theoretical and political projection of self which blinds us
to the other. At issue is not so much information, but insight.
It is likely that Western Sovietologists know more facts about
the workings of the Kremlin and the Soviet system in general
than the native post-totalitarians. But they, rather than we,
know the system from the inside and profoundly understand
and experience its logic. They provide a unique means to
understand its limits and elasticity, and they must live with its
consequences.

People throughout the Soviet block and beyond are realistically enthusiastic about the changes that Gorbachev has initiated. The realism is based on an understanding of the profound
limits of the changes which we have observed. If we distinguish
between totalitarian and nontotalitarian democratic-liberal
orders on the grounds of public freedom and democracy, as
the analysis above strongly indicates we ought to, then we
should not simply be satisfied that Gorbachev is a liberal
Communist. We must recognize that fundamental enlightenment ideals are being further obfuscated by his neototalitarian
state. This, of course, does not mean we should begin ranting
and raving about the evil empire. But it does mean that when
we deal with practical problems such as disarmament, increased trade, and officially sponsored cultural exchange, we
should not lose sight of the differences between democracy as
an ongoing political project open to informed contestation by
a broad array of citizens, and democracy as an official policy
in a totalitarian cultural context. We thus ignore at the peril of
our own democratic principles the democratic aspirations of
the post-totalitarians.

When there are people within the totalitarian orders who
fundamentally question it, we must not simply "realistically"

favor and follow the views of "liberals" within the system
who accept it and benefit from its continuation. Michnik, not
Jaruzelski, most accurately reveals the Polish democratic position on perestroika. It is Sakharov's, not Gorbachev's, views
on the validity of Soviet reforms which we should take most
seriously from the viewpoint of liberty.

When dealing with the Polish and Soviet (neototalitarian)
states, we must and should seek to understand Jaruzelski's and
Gorbachev's positions, reaching common agreements and ac-
commodations. But we must not confuse the geopolitically
necessary with the political good. When Western officials
quickly expressed an understanding, if not a support, of Jaruzelski's war on the Polish nation, Western European politics
reached quite low. While they did not support the repression
directly, as the United States often has in Latin America, they
clearly revealed an acceptance of the idea that the other Europe must eternally be the land of the un-free. This when some
of the most cogent political advocates of democracy and liberty, and most profound cultural critics and imaginative writers, are from that other Europe. Here we have an indication of
not only a faulty geopolitics but an unsteadiness in modern
democratic commitment.

Thus, as important as the political insights derived from the
post-totalitarians are, probably the most profound significance of the post-totalitarian mind for us is cultural. They, the
post-totalitarians, speak to us in the West not only about their
lives, but about ours, about how we understand the modern
human condition.

At crucial points in our inquiry, we observed similarities between totalitarian and modern nontotalitarian life. We have
noted how localized Newspeak is used by government officials
such as Alexander Haig, how positivistic sciences (such as be-
haviorism and dominant modes of policy analysis) obliterate
the problematic connection between past and future, as do the
totalitarians, how ideological thinking penetrates our political
ideas and actions (e.g., those of Reagan, Kirkpatrick, and
Podhoretz), and how kitsch currently forms varieties of West-

ern leftist and American political culture. In order to understand the totalitarian object, the differences between them and us rather than the similarities have been emphasized. The project of the inquiry was to clarify the nature of modern tyranny in order to analyze its political and literary alternatives. Yet in that the alternatives are formulated not only against tyranny, but specifically against the complex form of modern tyranny, they speak to us, as moderns, quite directly. They highlight the darkest underside or our life. Here, then, we explore the similarities, not to equate totalitarianism with modernity, but to examine the underside of the modern project in the search for alternatives.

Postmodernism and Post-Totalitarianism?

Are the alternatives modern or postmodern? Whether postmodern forms, cultures, epistemologies, politics, and societies exist and/or ought to be promoted is an issue of many contemporary debates. The debates ambivalently take on a number of fundamental issues. Habermas calls for a continuation of the modern project of enlightenment and locates a neoconservative, postmodern thrust in critiques of the project.[2] Lyotard starts with a critique of modernity and its superrationalism, but seems to label any defense of reason in politics as totalitarian, or potentially totalitarian.[3] Daniel Bell celebrates the passage of industrial (i.e., modern) society with its logic of production and physical labor to postindustrial society with its logic of information and mental labor, but criticizes the modern culture as the adversary culture, for undermining the normative basis of modernity (i.e., the work ethic).[4] People such as Andreas Huyssen and Hal Foster "map the post-modern,"[5] distinguishing positive pluralism from negative relativism., and progressive from reactionary use of new cultural forms. Zygmunt Bauman sociologically explains away these debates, accounting for them as products of displaced intellectuals who no longer play key ideological and utopian roles in political and cultural life.[6] On the other hand, Ferenc Feher seriously considers Bauman's position, but finds it wanting because it is sociologically reductive and does not confront the common experience of being after—being not only after premodern religious certainty, but after the scientific, political, and aesthetic certainties of enlightenment and modernism.[7]

From the point of view of our inquiry, these debates are insufficient, because the participants, for the most part, have not self-consciously and directly confronted twentieth-century horrors and the connection between these horrors and modern life. For us a chief, if not the chief, "being after" is being after the fact of modern barbarism.

The postmodernists sense an end of an era, a fin de siècle, but do not link their sensibility to the depth of twentieth-century tragedy. Instead, they construct elaborate theories which cancel rather than reveal. On all sides of the debate, they present symptoms of the problem rather than a proper analysis leading to a solution. Arendt explains:

> When we think of dark times and of people living and moving in them, we have to take [the] camouflage, emanating from and spread by the "establishment" . . . also into account. If it is the function of the public realm to throw light on the affairs of men by providing a space of appearances in which they can show in deed and word, for better and worse, who they are and what they can do, then darkness has come when this light is extinguished by "credibility gaps" and "invisible governments," by speech which does not disclose what is but sweeps it under the carpet, by exhortations, moral and otherwise, that under the pretext of upholding old truths, degrade all truth to meaningless triviality.[8]

The discussion about postmodernism indeed seems to sweep the facts of totalitarianism under the carpet, primarily through extreme theoretical abstraction. Evolutionary schemes, sophisticated historical materialism, and apparently purposely obscure notions of epistemological shifts are used abstractly as the keys to understanding the second half of the twentieth century without confronting the uniquely definitive cultural form of the century—totalitarianism. For Bell and Touraine, postindustrial changes in the basis of the production of wealth and inequalities, emanating from sources ranging from industrial production to information processing, define the significant parameters of social change.[9] For Habermas, as an antipostmodernist, the development of late capitalism (i.e., the welfare state) and postcapitalism (i.e., Soviet-type societies) defines the fundamental modern structures of domination, to be resolved by modern enlightenment means.[10] For Derrida and Lyotard, the quintessential postmodernists, it all comes down to linguistic games.[11] Concentration camps, mass terror, the depopulation of cities, and the pervasiveness of ideological thinking sometimes may find passing comment, but in that they are not manifestations of some key idea—from technological innovations through historical materialism and linguistic breaks—they are not analyzed directly. And when they are addressed, they often serve ideological purposes.

Thus, for example, for Bell, anything other than modern liberalism is apparently dangerously totalitarian, and for Lyotard and like-minded French poststructuralists and new philosophers, principled attempts to introduce rationality into politics are likewise totalitarian. Dangers loom, but are not investigated. From the point of view of the post-totalitarians, we are in a position to investigate.

The Danger of the Conflation of Spheres

A central social consequence of totalitarian culture is societal dedifferentiation. As we have seen, not only are past, present, and future explained by a key idea, separate spheres of life— art, religion, economics, politics, science, etc.—all are controlled and directed by key ideological principles. Though in the case of nazism the key idea was racial theory, a deformed anthropology, and in the case of Soviet Marxism the key was class theory, a deformed theory of history, in both the consequence for the social structure was the conflation of all societal life with ideology. The same process can be observed today in the world of Islamic fundamentalism.[12] Using a radical, and in fundamental ways antitraditional, interpretation of Islam, a modernizing society is being restructured.

The restructuring and dedifferentiation of the totalitarians are foreign to us. We take the benefits of the relative autonomy of the separate societal spheres and the political liberal guarantees of autonomy for granted. Autonomous culture and politics appear so natural that political and cultural go unappreciated by all sorts of thinkers and activitists, so much so that some postmodernists cannot even distinguish liberal from totalitarian orders.

This problem is not only on the Left. People like Milton Friedman advocate the free market as the answer for all economic and noneconomic problems.[13] For such laissez-faire liberals, nowadays called conservatives, economic growth and social justice, mass entertainment and art, scholarly distinction and democracy are served by market logic. When Edward Banfield criticizes extramarket support of the arts, for example, he does not distinguish the logic of cultural expression and freedom from marketability. He, in effect, approves of the economic colonization of the cultural realm (as Habermas would put it). He confuses cultural excellence with what sells.[14]

Artistic autonomy in this way can be seriously compromised. If artists were always forced to produce the works which satisfy the cultural demands of the broadest possible audience, the arts as we know them would come to an end. Remembrance and appreciation of the full range of the works of the past would not be promoted in museums; rather there would be simply a series of blockbuster exhibitions. Foundations would not support the artistically challenging, but the most easily satisfying. No special, i.e., extramarket, effort would be made to maintain alternative galleries, theaters, and publishers. The culturally free and innovative would become identical with the marketable.

That this is not the case attests to the relative autonomy of cultural activities and institutions from the market. They are not completely free of the market, nor from often wrongheaded government policies, but they develop without complete dependence upon them. When conservatives promote the extension of the market to cultural activities, they act without a full cognizance of the dangers. This is most evident in the foolish ideas concerning privatization of public schools. Their advocates assume that the educational needs of the handicapped and the impoverished, of the ignorant and the illiterate, of the remotely rural and of the devastated centrally urban would be satisfied by fostering competition among schools for the parental dollars of the affluent and the parental vouchers of the poor. Since the freest competition allows for the greatest possible productivity, they argue (though this is far from proven) that such competition will also promote the best in education. What they do not take into account is that parents often do not have sufficient education themselves to make sound judgments about the quality of education, and that indicators of educational quality are notoriously difficult to interpret. What prevails now in the educational market is often not the educationally sound, especially for the disadvantaged.

While contemporary conservatives would reduce many judgments to the market, and this has been a long-term position (for example, Reagan's favorite past president, Calvin Coolidge, declared that the business of America is business), there are those, most often on the Left, who conflate their politics with culture. Indeed, a central characteristic of "advanced" politics and culture is the identification of the arts and sciences with political positions and social characteristics. Some, from the constructivists to the surrealists, use this identification to claim an essential political role for the arts— fostering the revolution, leading it, constituting it, or even realizing it. Others use the identification as grounds for criticizing or even silencing the arts and sciences—from Zhadanov's and Lysenko's cultural polities to Lionel Trilling's and Daniel Bell's condemnations of modernism as adversary cultures and unproductive (or even antiproductive) criticisms.[15] The positions of the avant garde and the anti–avant garde obviously have telling differences, but they share a general strategy of interpretation—the significance of the arts and sciences is imputed to be not artistic or scientific, but political.

Thus, the politics of avant garde and anti–avant garde culture and the cultural policy of vanguard politics make up a semiotic whole. Though they often oppose each other, they share a mode of politically interpreting culture. The present-day Left and Right in the nontotalitarian modern world do not sufficiently appreciate the importance of guarding against social, political, and cultural dedifferentiation. They have not learned what the post-totalitarians have, the remarkable fragility in the modern world of independent cultural institutions.

Unfortunately, various sociologies of culture reinforce this ignorance. They take as scientific the explanation of cultural products and practices through sociological facts. Knowledge is explained (away) by its purported class or institutional background (in Marx's *German Ideology,* Mannheim's "Conservative Thought," and Bourdieu's *Distinctions*).[16] Religion, literature, and the arts are demonstrated to reflect social structure (in Durkheim's *Elementary Forms of Religious Life,* Lukacs's *Historical Novel,* and Lowenthal's *Literature and the Images of Man*).[17] Though there are important differences among these and other sociological approaches, they share a general strategy of explanation. The works of the arts and sciences and religious practice are explained not by the arts and sciences and religion, but by something else, and usually the something else has political significance. When the great sociologist of knowledge Karl Mannheim demonstrates the class character of nineteenth-century German conservative thought, he is in effect dismissing the political significance of the thought without confronting its reasoning. Conservative thought is based in the old aristocracy; therefore it is irrelevant.[18]

The problem with such interpretations is their very strength and ambition. Cultures of great variety are interpreted around the same theme—their social basis. This becomes the deep structure of history: culture reduced to its social life and to politics. From the point of view of post-totalitarianism, problems, i.e., the problems arising after totalitarianism, are evident. Master concepts of history and culture are suspect. Cultural distinctions and differences between human endeavors are obscured.

Politics, science, and art as vocations must be understood as related but distinct vocations. Along with Max Weber, we not only observe the historical phenomenon of the separation of spheres of life in modernity, i.e., social differentiation (the desacralization of politics, the depoliticization of economics, and the emerging autonomy of the arts and sciences), we as well judge that such separation serves normative purposes. Only then can the promise of the Enlightenment be fulfilled.

Weber and Habermas (as his student in this regard) take this position from the point of view of Western historical experience in a fairly distanced, cool, scholarly fashion—not at all a fault.[19] They observe how the fruits of the Enlightenment—the development of Western science and scholarship, economic and political liberalism, and the promise of political wisdom in mass societies—require the relative autonomy of spheres of life. Weber called for the specialized vocations and logics of science and politics as a way to realize Western ideals in the aftermath of World War I and amidst the chaos of a social revolution. Habermas warns that the logics of political and economic domination may colonize and overwhelm spheres of public deliberation, inquiry, and creativity. For both, cultural autonomy (spheres of life, as Weber put it, or the life world, for Habermas) is threatened by dedifferentiation—the inappropriate extension of political zeal or economic calculation into nonpolitical economic life.

After the experience of totalitarianism, the dimensions of the threat are evident. The urgency and the severity of the problem are clear when we reflect upon totalitarian experience. In the case of Lysenko, we saw how the use of tendentious political criteria overwhelmed genetics as an independent discipline, murdering both the science and the scientists. In the case of the young Polish social scientist, we saw how total-

itarian relationships persist in daily cultural life without terror. The very existence of independent culture and cultural
accomplishment is at stake, not only for "them," but also
for "us," if we do not appreciate the importance of cultural
autonomy.

The Danger of Complete Theories

Totalitarian culture, with its key idea, not only conflates
spheres, it as well brings all of them tightly together in a neat
package. It presents a central theory, deduced from the key
idea, which explains everything. Such packaging is inimical to
the post-totalitarian mind. The very form of Kundera's novels,
for example, is intentionally fragmentary. Chapters come together not as unities, but in tension. Not only is there no uni-
form story line, but the voice changes, and the literary form
alternates between confession, fiction, and philosophical aphorism. As Kundera tells us, each of his characters represents his
own unrealized conflicting potentials. Instead of an underlying theme revealing a great truth, there are, in Kundera's
novels, conflicting fragments which lead to questions.

As we have seen, the political essays of Michnik and Havel
exhibit a similar quality. The complete truth in systematic detail is not presented. Rather, reasonable insights and limited
truths about specific issues are investigated. Michnik's approach to history and Havel's drama do the same. These
works stand in contrast to complete explanation and accounts
(the systematic treatises and global theories so fashionable
in the West), not because of the modesty of the thinkers, nor
because of the lack of ambition, but out of a kind of post-
totalitarian principle. Yet there is something paradoxical here,
a paradox which reveals my theoretical position in this essay
and clarifies its subject matter—the post-totalitarian mind.

I have argued for the continued saliency of totalitarianism
as a concept for understanding the politics and culture of our
century. I have, primarily by following Arendt, used it to specify the particular modern form of tyranny and barbarism. Yet,
the concept has been rejected by many sober observers be-

cause it is too totalistic, attempting to explain too much with
too little, and I, following post-totalitarian insight, am quite
critical of totalistic concepts. But despite this insight, I am also
following Michnik, Konrad, Havel, Baranczak, and their
many colleagues in the other Europe by employing the term to
explain their world.

The paradox can be resolved when we recall that the notion
of totalitarianism does not refer here to a total system, but to
a total culture which promotes and justifies horrendous actions, though the culture and the action do not constitute a
complete social, political, economic, or cultural system. Totalitarianism is not characteristic of a system, but a characteristic
set of actions which add up to modern barbarism and tyranny. The structure of the enforced culture is totalistic even if
it is never realized. The cultural structure purports complete
certainty and commitment to a utopian teleology even when
that is not the practical intention of totalitarian leaders such
as Jaruzelski and Gorbachev.

Opposed to totalitarianism are various forms of publicity,
as explained in the early chapters of this inquiry. Arendt's *Origins* tells the story of the slow retreat of publicity, the retreat of
the political capacity for action in Western civilization. Here I
have told the story of the resurfacing of the public realm. Neither her inquiry nor mine is systemic. Arendt did not analyze
the cause of totalitarianism's emergence and reproduction.
Rather, she highlighted moments in European history and factors of contemporary experience which eroded the capacity
for political freedom and action. These moments and factors—anti-Semitism, imperialism, the emergence of mass society, atomization, the privatization of politics, the emergence
of ideological movements—did not *cause* totalitarianism.
They undermined the capacities to act politically and think
critically. But since these capacities are inherently human,
Arendt's is not a straightforward account of the inevitable decline of the West. She knew alternatives and resistances were
always possible. We have observed the development of political and cultural resistance and of tyrannical resilience.

Such an approach to theory and history contrasts markedly with a great deal of contemporary social science. Systemic thinkers such as Talcott Parsons and Jurgen Habermas[20] explain history and contemporary social structure as complete (evolving) systems, as totalities. For Parsons, the modern societal community and its core values are articulated through a complex differentiated and reintegrated set of social systems and subsystems. Each component part of a social order is explained by its relationship with the other parts and with the core values. Thus, all structures of the system function to support the whole. Habermas presents an alternative scheme. For him, the core is the economic system. The account is primarily of crises and changes, and secondarily of social order. He shows how crises in "advanced capitalism" are articulated through the economic, administrative, political, and psychocultural systems, in that order. The development of fundamental changes, i.e., crises, in each system yields changes in the other systems, leading to further crises. The anticipation is that revolutionary change will ensue when all the systemic crises cannot be resolved within the existing mode of domination. Again, each part of the system supports (and undermines) other parts. The theory seeks a complete explanation.

Parsons's and Habermas's theories are in many ways the opposing alternative approaches to social science today. At its center, Parsons's theory draws upon Weber and Durkheim; Habermas's draws on Weber and Marx. Parsons is primarily concerned with social order; Habermas with social transformation. Parsons is fundamentally an idealist; Habermas a materialist. But despite the fact that their theories are opposing analytical systems, they share a common flaw from the point of view of our inquiry. The theories present unified systemic explanations (models) of social, political, and cultural life. Human actions are primarily interpreted as the working out of systemic processes, not as independent, pluralistic actions. Both theorists do, of course, build independent human action into their systems. But by situating such action in an overall system, they tend to overlook its complexities and ambiguities.

There are, of course, important differences between Parsons and Habermas. In Parsons social action becomes a component part of the system and therefore is not politically problematic. In Habermas's recent work, the problem of the colonization of the life world (the world of independent human action) by system imperatives is a central concern. Yet the highly abstract rendering of this concern, without an accounting of the uniqueness of actions on their own terms, focuses attention on systems and not on the human capacity for free action. Distinctive actions, then, in both theoretical systems are overlooked.

Such theories can strangely affect the way we conceive of political ethics. Taken to extremes, systems theory can provide a way to demonstrate that appearances are not realities, that moral choice and political judgment are not necessary, and that individual responsibility is an illusion. Some classic examples from the sociological literature demonstrate these points. The corruption of machine politics becomes, in the hands of Robert Merton, a student of Parsons, functional for the social system as a latent form of social welfare;[21] suicide and law, for Durkheim, a "teacher" of Parsons, are not matters of existential choice and societal judgment, but matters of group cohesion;[22] and as David Matza has shown, as a critic of systematic explanations of deviance, functional explanations of juvenile delinquency explain away responsibility for freely chosen acts, and ironically, the currency of these explanations encourages delinquency, since without a sense of personal responsibility there is little self-restraint.[23]

Within total theories, conceived system needs have explanatory priority. The appearance of corruption is only a particularity. Since the systemic needs of social welfare are served, appearance is not the deep reality. Even when people give highly individual reasons for acts of desperation, suicide is shown to be most highly correlated with the strength of moral codes; therefore the reality behind the individual act is a systemic social reality. Matza shows how individual acts of delinquency are encouraged by such explanation. Since appearance is not reality, responsibility is not involved.

Habermas's tradition of inquiry—the tradition of Marx, historical materialism, and critical theory—is especially vulnerable when it comes to the deflection of responsibility, the impaired capacity of political and moral judgment, and the loss of appearances to underlying realities. Habermas himself does try to free his inquiry from such vulnerability. Indeed his concern with the public sphere, communicative action, and discursive truth present important advances in, if not breaks with, Marxism and critical theory by attempting to include in the Marxist tradition a grounds for democratic deliberation and moral judgment. In *The Theory of Communicative Action,* he deliberately attempts to avoid the Hegelian totalisms of his Marxist and critical-theory predecessors (specifically Adorno). He develops an action-and-systems theory, hoping to retain at a higher level of abstraction a systematic analysis of the state and the economy and their impact upon everyday life. Yet, in my judgment, the end result is that the distinctive characteristics, richness, ambiguities, and ironies of cultural, political, economic, and social life are lost. The theoretical and practical problems raised by Marxism and critical theory are only apparently avoided by this most powerful critical thinker. He substitutes one systems theory for the totalism of Marxism. But he does not address the experience of human life, where the real conflicts among politics, economics, and culture are situated. He ignores such situations through abstraction. Now we ought to address a much more demonic ignorance—the ignorance of Stalinism. A difficult and sensitive problem remains to be considered: is there a necessary relationship between Marxism and totalitarianism?

From Marxism to Stalinism?

It should be clear at this point that I do believe there is an important connection between Marxism and Stalinism. To assert otherwise is to deny simple facts of European history. Some of the fundamental characteristics of totalitarianism are also fundamental to Marxist theory and politics. Not only Stalin but also Marx had at his disposal the key to human history—

class conflict. Not only Stalin but also Marx knew how to deduce from the key to total explanations of the human world.
For both Marx and Stalin differences of opinion and judgment, further, were interpreted by the key. For Marx, other
philosophers become ideologists; socialists with different programs become utopians or worse. For Stalin, it is all worse—
purges, mass starvations, and the gulag. Both Marx and Stalin
had the political truth, and when the truth was imposed by
Stalin, and Lenin before him, the results were disastrous.

But to say there is a connection between Marx and Stalin is
not to assert that the connection is necessary. Lenin is the central link. Though his elitism and the special role he assigned to
intellectuals to foster a revolutionary vanguard party (overcoming the trade-union consciousness of workers) can be
found in the political writings of Marx and Engels, he added
the crucial notion that there is a stark, black-and-white choice
between socialist and capitalist ideology, between liberation
and continued exploitation. He wrote:

> Since there can be no question of an independent ide-
> ology formulated by the working masses themselves
> in the process of their movement, the only choice is—
> either bourgeois or socialist ideology, and in a society
> torn by class antagonisms, there can never be a non-
> class or an above-class ideology. The spontaneous de-
> velopment of the working class movement leads to its
> subordination to bourgeois ideology. Trade unionism
> means the ideological enslavement of workers by the
> bourgeoisie.[24]

Armed with Marxism as the means to the historical truth,
Lenin's vanguard not only knew the working class's interest
better than the working class left to itself; the working class's
understanding of its own interest was defined as bourgeois
ideology. When such an approach to politics comes to power,
differences of opinion become treacheries, alternative political
principles become opposing ideologies, and unity becomes a
political requirement. Terror follows naturally.

Yet, to state the obvious, not all Marxists are Leninists. Fur-

ther, many Marxist political activists and scholars do not approach Marx's writings as a new gospel to be confirmed in
research and enforced in politics, as it has been in the Soviet
Union. Clearly, many Marxists are not in any way Stalinists.
Their research tells a great deal about the development of the
modern state and economy, about social class relations, philosophy, the arts, and language. Marxist inquiry is one of the
central intellectual traditions in the modern social sciences.
But as with the Parsonian tradition, from the viewpoint of
post-totalitarianism, there are central problems in the tradition, particularly in its approach to the independence of politics and culture and in its general method of theorizing.

The fundamental problem is the idea of totality, as already
indicated. Marxism in its many varieties is a complete theory
of social order and transformation. Marxists argue about the
relative priority of class relations, mode of production, base
and superstructure, determinism, voluntarism, dialectical materialism, and historical materialism, among other concepts.
But regardless of these differences, Marxist theory seeks a
complete explanation. This makes the theory relatively insen-
sitive to human plurality, societal differentiation, and the autonomy of culture and politics. In orthodox approaches, all
human activities are explained according to fundamental laws
of the mode of production or are related to the dynamics of
class struggle and capital formation. Such laws and dynamics
are viewed as the realities behind appearances, as being the
underlying reality.

Neo-Marxists of various sorts share with anti-Marxists
an understanding that economics or economically derived
variables—capitalist productive forces and capitalist social
relations of production—explain too much too directly in orthodox Marxism. Even Lenin, in his tactical use of nationalism and the peasantry, broke with orthodoxy.[25] Yet from the
point of view of post-totalitarianism, such breaks and such
criticism do not get to the heart of the matter. The problem
goes beyond Stalinism, Leninism, and unidimensional social-
scientific explanation. It has to do with the normative and sci-

entific core of Marxism, a core it shares with a great deal of non-Marxist and anti-Marxist inquiry. The central issue is that of social-scientific reductionism in the service of a theoretical hubris.

The problem of reductionism involves more than economic determinism or over-reliance on economic factors for social-scientific explanation. The central issue, rather, is the confusion of correlation with explanation, and the confusion of correlative explanation with complete explanation. Solidarity emerged when the Polish economy collapsed. Is Solidarity explained by the collapse? Abstract expressionism dominated the art market with the ascendancy of the United States as a superpower after World War II. Is the art completely explained by the geopolitical facts? The mass democracy and capitalism emerged in the same societies. Is the democracy explained by the capitalism? Not only would Marxist analysis have us affirmatively answer each of these questions, so would a great deal of non-Marxist social science. Master concepts and structures are identified, be they class or normative structures, and these explain other phenomena.

This form of explanation undermines an appreciation of human plurality, a first principle of the post-totalitarian mind. As we have observed, Daniel Singer does not explain Solidarity by its members' aspirations, by the way they become involved in it, or by how the movement crystallized around aspiration and involvement, but by external conditions which may have fostered the social movement. Similarly, Serge Guilbert explains the abstract expressionists not through an analysis of their works, nor through a study of the relationships among themselves and their teachers, peers, and predecessors, but by observing the correlation between their rise to prominence and the rise of American world hegemony, the emergence of McCarthyism, and the disenchantment of certain American leftist critics.[26] And generally Marxist and neo-Marxist critiques of bourgeois democracy, from Lenin's to Marcuse's, are based not on a consideration of political principles and norms as revealed in the history of political thought and action, but on the simple correlation of the emergence of modern democratic regimes with the rise of the bourgeoisie.

From the point of view of post-totalitarianism, such intellectual practice is highly suspect. Michnik knows that Dmowski was a cryptofascist, but seeks to illuminate his political astuteness. Kundera tells us stories of erotic and political adventure, but unlike Marx and Freud, he tells the stories as parallel but independent developments. Havel's crucial notion of living in truth is based upon existential independence. The fable of the greengrocer reveals not that the petit bourgeoisie can oppose proletarian rule, but that individuals can choose different paths, based upon their understanding of personal and political principles. Thus, we see Michnik's great concern for human dignity, not because of circumstances, but often despite them.

We should note how these positions of the post-totalitarians differ greatly from various anti- and neo-Marxists. Michnik finds virtue in certain Communist politicians and thinkers as he does in certain right-wing political-cultural traditions and in the Catholic tradition. Hannah Arendt, a fundamental critic of Marxism, wrote a touching tribute to one of the most orthodox of Marxists, Rosa Luxemburg.[27] Kundera morally equates anti-Communism and anti-Marxism with Communism and Marxism as political kitsch. Yet, despite this lack of theoretical antagonism, the post-totalitarians do not use or build upon Marxist insights or complete Marxist theories as do neo-Marxists. Bringing the state back in, as is the fashion among comparative sociologists,[28] is not the project. A more complete theory of determinations is not their end; rather, they seek more enlightened autonomous thought and action.

Social and political truths derived from theoretical systems present real dangers. If our theories explain the link between past and future, even without Stalinist brutality there is no room for free action. The consensus of social scientists is that the link cannot be maintained with absolute certainty; thus studies most often utilize statistics and probabilities. But the use of these procedures keeps alive the notion of a scientific truth (now probabilistically defined) in social and political

life. Thus there can be a technocratically derived proper policy, not a result of public deliberation amongst citizens, but
defined by science. It is the *official* certainty of the linkage between truth and politics which distinguishes totalitarianism
from policy science. But the crucial point is that social inquiry
which seeks or asserts scientific truths about the human world,
and seeks to base our actions on these truths leaves little room
for autonomous action, cultural or political. It is this attribute
of Marxism, which it shares with a great many non-Marxist
studies, which is also a fundamental aspect of Stalinism. But
Stalinism, requiring brutal enforcement by the Party-state,
is not a necessary aspect of Marxist, neo-Marxist, or anti-
Marxist theories. Such enforcement, a hallmark of Stalinism,
also brutally proceeded on anti-Marxist, anti-Communist
grounds in Germany—thus Soviet Russia's and Nazi Germany's identity as totalitarian orders.

Legitimation through Cynicism

While post-totalitarian works and experiences starkly reveal
the aforementioned totalitarian potentials and weaknesses
in our own theories, the daily experiences of totalitarianism
without terror, and the post-totalitarian critiques of these,
speak directly to problems in our everyday political culture.

We analyzed how the conflation of truth with force makes
possible an odd sort of legitimation through disbelief. Such
legitimation sociologically extends the use and viability of
Newspeak, enabling totalitarianism to exist without terror.
When conflated with force, believed truth disappears from
public life. People cynically use the officially true rhetoric to
get on with their lives. Living in truth, in Havel's sense, then
becomes a political act of defiance. The literature of such defiance is of great political and cultural significance both within
the totalitarian orders and beyond. This literature, as we have
observed, is directed to "us" as well as "them." It is a modern
literature, addressing specifically modern problems. Primary
among these problems is rampant cynicism as an element of
sociological structure.

Legitimation through cynicism should be considered along

with Max Weber's rational-legal legitimation as a distinctive modern means of moving from force to authority. Weber proposed three types of authority: charismatic, traditional, and, the modern type, rational-legal authority. Appeals to the special qualities of the leader, the ways of the past, formal laws, and means-end relationships facilitate the likelihood that subordinates will follow the commands of their superiors. He demonstrated that distinctive types of society, state structures, and cultures emerge from the different types of legitimation. What we have found in today's totalitarianism is an extreme form of a fourth type of legitimation—legitimation through disbelief. It uses Newspeak, promotes modern tyrannical social relations, and suggests its opposition—the cultures and politics of living in truth.

Signs of legitimation through cynicism are ubiquitous. Many of our public communications are colored by varieties of Newspeak. In formal bureaucratic organizations, speech is constructed to deflect responsibility and to minimize the moral and political dilemmas of daily life. Applications are processed, not judged. Issues are prioritized, not ranked. Not only blacks but women are euphemistically called minorities. Bombs have become destructive devices. Our Ministry of War is the Defense Department.

When a welfare recipient meets a welfare worker, they may both know that they are exchanging socially compliant behavior for financial support. But the welfare worker speaks to his client as if support will yield changed social status, as if compliance is a form of rehabilitation. In fact therapeutic and professional jargons in such cases are often disbelieved by both parties, but their use sustains the desired social interaction.

When a bank or university embarks on an affirmative action hiring program, its members will assert a commitment to equal justice. They will speak not as members of institutions concerned about government contracts and supports, but as members of socially conscious institutions. Yet job applicants, the institutions themselves, and government observers are all cognizant of the instrumental nature of their actions. People wonder: Do Africans count as blacks? Are Spaniards Hispanics?

Our political discourse is saturated with obfuscations and irrational sentimentality. Candidates run on platforms dedicated to "making Americans proud again" or to undefined "new ideas." They say what their media consultants tell them people want to hear. People know that candidates pander to their prejudices. Yet electoral decisions are based on such media rhetoric. The candidates do not believe what they say. The electorate does not believe what it hears. Yet the democratic political process is legitimated by such elections. The "selling of presidents" in their speeches and in political advertising is a variation on Madison Avenue themes; the selling of our political leaders uses the methods of commodity sales.

If the concentration camp is the archetypical organization of totalitarianism, as Hannah Arendt observed, then television advertising is the archetypical linguistic center of legitimation through disbelief in our world. Words are used by the makers of television commercials to entice and obfuscate simultaneously. The makers of Anacin, an aspirin-based painkiller, advertise the "active ingredient doctors recommend most." On this ground they entice consumers to buy their product instead of aspirin. But of course the active ingredient it contains is aspirin.

The public is not stupid. It knows that such manipulation of words is part of the sociocultural landscape. It learns, therefore, to use words not as means of clear communication but for manipulation through obfuscation. The word is simply not to be believed.

Such learning begins early. Children's commercial television presents the most crass form of manipulation. Through camera angles and catchy tunes, small plastic objects, from fashionable dolls to the latest in toy tanks, are transformed into icons of happiness and adventure. Through the endorsement of cartoon characters, candy products become required breakfast treats. In fact, in recent years, in an era of deregulation, not simply the advertisements but entire broadcasts sell products in this fashion. Toy manufacturers produce series about their latest product lines. Because children cannot distinguish between an advertising claim and an objective product description, the manipulative aspects of television commercials are objectionable to many, even to those who generally support commercial culture. Yet the most radical and generally unrecognized problem is not the initial manipulation, but the lesson such manipulation teaches. Early on, children who regularly watch commercial television learn cynicism. They remember their disappointments with robots that could not really do anything, with dolls that were inflexible and awkward and not the epitome of beauty, with electronic baseball that had no relationship to the excitement of playing the real game. Some parents take solace in this, but in fact docility to authority is being taught. Children know that television lies (ironically this was a major slogan of Solidarity), but they also learn and do not question that the road to the good life is through the acquisition of consumer goods. They become weary objects of manipulation at six years old. They are manchildren in a (false) promised land.

Adults know that politicians all cheat. Public professions of principles by statesmen, corporate leaders, trade unionists, and even the clergy are to be disbelieved by the wise. Cultural, political, and moral ideals about the good, the beautiful, and the true are but facades. Such knowledge yields inaction. There is a sense that nothing can be done, and therefore the prevailing patterns of domination are accepted and persist. This is the pattern of legitimation through disbelief. It is clearly not the only form of legitimation in our world. It might in fact only account for a small, but crucial, portion of authoritative social relations. Its existence suggests that a new version of the final crisis of industrial capitalism, i.e., Habermas's legitimation crisis, is far from imminent, nor is Daniel Bell's neoconservative notion of the "cultural contradictions of capitalism" operant.

The totalitarian experience tells us that when power is first grounded on claims to absolute truth, it can then give way to a loss of truth and to legitimation through disbelief. This is not only their experience; it is to some extent ours. Habermas believes that crises in capitalist relations in the late twentieth century were accommodated by political manipulations of the market. Market rationality was supplemented by the reasoning of social welfare and state guidance of economic life (Keynesianism), and when economic problems developed again, Habermas suggested the legitimacy of capitalist relations and the state were undermined, which could lead to a cultural and motivational crisis of legitimacy for the entire system. Because he thinks systemically, he links the subsystems of economics, politics, culture, and motivation totalistically. Thus, he investigates the possibility of the transformation of the social formation. He fails to observe the ironies of legitimation. He fails to recognize that the social order can be sustained by disbelief as well as belief. Societal cynicism may be as strong a political force as societal belief.

Daniel Bell's cultural contradictions of capitalism present conservative concerns about the same diagnoses. He argues that there is a major contradiction between the work ethic and the hedonistic consumer ethic. Following Weber, he identifies the spirit of capitalism with the pursuit of wealth and work as ends in themselves. He emphasizes that hedonistic modern culture and consumerism undermine the cultural basis of the political-economic order, the work ethic. Hedonism undermines commitment to work. What Bell fails to realize is that the dynamic dissatisfactions of consumerism may yield an intensification of work.

Cultural cynicism may have become a key basis of acceptance of the social order as it exists. Weber imagined that the capitalist ethic would yield work and wealth as ends in themselves. What the child and adult learn in a society of Newspeak and cultural cynicism is consumerism as a proper end in itself, even when it does not bring satisfaction. People are taught in commercial media that the pursuit of the good life is the pursuit of consumer goods. When particular available goods do not satisfy (be they new versions of aspirin or a new or repackaged political candidate), both the cynical adult and the child within him do not question the pursuit, but look for other goods. People may know that this is futile, but they just as well may not know any other way to proceed.

Media Newspeak and its Alternatives

Jean Baudrillard observes the legitimation through widespead, media-enforced cynicism in apocalyptic terms based on technologized and social forms of mass communication.[29] In his theoretical world, the behemoth of the media overwhelms and infantilizes the masses. They, in turn, can reject their oppressors through super-resistance, silence, or superconformism— the mass participation of reconstructed minds. The masses observe their own individual consumerism as spectacle, or most playfully construct new spectacles. With a lost sense of the true or desire to pursue the true, they have no other choice. Yet, if Baudrillard used even the most elementary sociology, he would know that people in the West can turn the media off. This is a significant instance of a Western version of Havel's living in truth. Havel's greengrocer refuses to put up the sign "Workers of the World, Unite," which he knows to be the nonsense propagated by the regime that oppresses him. People in the West can turn off the media, seek a different education for themselves and their children, seek the truth and find literacy.

What I am referring to, of course, is not as simple as turning off a television set, just as becoming a nonconformist and dissident in today's Czechoslovakia is not as simple as refusing to put up a banal slogan. The remarkable mass popularity of books proposing fundamental educational reforms, such as Allan Bloom's *The Closing of the American Mind* and E. D. Hirsch's *Cultural Literacy*,[30] suggests a desire to re-develop means to seek the truth apart from media manipulation, through a rediscovery of cultural literacy. The appeal and relative popularity (to a much more literate and restricted audience) in the West of authors like Baranczak and Michnik, Havel and Kundera, and Haraszti and Konrad likewise indi-

cates that the search for alternatives to Newspeak is our
project as well as theirs. But ironically, our search may be
much more difficult.

When Havel contrasts living in truth with the official lie, the
choice is clear and well understood by his Czechoslovakian
audience. When Baranczak contrasts the words on the reviewing stands with those in the parlors, all Poles know well the
difference. But Allan Bloom's ideas about an open mind and
E. D. Hirsch's notion of literacy are manifestations of closed-
mindedness and philistine illiteracy. Both are based on rather
static notions of education and the Western tradition. Both
seem to serve a rather narrow ideological purpose. Bloom defends the saliency of the classics by railing against feminism,
affirmative action, and, with particularly intense venom, rock
and roll. Hirsch's notion of "what every American needs to
know" seems to be a shopping list for former Secretary of
Education William Bennett's conservative political agenda. As
Kirkpatrick's critique of totalitarianism ignores its connection
with modern societies in general, Hirsch and Bloom promote
a celebration of a static and often authoritarian or ideological
tradition as an answer to the problems of modernity without
considering modernity's promise. When people turn to such
thinkers to understand how our education has failed democracy and impoverished our souls,[31] they are substituting (as
Baranczak would put it), the words on the reviewing stands
for the words on the reviewing stands.

People read Bloom and Hirsch because they know that media Newspeak and culture have to be turned off. But the dogmatic form of Bloom's and Hirsch's argumentation is far from
a sound basis for alternatives. To most educators, Jean Jacques
Rousseau's and John Dewey's ideas are fundamentally different, if not opposite. Yet Hirsch denounces them both to his
readers as purveyors of the major problems in modern education. His proofs include: "The first chapter of Dewey's
[*Schools of Tomorrow*] . . . is sprinkled with quotations from
Rousseau."[32] Bloom, throughout his text, cites the authoritative wisdom of the ancients, as if Plato and Aristotle and the

authors of the Talmud agreed, to support his assertions. Un-
suspecting readers will be convinced by such arguments without knowing how controversial they are. People searching for
alternatives to their and their children's miseducation are
being further manipulated. Only now, they trust the manipulation. Many solutions to our educational problems are but
extensions of the problems. We proceed thus from cynicism to
dogmatic belief. The contrast with the form and substance of
the leading post-totalitarian writers could not be greater. They
present questions with a plurality of answers, not answered
absolutely. They challenge us to communicate, not to accept.

The Culture of Politics: Them and Us

In this inquiry, we have observed the emergence of an oppositionist alternative to Newspeak and the implications of this
alternative for official and unofficial culture and politics. In
this chapter I have attempted to suggest the broad implications in our study of the totalitarians and post-totalitarians
for an understanding of our own world. I close our inquiry by
analyzing the relationships among the post-totalitarian mind,
post-totalitarian plurality, and our political culture.

We have seen how the post-totalitarians have deconstructed
the totalitarian conflation of truth and politics. Central elements of totalitarianism were frontally reversed. Instead of
ideology, there was a reconsideration of the search for truth.
Instead of an assumption of the infinite malleability of the human world, there was a reassertion of the importance of
human dignity. Instead of terror, there was a fundamental
questioning of the role of violence in politics. Instead of political massification and enthusiasm, there was a search for
democracy and rational deliberation. On these matters the authors we have considered agree, though with somewhat different emphases. None of them is committed to an ideology or
an ideological critique (finding hidden dark forces behind political appearances), but the emphasis on truth is more apparent in Havel's and Michnik's work than in Kundera's. Though
none of them wants to assert that human beings ought to be

THEM AND US   223

molded in some ideologically defined image, Michnik distinguishes himself as the thinker most concerned with the rather
old-fashioned notion of dignity. Whereas Arendt questions
the conventional notion that politics is another means for
war, asserting instead that politics is the opposite of violence,
the whole Solidarity movement was committed to nonviolence
more for strategic and ethical reasons than for the theoretical
ones Arendt specifies. While the commitments to democracy
and rational deliberation are shared and emphasized by all the
thinkers we have considered, the exact meaning of democracy,
how it is to be realized, and the setting of deliberation and what
it is to consider are subjects of debate. The post-totalitarians
seem to agree on a field for a discursive culture of politics, but
there is a plurality of discourses within the field.

To understand the field of post-totalitarian political culture,
we closely analyzed the novels of Milan Kundera and the political and historical writings of Adam Michnik. The commonalities of their works were emphasized. But, of course,
there are important differences. Their very physical situations
indicate the dimensions of the differences. Kundera is an exile
in Paris. Michnik is a political activist in Warsaw, who wrote
most of his essays and books in prison. Michnik still believes
in the necessity of action. Kundera questions such necessity.
Michnik writes primarily occasional pieces which answer immediate political questions through historical, literary, and
political investigation. Kundera writes with a sense of a trans-
historical European mission which must separate itself from
immediate circumstance.

Such differences can and do lead to opposing judgments
about pressing issues among the oppositionists in the post-
totalitarian situation. Exiles tend to be more resolute about
maintaining independence from officialdom, more concerned
about purity, less understanding of compromise. Those who
remain are more nuanced in their judgment of the latest shifts
in oppositional strategy, more aware of changes in official policy, more concerned about those caught between the totalitarian powers and their opposition. The external opponents

often believe that those who remained are hopelessly naive
about the possibilities of change. The internal opposition believes that those who have left are needlessly apocalyptic.
These differences can clearly be explained sociologically. Apart
from the relative accuracy of such opposing judgments, some
of those in exile, especially when the exile was voluntary, have
a proclivity to despair and to develop a sense of the hope-
lessness of the present political situation. Those who remain
have to try to believe in a possible improvement in their situation if they are not to succumb to complete despair.

Some of the differences between Michnik and Kundera can
be explained in these terms. Indeed Havel, as a person in a
situation quite similar to Michnik's, has engaged in rather
heated polemics with Kundera on these points. Yet among
exiles the same polemics can be observed (on the Czech scene
between Kundera and Josef Skvorecky). And among those
who remain, polemics about the relationship between the authorities and independent society and about proper courses of
political, cultural, and economic action are both heated and
of crucial significance. What is most striking, however, is the
way in which the various views accommodate each other as a
matter of both cultural form and political commitment. Kundera and Michnik are men of deep convictions. Yet as we have
seen, their most fundamental commitments and the way they
articulate them lead not to declarations of absolute truths, but
to nuanced judgments open to alternative views.

In Central Europe, a fertile ground for totalitarianism,
where intolerance, suspicious jealousies, and hatreds have
been the material of politics, where modern barbarism reached
its peak, a new democratic political culture is emerging. As
should be clear to the reader by now, I have no confidence that
this political culture *must* in the end prevail. Even stronger
neototalitarian states may very well emerge. We can, though,
have hope, and our hopes will have greater substance if we
learn from those who have experienced and moved beyond
totalitarianism. It is ironic that in political orders where
democracy and its culture have been banished without pre-

totalitarian democratic political cultures, democratic commitments are becoming part of political culture. This teaches us
that past political culture is far from destiny. Rather, it provides opportunities for present actions through which the future can be shaped. Many earlier studies in political culture
treated it as an independent variable in predicting the success
of modernization, democracy, and capitalism.[33] Here we have
seen, in the dynamics of political culture, man's capacity to
begin anew (in the words of Arendt). But we should soberly
note that such promise also suggests dangers when we address
problems in our politics and culture, when we observe and
seek alternatives for political problems and cultural crises. We
cannot be assured that our democratic political culture will
persist forever. The post-totalitarian mind, as it articulates
democratic alternatives to Newspeak, should remind us of the
importance of democratic commitment, not as a basis for collective self-satisfaction, but as the grounds for critical appraisal of our world in terms of our own ideals.

Notes

Introduction

1. George Orwell's notion of Newspeak plays a key role in my analysis. See George Orwell, *1984* (New York: Harcourt, Brace and World, 1963), and chapter 3 below. The most distinctive characteristic of Newspeak, alluded to here, is that it is an official jargon with few external referents. It is meaningful primarily with reference to itself. Thus, Orwell depicts the patently absurd phrase "War is Peace" as typical of Newspeak.

2. Specifying the reason for the advanced position of Poland is outside the purview of this study. I have addressed this issue in both *The Persistence of Freedom: The Sociological Implications of Polish Student Theater* (Boulder, Colo.: Westview, 1981) and *On Cultural Freedom: an Exploration of Public Life in Poland and America* (Chicago: University of Chicago Press, 1983). Strong traditions of resistance, including a two-hundred-year history of oppositional culture, are central to the advanced state of Polish post-totalitarianism. For the best overview in English, see Norman Davies, *God's Playground* (New York: Columbia University Press, 1982).

3. Czeslaw Milosz, *The Captive Mind,* tr. Jane Zielonko (New York: Random House, 1951), 2.

4. Tadeusz Borowski, *This Way to the Gas Chambers, Ladies and Gentlemen,* tr. Barbara Vedder (New York: Penguin Books, 1976).

Chapter One

1. Herbert Spiro, "Totalitarianism," *International Encyclopedia of the Social Sciences* (New York: Free Press, 1979), 106–13.

2. James Burnham, *The Managerial Revolution: What Is Happening in the World?* (New York: John Day Company, 1941).

3. Hannah Arendt, *The Origins of Totalitarianism* (New York: Harcourt Brace Jovanich, 1951).

4. Ibid., 387.

5. See, e.g., Allan Kassoff, "The Administered Society: Totalitarianism Without Terror," *World Politics* 16, no. 4 (1964):558–75.

6. Chalmers Johnson, ed., *Change in Communist Systems* (Stanford: Stanford University Press, 1970).

7. See, e.g., Patrick Glynn, "Reagan's Rush to Disarm," *Commentary*, March 1988: 19–28, and Stephen R. Sturm, "Shades of Containment," *Commentary*, November 1986:33–39.

8. See Jeffrey C. Goldfarb, "Social Bases of Independent Public Expression in Communist Societies," *American Journal of Sociology* 83, no. 4 (January 1978):920–39.

9. Spiro, "Totalitarianism," 106–13.

10. See Bruno Bettelheim, *Surviving and Other Essays* (New York: Knopf, 1979).

11. See, e.g., Paul Hollander, *Soviet and American Society: A Comparison* (New York: Oxford University Press, 1973), esp. 110–17.

12. For a description of what I mean by a normatively animated political and social theory, see Michael Walzer's discussion of the community-based social critic in *Interpretation and Social Criticism* (Cambridge, Mass.: Harvard University Press, 1987).

13. See Carl Friedrich and Zbigniew Brzezinski, *Totalitarian Dictatorship and Autocracy* (Cambridge, Mass.: Harvard University Press, 1965).

14. Hannah Arendt, *Eichmann in Jerusalem* (New York: Viking Press, 1964).

15. For a sampling of the controversy, see Hannah Arendt, *The Jew as Pariah: Jewish Identity* (New York: Grove Press, 1978).

16. See Jeane Kirkpatrick, *Dictatorship and Double Standards: Rationalism and Reason in Politics* (New York: Simon and Schuster, 1982).

17. In addition, the contrast between autocracies in the third world (e.g., in Latin America in the seventies) and modern tyranny cannot be as easily maintained as neoconservative apologists assert. The conflation of force and reason in the form of a politics of rationalized fear was a hallmark of the dictatorial regimes of Argentina and Chile. Thus, much of the analysis in this essay may be applicable to such "authoritarian" situations. With minor qualifications, it is the totalitarian qualities of bureaucratic authoritarianism which link the right-wing, most often military, dictators with modern tyranny. Considering such comparisons has been an ongoing New School for Social Research project, a democracy seminar with centers in Warsaw, Budapest, and New York. This study is an outgrowth of the seminar, which has focused to date on the problems of totalitarianism and its democratic alternatives. The clear link between totalitarian culture and the Latin American politics of fear was illuminated in the seminar through a combination of informal talk with Juan Corradi and an examination of his forthcoming collection (with Patricia Weiss Fagan and Manuel Antonio Garreton), *Fear and Society: The*

Culture of Fear in the Authoritarian Regimes of the Southern Cone (Los Angeles: University of California, forthcoming).

18. Kirkpatrick, *Dictatorship*, 101.

19. Compare Edmund Burke, *Reflections on the Revolution in France* (Baltimore: Pelican Books, 1968).

20. This is most clearly spelled out in Hannah Arendt, *On Revolution* (Westport: Greenwood Press, 1982).

21. See Hannah Arendt, *Men in Dark Times* (New York: Harcourt Brace Jovanich, 1968).

22. Arendt, *Origins*, 479.

23. Kirkpatrick, *Dictatorship*, 97.

24. For the presentation of a most telling critique of Kirkpatrick and the neoconservatives, see Michael Walzer, "On Failed Totalitarianism," in *1984, Revisited* (New York: Harper and Row, 1983), 101–2. Using the dichotomy of totalitarianism and authoritarianism, he denies that the notion of totalitarianism is applicable to the understanding of post-Stalinist politics. Here I reject the neoconservative dichotomy, but nonetheless use totalitarianism as a critical concept.

25. Hannah Arendt, *Between Past and Future* (New York: Viking Press, 1968).

26. See Max Horkheimer and Theodor Adorno, *The Dialectics of Enlightenment* (New York: Herder and Herder, 1972).

27. Probably the best account by an outside observer is T. Gordon Ash, *The Polish Revolution: Solidarity* (New York: Vintage Books, 1985). For my overview, see chapter 5 below.

28. See, e.g., Talcott Parsons, *The System of Modern Society* (Englewood Cliffs: Prentice Hall, 1971).

29. See Barrington Moore, Jr., *The Social Origins of Dictatorship and Democracy* (Boston: Beacon Press, 1966).

30. Robert Nisbet, *The Twilight of Authority* (New York: Oxford University Press, 1975), and Jean-Francois Revel, *The Totalitarian Temptation* (New York: Doubleday, 1977).

31. This is analyzed in detail in chapters 2, 3, and 4.

32. Ferenc Fehrer, Agnes Heller, and György Markus, *Dictatorship over Needs* (London: Basil Blackwell, 1983), 237–63.

Chapter Two

1. For a theoretical discussion of civil society as a goal of political action, see Andrew Arato and Jean Cohen, "Social Movements, Civil Society and the Problem of Sovereignty," in *Praxis International* 4 (October 1984): 266–83.

2. See chapter 5 for the way a leading Polish historian and activist, Adam Michnik, uses history.

3. Arendt, *Between Past and Future*, 17–40.

4. The key philosophical problem of this book has to do with the intimate relationship between force and reason. Osborne Wiggins and I began exploring this problem of philosophical sociology in a series of courses—"Authority," "The Political and Social Philosophy of Hannah Arendt," and "Phenomenological Sociology"—at the Graduate Faculty of the New School for Social Research. This section draws from an unpublished paper we wrote, "Newspeak and the Politics of Force," which was an outgrowth of joint teaching and long fruitful conversations.

5. See Maurice Merleau-Ponty, *Humanism and Terror: An Essay on the Communist Problem* (Boston: Beacon Press, 1969), and idem, *Signs* (Evanston, Ill.: Northwestern University Press, 1964).

6. The "power of the powerless" really exists. See Vaclav Havel, "The Power of the Powerless," in *Vaclav Havel or Living in Truth*, ed. Jan Vladislav (Boston: Faber and Faber, 1986), 36–122, and chapter 4 below.

7. Michel Foucault, *Beyond Structuralism and Hermeneutics*, ed. Hubert Dreyfus and Paul Robinson (Chicago: University of Chicago Press, 1983), 218.

8. Michel Foucault, "What is Enlightenment?" in *The Foucault Reader*, ed. Paul Robinson (New York: Pantheon Books, 1984), 46.

9. Ibid., 222.

10. See Eli Sagan, *At the Dawn of Tyranny* (New York: Knopf, 1985).

11. Arendt, *Origins*, 123–304.

12. Arendt, *Eichmann* (New York: The Viking Press, 1970), 105.

13. Ibid., 106.

14. This is central to the works of Emile Durkheim, Georg Simmel, Max Weber, and Karl Marx. For a discussion of this point see my *On Cultural Freedom*.

15. Zhores A. Medvedev, *The Rise and Fall of T. D. Lysenko*, tr. I. Michael Lerner (New York: Columbia University Press, 1969), 28–29.

16. Ibid., 62–63.

17. Ibid., 107.

18. Ibid., 104–10.

19. Ibid., 132.

20. Ibid., 4–5.

21. Ibid., 4.

22. See Maurice N. Richter, Jr., *Science as a Cultural Process* (Cambridge, Mass.: Schenken Publishing Co., 1972).

23. See Feher et al., *Dictatorship over Needs*.

24. I was the friend.

25. Z. Medvedev, *Rise and Fall,* 107.

26. See Milan Kundera, *The Unbearable Lightness of Being,* tr. Michael Henry Heim (New York: Harper and Row, 1984), analyzed in chapter 4.

27. Jadwiga Staniszkis, *Poland's Self-Limiting Revolution* (Princeton: Princeton University Press, 1984). This work is analyzed in detail in chapter 5.

28. Orwell, *1984,* 254–55.

29. Jurgen Habermas, *The Theory of Communicative Action,* 2 vols. (Boston: Beacon Press, 1984, 1987).

Chapter Three

1. The following section is taken from my essay, "Student Theatre in Poland," *Survey* 22, no. 2 (1976):155–78. References to student theater in the remainder of the book draw upon research I conducted in the seventies on theater in Poland and Eastern Europe.

2. See Thomas Kuhn, *The Structures of Scientific Revolutions* (Chicago: University of Chicago Press, 1962), and Richter, *Science as a Cultural Process.*

3. For a systematic comparison of this sort of issue see my *On Cultural Freedom.*

4. See T. S. Eliot, *The Sacred Wood* (New York: Harcourt, Brace, Jovanich, 1950).

5. The following three sections on cultural traditions, official ideology, and cultural institutions are from my "The Social Bases of Independent Public Expression."

6. Quoted in Philip E. Mosely, "Social Science in the Service of Politics," in *Soviet Society,* ed. Alex Inkeles and Kent Geiger (Boston: St. Martin's Press, 1961).

7. See George Denicke, *Links with the Past in Soviet Society,* External Research Office of Intelligence Research, Department of State, Series no. 84 (Washington: GPO, 1950).

8. See Karl Mannheim, *Ideology of Utopia* (New York: Harcourt, Brace and World, Inc., 1936), and Clifford Geertz, "Ideology as a Cultural System," in *Interpretation of Culture* (New York: Basic Books, 1973), 219. For an excellent reconsideration of Mannheim through Geertz, see Paul Ricoeur, *Lectures on Ideology and Utopia,* ed. George H. Taylor (New York: Columbia University Press, 1986).

9. Milovan Djilas, *The New Cities* (New York: Praeger, 1957).

10. See Jacek Kuron and Karol Modzelewski, "Open Letter to Members of the University of Warsaw Sections of The United Polish Workers Party and The Union of Young Socialists," in *Revolutionary Marxist Students in Poland Speak Out* (New York: Merit, 1968); Leszek Kolakowski, *Toward a Marxist Humanism* (New York:

Grove Press, 1968); and Adam Schaff, *Marxism and the Human Individual* (New York: McGraw Hill, 1965).

11. See Roy Medvedev, *Let History Judge: The Origins and Consequences of Stalinism* (New York: Knopf, 1971), and Z. Medvedev, *Rise and Fall.*

12. And this has been a long-term, ongoing process. See, e.g., P. E. Mosely, "Social Science"; Harrison Salisbury, "Literature: The Right to Write," in Salisbury, ed., *The Soviet Union: The Fifty Years* (New York: Signet Books, 1968), 124–45; idem, "Theater: The Naked Truth," ibid., 146–57; and Hilton Kramer, "Art: A Return to Modernism," ibid., 158–74.

13. See Eugene Rabinowitch, "A Survey of Russian Science," in *Soviet Society,* ed. Alex Inkeles and Kent Geiger (Boston: Houghton Mifflin, 1961), and Mark Zaitsev, "Soviet Theater Censorship," *The Drama Review* 19, no. 2 (1975):119–28.

14. R. W. Dean, "Gierek's Three Years: Retrenchment and Reform," *Survey* 20, nos. 2 and 3 (1974):59–76.

Chapter Four

1. Aleksander Solzhenitsyn, *The First Circle* (New York: Harper and Row, 1968), 483.

2. Cited in Arendt, *Origins,* p. 307.

3. Arthur Koestler, *Darkness at Noon* (New York: Macmillan Co., 1941); Merleau-Ponty, *Humanism and Terror;* Herbert Marcuse, *Soviet Marxism* (New York: Columbia University Press, 1968); Arendt, *Between Past and Future.*

4. Max Weber, *Economy and Society* (Berkeley: University of California Press, 1979).

5. George Orwell, "Politics and the English Language," in *A Collection of Essays by George Orwell* (New York: Harcourt Brace Jovanich, 1946).

6. George Konrad, *The Case Worker,* tr. Paul Aston (New York: Harcourt Brace Jovanich, 1978), 52.

7. The Taganka Theater, under director Yuri Lyubimov, was for two decades a challenging political and aesthetic center of theatrical innovation, similar to the Polish theater analyzed in chapter 3. Lyubimov is now in exile.

8. First printed in English in *Manhattan Review* 2, no. 1 (1981):28.

9. Ibid., 35.

10. Arendt, *Origins,* 479.

11. Miklos Haraszti, *The Velvet Prison,* tr. Katalin and Stepen Landesmann with the help of Steve Wasserman (New York: New Republic Books, 1987), 97.

12. I conducted this interview.
13. Vaclav Havel, "Power," 43–44.
14. Ibid., 45.
15. Ibid., 55.
16. Konrad, *The Case Worker.*
17. Vaclav Havel, *The Memorandum,* tr. Vera Blackwell (New York: Grove Press, 1980).
18. Havel, "Power," 43–44.
19. "Doing without Utopias: An Interview with Vaclav Havel," tr. A. G. Brain and E. Blair, *Times Literary Supplement* no. 4373, 23 January 1987, 81–83.
20. Milan Kundera, *The Farewell Party,* tr. Peter Kussi (London: Penguin Books, Ltd., 1977), 68.
21. Ibid., 68–69.
22. Ibid., 67–68.
23. In Arendt's sense; see chapter 2 above and her *Eichmann in Jerusalem.*
24. Milan Kundera, *A Book on Laughter and Forgetting,* tr. Michael Henry Heim (New York: Penguin Books, 1981), 3.
25. Ibid.
26. Ibid., 22.
27. Kundera, *The Unbearable Lightness of Being,* 254.
28. Ibid., 278.
29. Ibid., 257.
30. Ibid.
31. Ibid., 93.
32. Ibid.
33. See Kundera, *Life is Elsewhere,* tr. Peter Kussi (New York: Penguin Books, 1986).
34. Kundera, *Laughter and Forgetting,* 61.
35. Kundera, *Laughable Loves,* tr. Suzanne Rappaport (New York: Penguin Books, 1975).
36. See Kundera, *The Joke,* tr. Michael Henry Heim (London: Penguin Books, Ltd., 1982).
37. Norman Podhoretz, "An Open Letter to Milan Kundera," in *The Bloody Crossroads* (New York: Simon and Schuster, 1986), 167–83.
38. Kundera, *The Unbearable Lightness of Being,* 176.
39. Ibid., 47.
40. Ibid., 177.
41. Ibid., 222.
42. Ibid., 221.
43. See T. Garton Ash, "Does Central Europe Exist?" *New York Review of Books,* 9 October 1986.

Chapter Five

1. I have drawn from three of my previously published papers in composing this chapter: "Tyranny of Theory? Confronting Solidarity," *Sociological Forum* 2, no. 2 (Spring 1987):422–31, © 1987 by Eastern Sociological Society, all rights reserved; "Letters from Prison and Other Essays," *New York Law School Journal of Human Rights* 5, no. 1 (Fall 1987):213–28; and "1984: Poland, Public Freedom and Human Rights," *The Journal of Applied Behavioral Science* 20, no. 4 (1984):455–69, © 1984 by NTL Institute. They are reprinted here with permission.

2. Daniel Singer, *The Road to Gdansk* (New York: Monthly Review Press, 1981), 156.

3. Ibid., 235.

4. Ibid., 62, 198.

5. Ibid., 191.

6. Ibid., 232.

7. Jadwiga Staniskis, *Poland's Self-Limiting Revolution* (Princeton: Princeton University Press, 1984), pp. 38–72.

8. Ibid., 150–221.

9. Ibid., 222–47.

10. Ibid., 248–77.

11. Ibid., 278–312.

12. Staniszkis uses the ideas of Western critical theorists to be critical of the socialist order. For the discussion of new forms of corporatism, see Phillip Schmitter, "Still the Century of Corporatism?" *Review of Politics* 36 (January 1974):85–131. For repressive tolerance, see Herbert Marcuse, "Repressive Tolerance," in Robert Paul Wolff, Barrington Moore, Jr., and Herbert Marcuse, *A Critique of Pure Tolerance* (Boston: Beacon Press, 1965), 81–117. For artificial negativity, see Paul Piccone, "The Crisis of One-Dimensionality," *Telos* 35 (Spring 1978):43–72.

13. Alain Touraine, *Post-Industrial Society* (New York: Random House, 1971); idem, *Self-Production of Society* (Chicago: University of Chicago Press, 1977); idem, *The Voice and the Eye* (New York: Cambridge University Press, 1981).

14. Alain Touraine, *Solidarity: The Analysis of a Social Movement, Poland 1980–81* (New York: Cambridge University Press, 1983).

15. Ibid., 19.

16. Ibid., 34.

17. Ibid., 67–68.

18. Ibid., 113.

19. Arendt, *Between Past and Future*, 145.

20. Hannah Arendt, *The Human Condition* (Chicago: University of Chicago Press, 1968).

21. Paul Ricoeur, "Action, Story, History," *Salmagundi* 60 (1983): 60–72.

22. For a more detailed account of recent Polish history see Abraham Bromberg, *Poland: Genesis of a Revolution* (New York: Random House, 1983); Jakub Karpinski, *Countdown* (New York, Kowz-Cohl, 1982); and Neal Ascherson, *The Polish August* (New York: Viking Press, 1982).

23. Hannah Arendt, *Crisis in the Republic* (New York: Harcourt Brace Jovanich, 1972), 143.

24. The following account of the Solidarity experience on pages 134–40 is an excerpt from an unpublished paper I wrote with Elzbieta Matynia. She was an eyewitness of much which is described here.

25. Adam Michnik, *The Church, The Left: A Dialogue* (Chicago: University of Chicago Press, forthcoming in English).

26. Adam Michnik, "The New Evolutionism," in *Letters from Prison and Other Essays* (Los Angeles: University of California Press, 1986), 135–48.

27. Michnik, "Why You Are Not Signing . . . ," "Why You Are Not Emigrating . . . ," "The Polish War," "On Resistance," "A Letter to General Kiszczak," "About the Elections," "Letter from the Gdansk Prison, 1985," in ibid., 3–99.

28. Michnik, "On Resistance," in ibid., 51.

29. Michnik, "Darkness on the Horizon," in ibid., 117–23; "Why You Are Not Signing . . . ," in ibid., 3–15; "A Letter to General Kiszczak," in ibid., 64–70.

30. Michnik, "The Polish War," in ibid., 25–26.

31. Ibid., 28.

32. Ibid., 40.

33. See discussion of Vaclav Havel in chapters 4 and 6.

34. Michnik, "A Letter to General Kiszczak," in *Letters,* 66–67.

35. Adam Michnik, *From the History of Honor in Poland* (in Polish, underground).

36. Michnik, "Maggots and Angels," in *Letters,* 160, 162–63.

37. Ibid., 168.

38. Michnik, "Shadows of Forgotten Ancestors," in ibid., 221–22.

39. Michnik, "Conversation in the Citadel," in ibid., 306–7.

40. Ibid., 330.

41. The three essays cited here are translated and collected in ibid.

Chapter Six

1. This was the special contribution of "The University in Exile" of The New School for Social Research. See Peter M. Rutkoff and William D. Scott, *New School: A History of the New School for Social Research* (New York: The Free Press, 1986).

2. At a special seminar on Polish and Russian theater sponsored by the National Endowment for the Humanities in July and August 1979, this was the judgment of the participants. It could even be called the major finding of the seminar.

3. Haraszti, *The Velvet Prison*, 156.

4. For depictions of the historical Central European intellectual, see, e.g., Elias Canetti, *The Play of the Eyes* (New York: Farrar Straus Giroux, 1986), *The Torch in My Ear* (New York: Farrar Straus Giroux, 1982), and with Joachim Neugroschel, *The Tongue Set Free: Remembrance of a European Childhood* (New York: Seabury Press, 1979); and Czeslaw Milosz, *Native Realm: A Search for Self-Definition* (Garden City, N.Y.: Doubleday and Company, 1968).

5. Arendt, *Human Condition*, 50.

6. Ibid., 51.

7. Adam Michnik, "Klopot," in *Obecnosc Leszkowi Kolakowskiemu w 60 roznice yrodzin* (London: ANEKS, 1987), 98–219.

8. This is not to excuse Kundera for his misogyny. The point is that he does not reduce politics to sex or sex to politics, not that he is necessarily correct about either.

9. See Arendt, *Origins*, 250–66.

10. See "G.O.P. Senate Unite, Call Metzenbaum a Communist Ally," *New York Times*, 30 July 1987, p. 1.

11. See *Taking the Stand: The Testimony of Lieutenant Colonel Oliver North* (New York: Pocket Books, 1987). A major difference between the logic of Communist totalitarianism and the totalitarian logic of Western anti-Communists is that the anti-Communist script can be quickly reversed and rapidly forgotten. Thus Nixon and Reagan, who launched their political careers with anti-Communism, became advocates of "detente" and the "new realism" in their late careers.

12. Kundera, *The Unbearable Lightness of Being*, 212.

13. N. Podhoretz, "An Open Letter to Milan Kundera."

14. See Michnik, *The Church, the Left.*

15. See Michnik, *Letters,* and chapter 5 above.

16. Such as General Kiszczak; see chapter 5 above.

17. Claude Lefort, *The Political Forms of Modern Society* (Cambridge, Mass.: MIT Press, 1986).

18. George Konrad, *Anti-Politics,* tr. Richard E. Allen (New York: Harcourt Brace Jovanich, 1984).

19. George Konrad and Ivan Szelenyi, *The Intellectuals on the Road to Class Power,* tr. Andrew Arato and Richard E. Allen (New York: Harcourt Brace Jovanich, 1979).

20. See, e.g., Daniel Bell, *The Coming of Post-Industrial Society* (New York: Basic Books, 1978).
21. Arendt, *Between Past and Future*, 257.
22. Baranczak, "These Words," and see chapter 4.
23. Arendt, *Between Past and Future*, 259.
24. See Michnik, "The New Evolutionism," in *Letters*, 139.
25. Ibid., 142.
26. Ibid., 144.
27. Ibid., 136.
28. Ibid., 137.
29. Ibid., 137.
30. Ibid., 140.
31. "Gorbachev: The View from Warsaw," an interview with Jacek Kuron, *Harper's Magazine* 275, no. 646 (July 1987):26–27.
32. Private interview with Pawel Spiewak, June 1987.
33. "Gorbachev," 26–27.
34. In June 1987 I had the opportunity to speak to a broad representation of the Polish democratic opposition. Without exception they held this point of view.
35. In personal conversation with Bielecki, June 1987.

Chapter Seven
1. The analysis of post-totalitarianism in the Soviet bloc draws upon discussions I had with political activists and intellectuals from Poland, Czechoslovakia, Hungary, and Romania during trips to East Europe in December 1984, May and June 1985, and May and June 1987, as well as in the ongoing Democracy Seminar at the New School for Social Research.
2. *New York Times*, 24 August 1987, 1.
3. As of this writing (August 1987), Joseph Brodsky has just received the Nobel Prize for Literature. Simultaneously, there has been discussion concerning the possible official publication of his poetry. Such publication would represent a significant escalation of glasnost.
4. Interview with the author, June 1987.
5. For a distinction between social and political control, see Morris Janowitz, "Sociological Theory and Social Control," *American Journal of Sociology*, Vol. 81, no. 1 (July 1975):82–108.
6. See Daniel Chirot, "The Corporatist Model and Socialism," *Theory and Society* 9 (March 1980):363–81.
7. Johnson, *Change in Communist Systems*.
8. Haraszti, *The Velvet Prison*, and Staniskis, *Poland's Self-Limiting Revolution*.
9. Michnik, "The New Evolutionism," in *Letters*, 142.

Epilogue

1. My original intention was to use Teresa Toranska's account of Polish Stalinists in *Them* as a starting point for this epilogue. In reading her reportage, it struck me that the Stalinists' odd frame of mind had a remarkable resemblance to problematic Western social and political theory. I work this out here without direct reference to the Polish Stalinists, but with Toranska's outstanding book in mind. She depicted "them"; I analyze how they are part of "us." See Teresa Toranska, *Them: Stalin's Polish Puppets* (New York: Harper and Row, 1987).

2. Jurgen Habermas, "Modernity—An Incomplete Project," in *The Anti-Aesthetic: Essays on Post Modern Culture,* ed. Hal Foster (Port Townsend, Wash.: Bay Press, 1983). For a cogent discussion of the varieties of post-modernism and their political meanings, see Blaine McBurney, "The Post Modernist Transvaluations of Modernist Values," *Thesis Eleven* 12 (August 1985):94–109.

3. Jean-Francois Lyotard, *The Post-Modern Condition* (Minneapolis: University of Minneapolis Press, 1984).

4. Daniel Bell, *The Coming of Post-Industrial Society,* and idem, *The Cultural Contradictions of Capitalism* (New York: Basic Books, 1976).

5. Andreas Huyssen, "Mapping the Postmodern," *New German Critique,* 33 (Fall 1984):5–52, and Foster, ed., *The Anti-Aesthetic.*

6. Zygmunt Bauman, *Legislators and Interpreters: On Modernity, Post-Modernity and Intellectuals* (Ithaca: Cornell University Press, 1987).

7. Ferenc Feher, "The Status of Post-Modernity," forthcoming in *Philosophy and Social Criticism.*

8. Arendt, *Men in Dark Times,* viii.

9. Alain Touraine, *The Post Industrial Society* (New York: Random House, 1971), and Bell, *The Coming of Post-Industrial Society.*

10. Jurgen Habermas, *Legitimation Crisis,* and *Theory of Communicative Action.*

11. Lyotard, *Post-Modern Condition,* and Jacques Derrida, *Writing and Difference* (Chicago: University of Chicago Press, 1978).

12. Said Arjomand, "History, Structure and Revolution in the Contemporary Shiite Tradition," *International Political Science Journal,* forthcoming 1989.

13. See, e.g., Milton Friedman, *Capitalism and Freedom* (Chicago: University of Chicago Press, 1962).

14. See Edward Banfield, *The Democratic Muse: Visual Arts and Public Interest* (New York: Basic Books, 1984). I analyze closely the relationship between the market and cultural autonomy in *On Cultural Freedom.*

15. Lionel Trilling, *The Liberal Imagination: Essays on Literature and Society* (New York: Harcourt Brace Jovanich, 1979); and Bell, *The Cultural Contradictions of Capitalism.*

16. Karl Marx and Friedrich Engels, *The German Ideology,* ed. C. J. Arthur (New York: International Publishing Co., 1970); Karl Mannheim, "Conservative Thought," in Paul Kecskemeti, ed., *Essays on Sociology and Social Psychology* (New York: Oxford University Press, 1953), 74–164; and Pierre Bourdieu, *Distinctions: A Social Critique of the Judgement of Taste* (Cambridge: Harvard University Press, 1984).

17. Emile Durkheim, *The Elementary Forms of Religious Life* (New York: The Free Press, 1965); Georg Lukacs, *The Historical Novel* (University of Nebraska Press, 1983); and Leo Lowenthal, *Literature and the Images of Man* (New Brunswick: Transaction Books, 1985).

18. Mannheim, "Conservative Thought."

19. Habermas, *Legitimation Crisis;* and Max Weber, "Science as a Vocation," in *Max Weber's Essays in Sociology,* ed. H. H. Gerth and C. W. Mills (New York: Oxford University Press, 1946), 77–156.

20. In the discussion that follows, I am drawing primarily upon Talcott Parsons, *The Social System* (New York: Free Press, 1964); and Habermas, *Legitimation Crisis.* These works are the ones in which their systems theory problematic is most clearly presented. The discussion here should not be viewed as an overall critique of either theorist's work. Rather, it is a critique of a type of theorizing that each employs to varying degrees and in different ways.

21. Robert Merton, *Social Theory and Social Structure* (New York: Free Press, 1966).

22. Emile Durkheim's is one of the major classical European social theories upon which Parsons bases his work. See Talcott Parsons *The Structure of Social Action* (New York: Free Press, 1949). For Durkheim on suicide, see *Suicide* (New York: Free Press, 1966).

23. David Matza, *Delinquency and Drift* (John Wiley and Sons, Inc., 1964).

24. Quoted in Leszek Kolakowski, *Main Currents of Marxism,* vol. 2 (Oxford: Oxford University Press, 1978), 387.

25. See ibid., 398–405.

26. Serge Guilbert, *How New York Stole the Idea of Modern Art: Abstract Expressionism, Freedom and the Cold War* (Chicago: University of Chicago Press, 1983).

27. Arendt, *Men in Dark Times,* 33–56.

28. Peter B. Evans, Dietrich Reuschemeyer, and Theda Skocpol, *Bring the State Back In* (New York: Cambridge University Press, 1985).

29. Jean Baudrillard, *For a Critique of the Political Economy of the Sign* (St. Louis: Telos Press, 1981); and "The Ecstasy of Communication," in *The Anti-Aesthetic,* ed. Foster, 126–34.

30. Allan Bloom, *The Closing of the American Mind: How Higher Education Has Failed Democracy and Impoverished the Souls of Today's Students* (New York: Simon and Schuster, 1987); E. D. Hirsch, *Cultural Literacy: What Every American Needs to Know* (Boston: Houghton Mifflin Company, 1987).

31. The paraphrase comes from Bloom's subtitle.

32. Hirsch, *Cultural Literacy,* xv.

33. Classic examples are Gabriel Almond and Sidney Verba, *The Civil Culture: Political Attitudes and Democracy in Five Nations* (Princeton: Princeton University Press, 1963), and Robert Bellah, *The Broken Covenant: American Civil Religion in a Time of Trial* (New York: Seabury Press, 1975).

Index

242

208, 210; and science, 45–47; on
sex and politics, 164; and Sta-
linism, 210–12. *See also*
Marxism
Marxism, 65; and Habermas, 208,
210; and independent expression,
72–75; and Lysenkoism, 40–45;
and Stalinism, 210–15; and totalitarianism, 5–6, 119–29; and
truth, 89–90
Matejko, Aleksander, 79
Matza, David, 209
Media: on dissident writers, 97–98;
and Newspeak, 57, 220–22; in
Poland, 134, 139–41
Medvedev, Roy, 74
Medvedev, Zhores A., 41, 45–
47, 74
Memorandum, The (Havel), 106
Merleau-Ponty, Maurice, 90
Merton, Robert, 209
Michnik, Adam, xvii, xxvii, 118,
119, 131, 142–57, 162, 170,
178, 185–86, 195, 198, 207,
220–21; *The Church, The Left*,
143; "Conversations in the Citadel," 153–56; on democracy,
142–44, 166–67; on Dmowski,
153–55, 164, 214; fragmentary
style of, 206; *From the History of
Honor in Poland*, 148; "In the
Shadows of Ancestors," 152–53;
and KOR, 128, 143; Kundera
compared with, 222–24; letter to
Kiszczak, 146–48; "Maggots and
Angels," 156; and Marxism, 214;
"The New Evolutionism," 143,
157, 167, 171–74, 195; "On Resistance," 156–57; on papal visit
and religion, 148–52, 164; on
Pilsudski, 152–53, 164; on Soviet reforms, 189; "A Year Has
Passed," 156
Mickiewicz, Adam, 70
Milosz, Czeslaw, 137; *The Captive
Mind*, xxi–xxiv, 148
Modernity, 130; and glasnost, 187–
88; and postmodernism, 199–
201, 203; and totalitarianism,

8–9, 14–18, 23–29, 36–39, 47,
66–68
Modzelewski, Karol, 73–74
Mrozek (dramatist), 71
Music, 113, 221

National Democracy (movement),
154–55
Nazism, 5–8, 14–15, 37–38, 161,
182, 201, 215.
Neoconservatism, 15–17, 24–25,
36. *See also* Conservatism
Neopositivism, 173–77. *See also*
Positivism
Neototalitarianism, 186; Gorbachev
regime as example of, 186–95,
197
New Dealism, 6–7
"New Evolutionism, The"
(Michnik), 143, 157, 167,
171–74, 195
Newspeak, 3, 106, 110, 155, 179,
180, 181, 198, 225; and embedded culture, 82; and glasnost, 189–
94; and legitimation through disbelief, 90–91, 215–20; of media,
220–22; Orwell on, 18, 19, 48–
49, 54, 56, 57, 91, 94, 227 n. 1;
and post-totalitarianism, 87–88,
161, 162; role of, in totalitarianism, 39, 48–60, 169–70
1984 (Orwell), 18, 19, 48–49, 54,
56, 57, 60, 94, 227 n. 1
Nixon, Richard, 68, 165–66,
236 n. 11
North, Oliver, 166

Oedipus, 115–16
"On Resistance" (Michnik), 156–57
Openness. *See* Glasnost
Origins of Totalitarianism, The
(Arendt), 8–10, 14–15, 101–2,
163, 207
Orwell, George, 91; *1984*, 18, 19,
48–49, 54, 56, 57, 60, 94, 227 n. 1

Painting: abstract expressionist,
213; Newspeak and criticism of,
57–58